To Norman
Best Wishes
Sheila Ward

STARTING
AGAIN IN
EGOLI

Also by the same author:

Beyond White Mischief—The memoirs of a Tea Planter's wife

Contact Sheila at:
sheilaward@uwclub.net

STARTING AGAIN IN EGOLI

SHEILA WARD

authorHOUSE®

AuthorHouse™ UK Ltd.
1663 Liberty Drive
Bloomington, IN 47403 USA
www.authorhouse.co.uk
Phone: 0800.197.4150

Cover design by Malcolm Cook

Published by AuthorHouse   05/29/2013

ISBN: 978-1-4817-9650-7 (sc)
ISBN: 978-1-4817-9651-4 (hc)
ISBN: 978-1-4817-9652-1 (e)

Dedicated To My Family and Friends

Synopsis for Starting Again in Egoli

In South Africa in 1965 I left my husband and three children and moved to Johannesburg (known by the Zulus as Egoli) where I hoped to return to the theatre. His mistress moved in with him after I left. I had promised not to fight for custody but that was under duress. I found a lawyer and was able to arrange to visit the children. He later advised me to drop the fight because my husband would leave the country.

I was trained at RADA, went into repertory, toured, then met my ex RAF husband. We married and flew out to Kenya. (See "Beyond White Mischief" The Memoirs of a Tea Planter's Wife).

In Egoli I found a job in a department store, then an office, hospital reception and more offices. In between I started acting again, radio plays, stage plays and TV. I also wrote plays and short stories. Our divorce was finalised, I met my second husband, became a Buddhist and had a baby. He was 12 years younger than I, so when his wandering eye lighted on another we divorced. Married for a third time, after two years discovered he was an alcoholic, but we remained good friends. I returned to UK in 1999.

Eleven years of marriage, three children . . . successive emotional blows had driven me to leave them. My husband's new mistress would soon replace me. Children are wonderfully adaptable, that's what I told myself, during the endless days and sleepless nights of longing to see and hold them. They were better off without me, I had become a nervous wreck.

Now I had come to Egoli, city of gold. That is what Zulus call Johannesburg.

There are so many deep mines, in certain places, a house can disappear overnight into a bottomless pit without any warning. In August 1965 when I arrived it was the commercial hub of South Africa. We were ruled by the Volk, the Afrikaner white majority. Yet it was really two cities. Soweto-or South West Township, lay alongside the wealthy areas, a festering scatter of makeshift huts. No electricity, sewage, or running water, unless you counted the occasional stand pipes.

Trained as an actress at RADA and in repertory theatres, when I married my tea planter I had no idea how lonely life in the bundu (wild) could be. (*See "Beyond White Mischief The Memoirs of a Tea Planter's Wife".*) Now I had finally left him I thought I could go back to acting again . . . . but where do you start in a strange city? You have to have that magic word – Contacts!

Standing all day at the Gift Department in Stuttafords was tiring enough, then walking home up a series of steep hills I would pass out on my bed, then have to wake up to have supper, the only proper meal of the day. The hardest part of my job was getting used to South African currency, the decimal system, giving the right change and cashing up at the end of the day. I enjoyed selling gifts, though, and my Buyer, Mrs Sharp, suited her name, and chivvied me into a semblance of efficiency.

I wrote to my daughter Jane trying to explain in simple terms, that a nine year old could understand, why I had left, and that I would try to visit them soon. The children had seen the way he treated me. She was marvellous, took on the responsibility of keeping order between Michael and Roger, who were always squabbling. She mediated between them and their father, who could deny her nothing. They all three wrote to me, sad little letters, when would I come home?

1

A few weeks after arriving in Jo'burg, I remembered Bill Fourie, the young piper from the Transvaal Scottish and rang him at work. He sounded strange, not at all willing to see me. However, we met at a nearby pub.

"I wrote to you – Poste Restante as you suggested. Your husband read my letter, and now I'm banned from ever going back to Barberton with them. He nearly got me sacked. I had to promise never to see you again! "He was nearly in tears". My God, what did you say?"

"Just that I liked you, wanted to see you again nothing explicit".

"Bill, I'm so sorry, I left so suddenly". Then I explained the events that had led up to me leaving. Peter obviously thought I had planned to meet up with Bill, but I had forgotten about him. We didn't meet ever again, we really had very little in common.

Gradually, I rose in the ranks, became a Supervisor on Gifts and then I moved on to Cosmetics. The Buyer there was an ex-actress, a lovely understanding person. Worked in the Fashion Department and then ran my own Young Leather Look section. Next the Crockery Department, where pushing heavy skips gave me a slipped disc and I had to wear a corrective corset for a while. When I became Supervisor of the Lifts I wondered if I'd reached the end of the line!

It was fun being on the Entertainments Committee, helping to Organise Dances, I even won a prize, dancing the Charleston! I met a piquant Portuguese girl, Olga Caroto, while working in Cosmetics and she had been trained in Paris and had a marvellous sense of humour. We both used to give bottle parties with different themes. It was like being a student again.

My first priority after settling into the new life was to find a lawyer. Although I had promised Peter I would not fight for custody of the children – that was when I was under duress. A lawyer would surely back me up? Angus McNair was suggested to me by a friend, and he proved to be an ideal person. He arranged for me to visit the children in Barberton several times, and to apply for custody. The Murrays let me stay at the Impala Hotel at a reduced rate. While chatting to Dan I learnt more about P's drinking habits, surely he should not have custody? Penny moved in with P soon after I left, they both spoiled her four year old son, Guy, to the detriment of his own children. She had seemed a nice enough woman, but apparently thought P had plenty of money, whereas he in turn believed she was well off! Not true!

At the end of the year Angus advised me not to pursue the custody application. He believed that P was so vindictive that if I was awarded custody he would leave South Africa and refuse to pay child support. He asked how I would be able to look after three children in a one-roomed flat? I had moved into a flat in Lake Success, Pietersen Street.

They spent one weekend with me and it was purgatory – the boys were whining and bored, the only place they could play was nearby Joubert Park, a haunt of tramps and drunks, not to mention perverts. Whereas P had a lovely new house, horses to ride, pets, and school friends could come and stay. So the divorce went through unopposed and he got custody. Jane wrote to me that the German nuns at St Peter's boarding school beat Roger for wetting his bed. Poor little soul, his father treated him with suspicion, then I left, no wonder he wet his bed. Then he got German measles and the nuns neglected him . . . , I felt so helpless, miles away, having no money, being unable to drive.

Alistair Yuill lived in the same block, and took me out a few times, what a charmer but he was ten years younger than me, so there seemed to be no future in an affair. I met George Moore, an elderly actor, who became a good friend. I overheard his daughter Pam say I was one of his "lame ducks", however, I like to think he enjoyed my company. He introduced me to many actors, took me to plays and films, He was involved with Bob Courtney in the show "Pick-a-Box" which was very popular on Springbok Radio. He had been a Diplomat in the Far East, his flat was decorated with Chinese artefacts, Ming vases, and a large jackal kaross covered his bed.

February 13th 1967 – Mummy arrives. Alistair gives me a lift to the airport to meet her. She means to comfort me in my despair . . . , or perhaps help with the children, but I remember the last time she came to Kenya and caused such upheaval. At least Peter is no longer around, she can only quarrel with my choice of escorts, which she does! Alistair is too young, George is too old. Quote" He's old enough to be <u>my</u> boyfriend!"(She is 67).

Wed March 8th – First night of "Black Chiffon". Bank Players are a really good amateur group. I play Brian Rabjohn's fiancée. It's a start & feels good to be back on a stage again.

Thur 23rd – Children arrive for Half Term. Sat 25th – Take them to the Rand Show at Milner Park and it rains, of course, but they have a good time going on all the rides at the Funfair. On Sunday, George takes us all to the Zoo, and the War Museum, the boys love that.

Mon 27th – End of Half Term, they have to go back to school, so sad. George & I take Mummy round "Artists in the Sun" at Zoo Lake. She has done quite a few oil paintings since she's been staying with me. April 3rd – Her return ticket is up, she decides to fly home. We've had a few disagreements and she can be a bit tactless.

Thur June 1st – *The divorce is final.* Opening night of "Any Other Evening". Sat 12th – the children come to stay. Barney, an artistic type with a shock of frizzy hair, takes us boating on Wemmer Pan (dam). They love it, have a picnic. Mon 14th – Take them to the Zoo and boating on Zoo Lake, with Val Donald & Tommy. A braai with Val & Gavin. Mon 21st-I paint Michael in oils. Wed 23rd – Go to see Brickhill Burke's "Minstrel Scandals", All done in Blackface make-up.

They love it. Sun 27th – Have to take them back to P. and a big wrench, we had such a lovely time together.

Sun 3rd Sept – Tubby takes me to the Jazz Club. He's plump, bearded, very "hip". Has no visible means of support! When I ask him what he wants to achieve in life, he says mysteriously, "a big wheel". Tues 5th – We see "A Man and a Woman". Loved it, so sad, adore the music. Party at Tubby's and 'hopheads' galore. Thur 28th – George's lecture about acting, it's very good, but only 18 people come. Sat 7th October – Meet Jenny at the Chelsa Coffee Bar in Jeppe Street. It was like a club, we all used to meet there. We discussed the idea of us sharing a flat. A few of us go on to a Gay club,

Connections. There's a transvestite in the Ladies Room, horrors! I rush out and have to hold it in, till we find somewhere else!

Am earning very little at Stuttafords and start working evenings at Exclusive Books in Hillbrow. Sat 21ˢᵗ – Visit Olga, she's now working at Renato's, a sex-mad hairdresser, doing make-up for his clients. It's his birthday, champagne and cake for all.

Thur 16ᵗʰ November – *Peter marries his live-in mistress, Penny Rogers.*

Thur 23ʳᵈ – Jane & Michael's Birthdays. I move to Anchor House, a flat near work. Jenny & I decide not to share. Sat 25ᵗʰ – Mary Phillips brings the children. I'm overjoyed to see them so unexpectedly. She is a kind hearted woman, the wife of Ted, a cricketing friend.

1968 – *This part of my diary was damaged when water seeped through a tiny hole in my tin trunk, so this is from memory.*

Went to see "Dr Zhivago" film with a new boyfriend. When a train is going through the snow plains it stops momentarily at a station, where a mother tries to throw her baby up to helpers on the train. I found myself straining to catch the baby, halfway out of my seat. Astonished faces brought me back to reality as my new friend pulled me back.

How could I explain recurring fear from the loss of a child . . . , at the end of the film I kept the whole row waiting, as I zipped up my long boots. He was not impressed by this odd person and did not see him again.

I meet an Aussie, John Brodie, who seems a nice, dependable sort of man. We start going out. His friend was actor Peter Tobin, a dashing man-about–town. We lead a social life, which puts a strain on my minimal wardrobe. Fortunately, am able to buy clothes with a discount from work. We'd got to the stage of his asking me to marry him and I was seriously considering the idea, but then we went away for a weekend. When we got back he asked me what had happened? I thought he was joking, but he was deadly serious.

Peter Tobin then informed me, that John had a bad memory. I had not survived one bad marriage to jump into another!

Now I moved again, into Anstey's Building, only one street away from work. Although only a one-roomed flat on the ninth floor, it was a huge room with a lovely bay window and a separate bathroom and kitchen. I was still working at the Gift Dept, but was now a Supervisor. One day a large, spotty young man walked in, he seemed to be in a terrific hurry. I sold him a key case. Later, I met my friends for coffee at the Birdcage Café in the basement. The same man was sitting near us and he began listening to us, interrupting our conversation. I thought he was a crass, rude person, gave him a cold look, but he was undeterred. He had the cheek of the devil, but a kind of ingenuous charm with it.

After work he was waiting outside for me. I began to feel uneasy, how was I going to shake him off? We walked to the corner, I said goodbye, as I had shopping to do. Oh, he said, let me help you carry it. In the end he saw me back home, helped me unload the food, arrange chairs for the rehearsal. My new drama group, RAPS, were putting on Jo Orton's play "Loot". I was producer and they met at my flat. In the end he stayed and helped me. I was so tired, from standing all day and working 2 nights a week at the bookshop, that I actually fell asleep sitting up.

Leon said" Were we <u>that</u> bad!?" I blushed, at last they all left.

He turned to me, "By the way, my name is Bryan Kiely".

He went off home, to my relief. He'd just joined a commune house in Dundalk Avenue with his friend Carlo and both from Port Elizabeth.

Coming back from an evening out with George Moore, seeing "Butterflies Are Free" with Bruce Miller at the Brooke Theatre, Bryan rushed up to the car, pulled me out and said "Good evening, excuse me,""to George and manhandled me into to his car where Carlo sat. George was bemused, I was furious!

Always in a hurry, was Bryan.

Michael & Roger   *Jane*
1967 Wemmerpan   *Lowfeld Show*

Hamlet 1969   *Stuttafords Dance*
Gertrude Library Theatre   *Won Fancy dress prize*

The Three sisters 1969
Irina Olga Masha

He, Bryan was twelve years younger than me, we had very little in common, but it is very flattering to be the object of unconditional love, after years of contemptuous treatment.

We began a relationship, with him helping me organise the rehearsals for "Loot".

We needed a body, the mother-in-law. My old friend, who ran the Window Dressing Dept. allowed me to smuggle an old dummy out of Stuttafords in separate pieces, arms first, then legs, then torso and reassembled her in my flat. She had bright blue staring eyes and a rosebud mouth in thirties style. Her nose was chipped and her plaster hair sported marcel waves. A coffin had been made out of rigid foam and we lowered her in and positioned the lid over her. The lid was askew the next morning. There was a slight breeze, so I thought it had moved the lid. Still, it made me uneasy. For the next rehearsal, we dressed her in WVS navy uniform and stood her in one corner of the room. When I got back from work that day, she was in the kitchen . . . I was sure I had left her in the bedroom. I phoned Bryan and begged him to spend the night with me. Nothing happened, of course, but I was spooked. The next day we took her to the Scout Hall in Rosebank, where we put on the play.

I took her back, in various bags and the doorman was mystified. Later, I explained that it had been for a play and he nodded understandingly. I asked the caretaker at my block about the previous tenant of my flat? "Oh", he said, "I thought they told you".

"Told me . . . ? Er, she was a young girl, jumped out of the window".

I had felt dizzy looking over the balcony. Nine floors, I was now so nervous about being in the flat on my own that Bryan moved in with me. He was into all kinds of spiritual beliefs, said he would perform an exorcism to pacify the spirit of the suicide. It seemed to help. We were now very much in love. He snored a lot, smoked and coughed most of the night, so heaven knows how I managed to sleep!

He said his father was in the Army and drafted him into 'spying on drug users and sellers', when he was sixteen. In order to be accepted by them, he took drugs and became addicted to heroin. Just before I met him, he said he had "gone cold turkey" and cured himself of the drug on his own in a hotel in Bloemfontein. It took three days. This news really horrified me. I had never had anything to do with drugs before. What was I getting into? I looked at his arm there were little pinpricks inside the elbow. So I believed him. He said I must never be unfaithful to him, as he had people watching me all the time. He was an expert manipulator. Had I jumped out of the frying pan into the fire?

During the War, his sister was born and who was very sickly, as well as deaf and dumb. She had been delivered by an inexperienced medical student, using forceps. Bryan was very spoiled by his grieving mother, especially after Dawn died aged nine. He had a difficult time at school, as he was dyslexic and crashed a number of motor bikes in his teens, but she denied him nothing. He said, he was an expert swimmer and diver. He was caught in some fishing nets, got the "bends", when surfacing from a dive and it damaged his sinuses. That was why he was tone deaf, he said.

The next disclosure was that he had been initiated into African witchcraft by a witchdoctor in Port Elizabeth, when he was in his teens. He then tried a series of different religions, including Scientology, fell foul of them and was cast out, but now a Buddhist. He also said he was an expert in astral travel . . . well, how do you disprove something like that? All these revelations seemed even more far-fetched, when I later met his mother Yvonne Parnell. She was so sweet and ordinary. She felt our twelve year age difference would prevent a lasting relationship. Mrs Sharp, my mentor at the Gift Dept, was unequivocal in her disdain.

"Don't get involved with him, he has a bad skin, he will never be a success!"

Of course, I ignored her advice and asked to move to the Cosmetic Dept.

Bryan's stepfather was a difficult character, a typical "sea lawyer", very argumentative and jealous of his stepson. Yvonne met him, when she was running a seaman's mission club in Port Elizabeth. Eddie attacked Bryan once, hiding behind a door, then hitting him with a hammer, breaking some bones in his face, one being near his optic nerve, so that he would never go to the dentist in case he lost his sight. As a result, his teeth were in a shocking state.

Bryan had been an apprenticed to a jeweller and had been in the Army, but now he'd come to Jo'burg and wanted to start a new career as a photographer. He fully supported my desire to resume my acting career and encouraged my writing ambition, but in the meantime someone had to earn a living!

In 1968, I left Bank Players. They were an excellent amateur drama group, but they concentrated on popular middle-of – the road kind of shows and after twelve years of living in a thespian wilderness. I longed to perform in good classical plays, the kind of meaty stuff I had been trained to do. RAPS put on a production of "The Dybbuk" at the Library theatre. This strange play is about a bridegroom, who has a "Doppelganger", a ghostly double. It was well acted, very moving and I auditioned to join the group. We put on "Blithe Spirit". I played Mrs Bradman, the Doctor's wife in the dinner party scene. The Taub's were the main motivators, Clara Taub was very dynamic and a good actress, another actress, Shelagh Ray was semi-professional, as was Norman Coombes and most of the members were semi or mainly professional. PACT, the Performing Arts Corporation of the Transvaal, provided most acting opportunities, but the organisers were principally

Afrikaans and usually employed people who could speak English and Afrikaans, thus who gained more experience. Recently arrived actors were restricted in the jobs available to them. Pieter Toerien, a producer based in Cape Town, put on tours. Then there were the Springbok Radio and English radio

Photo taken by Humphrey

Rehearsing Olga in The Three Sisters 1969

programmes. I went to audition for various radio producers, Colin Fish, Jack Mullen, Douglas Bristow, John Boulter, Michael McCabe, Tim Bungay, Ziona Bonell and Margaret Heale. (Michael and Tim had moved down from

Kenya). Gradually, over the next years radio plays and series became my mainstay, in between shifts as a Receptionist in a Hospital and alternating with temporary office jobs. Joseph Sherman directed the next production, Tchekov's "Three Sisters". This was more like it! This version was translated by Stuart Helps' Russian wife, Nina. Jo went to great lengths to make it authentic in mood, with Russian music, particularly marches.

He was an eccentric character, droll, sometimes wickedly acidulous and was very thin, with a back problem, which mean't he had to wear a brace at all times. He taught English at Athlone Boys High. Paul Romanov, a descendent of the Tsar, was the stage designer.

Many of the large cast had Slavic connections. I was cast as Olga, the oldest sister, a teacher. Shelagh Ray played Masha, the bitter middle sister, Beverley Luyt, Irina, the youngest one. Humphry Ward played Fers, the old servant.

It was a long play, many thought it should have been cut, but we all felt it was a marvellous production and we had mainly good criticisms, except for, perhaps,

the length! We put it on at the Library Theatre in the centre of town and audiences were good, there was such a dearth of classical plays at that time and schools flocked to see it.

Bryan said one day, when I was complaining of being too tired to rehearse and trying to learn the long speeches was too much for me.

"One day you will look back on this and realise that it was the happiest time of your entire life"!

He was right. He had become a stage manager and was an integral part of the group. He was quite bossy, but in a jolly way, so that people tended to do things his way. His plan was to become a professional photographer, but suffered from a lack of equipment and was put on hold.

We married in a registry office on May 29th 1969. There were no wedding photos, as our Hungarian friend, Laci Novak, did not turn up with his camera!! We had no money, but we were very much in love. Olga and Carlo were witnesses and she got so much in the spirit of the thing, we had to restrain her from marrying Carlo! We went back to Anstey's Building and held a small reception. One of my friends promised to clean up afterwards, as we had to rush away to catch the train to Pietersburg to see the children. We caught it just in time. So our short honeymoon was spent listening to the rhythm of the wheels, quite inspiring!

The children were now at Capricorn School near Tzaneen, as Peter had moved to the tea estate there. They met us at the station and we had a lovely day. Bryan was casual and relaxed, quite unlike their father and they immediately warmed to him, being so much younger. We had a picnic and lay about chatting, then caught the evening train back on Sunday evening, so I could be at work on Monday. The flat stank of champagne, stale cigarettes and Gorgonzola! The ex-friend had let us down of course. I was still working at Stuttafords, but the elusive Buyer's position never came my way. Bryan thought I should look for another job, paying more money.

Bryan Keily

Started at Truworths, a good clothes shop for more money, but I wasn't happy after the "family" atmosphere of a big store and finally left and started working in an office.

In 1970, RAPS put on "Hamlet" at the Library Theatre. Jo was producing again and decided to make it a modern dress version. This was quite a departure from the norm, especially in Johannesburg. He cast me as Gertrude. I had to provide my own clothes of course, but luckily I'd bought a few outfits while I worked at Stuttafords. The Ball scene presented a problem, since I had no ball gowns! Had put on some weight since the stick-thin person I became after we arrived in Durban, from Kenya in 1964 . . . Anyway, I made a slim satin sheathe in a deep turquoise, borrowed a tiara and earrings from a jeweller friend and saved changing time by ditching the latter two during the bedroom scene.

Paul designed a stark, futuristic set on two levels with minimal change, relying on clever lighting. Michael Irwin played Hamlet, he was really good and went on to become a fine professional actor. Beverley Luyt played Ophelia, Leon Watson a devious Claudius and Richard Rowe played Polonius, as a fussy old diplomat. The criticisms were quite mixed, as a modern dress Hamlet was a bit go-ahead for the local critics! In my first fan letter, a Brakpan schoolgirl amused me, when she quoted a member of the audience saying about me, "She looks even lovelier when she's dead". A backhanded compliment! We did have enthusiastic audiences, augmented by the usual schools.

Bryan was getting more work, doing newspaper photography, but he had no studio and developed films in the bathroom. He seemed to get tip-offs about certain violent events, which made me suspect that his claims that he worked for the Government, might even be true. He knew I had left wing sympathies and was deeply appalled by apartheid policies, especially the Immorality Act, which made consorting with a person of another race illegal. Maybe he thought love would blind me to reality, or, on reflection, since we married quite soon after we met, that I would not be able to give evidence against him, if ever it came to that. His mother had moved up to Jo'burg and had accepted me since our marriage was a fait accompli. The strange thing was that, since he had grown a beard, most people thought Bryan was older than me. Eddie bravely began a Tenant's Association aimed at combating Chaim Wainer, the extortionate landlord, who owned many flats in Hillbrow. He preyed on pensioners, poor people and was universally hated. In the end he was forced to flee to the USA. So Eddie had some good points.

Bryan started running "The Troubadour", a club for folk singers in Noord St. Dawn Silver and Des Lindberg were a popular duo, who later put on successful productions. Mel, Mel and Julian were a fine trio. (Mel Green went to America, Mel Miller a comedian, Julian Laxton a fine guitarist), Francoise Hardy sang there (for free)!

She had been engaged to sing at the Colosseum, but came back to sing for us after the show. What a delightful person, so lovely and natural.

In 1970, we moved to a one-bedroomed flat in Clarendon Heights, a nice old block on the corner of Clarendon Circle, overlooking Pieter Roos Park. The rooms were spacious, with parquet floors and pressed steel ceilings. At first, we were idyllically happy, busy with RAPS and my office work. Bryan developing his films in our bathroom, although that could be awkward at times! Then Roger entered our lives. He was a know-all camera buff and taught Bryan a lot, but then he intruded to the extent that he moved in with us, sleeping on the balcony. It never seemed to occur to him that he was invading newly weds privacy. He also had the most unpleasant BO. He paid nothing towards food or rent, yet Bryan wouldn't hear of telling him to go. It was the first real snag in our unlikely marriage.

Pieter Toerien with Basil Rubin and JODS, was holding auditions for "Canterbury Tales". I landed the dual roles of the Nun and the Miller's Wife. Bryan somehow charmed his way into the production and became Stage Manager. Dear old Roger, whom I was hoping to leave behind, was his  Assistant! Jane was now sixteen years old, it was school holidays, so she became Maggie Gordon's dresser. Maggie played the Wife of Bath. A wonderful character, one of the old school. In fact, there were a number of well-known actors in the cast, Hugh Rouse, Gabriel Bayman, Rigby Foster, Ian Hamilton (Erica Roger's husband), Louis Ife, Deborah Witkin, Kerry Jordan, (who had been to RADA with me) and of course Billy Boyle, the charming Irish boy, who had played the lead in the West End production. Daniel Thorndike directed and Thomas Erskine was the Musical Director.

He stayed in a hotel with his window overlooking the Hillbrow Prison. Innocently, he took some photos of the internal yard, next thing two cops came and took him there for real. He was interrogated and clapped into jail. It was a time of tremendous political turmoil, with Nelson Mandela confined to

Robben Island and the Government on the look-out for so-called Communist plots. He was only released after Pieter had pulled a few strings.

We drove down to Cape Town in our clapped out old Citroen, which needed more oil than petrol and stayed at a B&B near the Foreshore and the Nico Malan Theatre. Opening night was a great success! The risque` tales, pretty dancing wenches and naughty songs attracted all kinds of people. We were fully booked wherever we went.

I fell in love with beautiful Cape Town! We visited the Castle and it's grim dungeons. Then we went up the cloud-capped table mountain by cable car. Sitting in the tiny restaurant, the view on all sides was breathtaking. Walking in the Gardens, near the Parliament Buildings had tame grey squirrels that would come up to you. Another day, we visited the magnificent gardens at Rondebosch, driving up to Cape Point, the tip of South Africa, where the Gulf Stream and the Atlantic meet. You can see two different shades of blue-green merging together. Every kind of Protea plant grows wild there and propagates only though fire dispersing the seeds.

On Christmas Day, we looked for somewhere to eat, but all the restaurants were closed. We drove to Simonstown, the naval barracks, then on to Fishoek, which was dry, no liquor was sold there. Stopped at a wayside café, great, they had turkey sandwiches!

That was our celebration lunch. I noticed brandy balls at the counter and ate a few, trying to get into the holiday spirit.

I started having problems with my knees, praying in some scenes, next dancing madly as the Miller's Wife and I had to make myself some foam knee pads. Once, my very long rosary broke and scattered all over the stage, they had to bring the curtain down, while we picked up all the beads. The dancers might have injured themselves. I sang harmonies with the Prioress, and joined in the main choruses, then as the Miller's Wife flirted like mad with one of the students, ending in the flat, stand-up bed copied from Chaucer's illustrations.

On Christmas Eve, the cast gave each other presents. Some of the women approached me about Roger and his aroma problem, should they give him deodorant? I said, yes, why not? But then Pieter decreed we should swop presents so that it was more of a surprise, which defeated the object. Who knows who got his present?

We had a terrible journey back to Jo'burg, stopping to put in oil and water every few miles, it was Bryan's will power which impelled us home. Opening night at the Civic Theatre was another triumph! We had our six week run extended due to public demand. Thank goodness Roger had to find other digs, even Bryan had had enough of him. Clarendon Heights was to be pulled down to make way for a high rise block, so we moved to a flat in De Villiers Street in town, opposite the Cathedral. A local Afrikaans schoolmaster took his pupils to see us, on the understanding that a great classic would be moral.

Two parts played in "Canterbury Tales"

He was so disgusted he marched them all out halfway through the show. Letters to the papers made a great furore, so even more people came.

Sometimes acting in a musical written in rhyming couplets can be trying, especially when another actor gives one the wrong cue, because making up fresh couplets on the spur of the moment is alarming. One or two of the older actors did this to me and I would have to paraphrase the answer, such as, "what you really meant to say was, etc.", because if I gave the wrong cue to the next speaker, the mistake would be continued all the way through the scene! Rigby Foster was one elderly actor playing, the Knight, who was well known for his vagueness. The story goes that while acting in Rhodesia (now Zimbabwe), he was asked to book a row of seats for the Queen Mother's party (she was touring in East Africa), but he forgot and when the 'Royal group' arrived for the show, a row of white farmers objected violently and refused to be turfed out of their seats.

Another evening at an after party, the wife of a multi millionaire in the throes of divorce, had been vilifying him to all and sundry. Rigby looked innocently at her and said, "you like him then?" That provided the laugh of the tour. Rigby never understood why they found it so funny. If you mentioned some article of clothing he wore, such as a brocade waistcoat, he would bridle, "Knitted it myself" Years later, he fell asleep while smoking and rushed into the bathroom, jumped into a bath of cold water to put out the flames, (he must have forgotten to empty it) and had a heart attack. Poor Rigby!

I was longing to extend my writing skills and joined Avonwold Publishing. I began writing book reviews and sent some of my stories to the SABC and also recorded a few as well. I sent this poem to 'The Star' newspaper in 1971. They didn't print it, either because it was lousy or that it might upset the 'verkrampte' Nationalists.

> In the park today
> The children play
> Black & pink,
> Brown & khaki
> They must be blind
> They don't see colour
> The children play together . . .
>
> Adults smile in the sun
> Life seems good
> For a moment
> Open the paper
> Headlined hate
> Leaps from the page
> The sun grows cold
>
> Now we fear again
> Colours show up
> In their difference
> But the children play
> They must be blind
> They don't see colour . . .
> Why can't we see like them?

17

Around the same time, I wrote the poem about children, I watched a prison vehicle passing. It was full of men singing in unison. Africans will always sing, they have wonderful voices, but these men were being imprisoned for living with their own wives, (forbidden in single miner's quarters), or for losing their passes, (which they were supposed to carry on them at all times). The next arrest would be for something worse, stealing for food, because they couldn't find a job. They sang because prison mean't free food, a roof over their heads, so prison was OK.

In 1971, Bryan was established with a small studio, photographic equipment and was beginning to make a name for himself, as a Press Photographer. We couldn't afford insurance, so when he was burgled, it was quite a blow. I had started a new job with the Professional Provident Fund, as a clerk. I still managed to fit in radio plays and I had gone for an audition to be an announcer, but they said I had to become a South African citizen – I was not prepared to lose my British passport!

It was agreed before we married, that we would not have any children, since I already had three. There was my age, (then 39 was considered very old to have a baby) and the fact I was Rhesus negative, but lo and behold, in spite of using all kinds of contraceptives, I became pregnant. Belinda Isis

"Bo" (Belinda)

Kiely was born at 9.30 pm at the Marymount Nursing Home in Kensington. Dr Chouler and the nuns were wonderful, but there came a point in the labour, when the intense pain was so exhausting, I found myself floating near the ceiling, looking down at the body of this poor woman, who was groaning in agony. I think I must have been dying, but something brought me back into my body. Perhaps the doctor gave me a painkiller? Years later, I asked her, but she didn't remember. Belinda was slightly jaundiced, but fortunately our blood group was the same as Bryan's, so she soon regained a rosy skin. Seven pounds at birth and had his brown eyes, hair and upturned nose. He could have watched the birth on close circuit TV, but chose not to. I didn't want him to anyway. There should be some mystique! He must have smoked several packets of cigarettes . . .

I weaned her at two months, because I had to go back to work, someone had to pay the rent. When she was six months old, Bryan and I were both out at work, her nanny Elizabeth had been drinking and dropped her on the floor. She was a devoted nanny, we couldn't believe it, but there was a dint above Belinda's left eye, I said we must take her to hospital right away, but he said, "No, she's not concussed, her eyes are focussing. There are no other signs of trauma". So, against my better judgement, we merely sacked a plainly drunk servant.

Belinda, (or 'Boo', as we called her), had always been a happy contented baby. I don't know if the fall made any difference, but I noticed she would scream when she looked at a little copy of my Nun's costume hanging on the wall. It had a blank face. You don't expect a baby of six months to have developed an imagination? It took a while for me to realise that the doll frightened her. We were sick of living in the centre of town, where the noise, pollution and crime had increased. We moved back to Hillbrow, to a fourth floor two bed roomed flat, Clarendon Heights, in Bruce Street. Yvonne, Bryan's mother lived nearby and helped us with baby sitting.

Jane was at school at nearby Barnato Park, she moved in with us, sharing a bedroom with Boo, who was teething by now. Not easy, as Jane was studying for exams. One day she picked up a pigeon nestling in Joubert Park. She kept it in a shoe box and fed it with an eye dropper. Amazingly it survived. Later she took it to an old school friend called Stuart, who was now a miner in Westonaria. He cared for it for a while and it used to fly back to visit him every year. He was very brave, had lost a leg in a railway accident, but rode his 1000cc motor bike everywhere & with his crutches attached to the bike.

I learned more about Bryan from his mother. When he was five he smeared the sofa and two chairs with Golden syrup, while she was out. He said it made them look nice and shiny! His grandfather was a red-haired Irish blacksmith, who joined the Afrikaners to fight the English during the

Boer War! He told me his forbears had been highwaymen and were the inspiration for the folk song" Whisky in the Jar".

In June 1973, I left PPS and started at John Orr's store, doing relief clerking in their office. Eleanor Anderson, the philanthropic wife of a Director of Anglo American, wrote a revue, which she put on at the Galerie Elysia in Biccard Street, Braamfontein, JHB. We joined Lance Lockhart Ross, a Baron and a descendant of the Royal Stuarts, his lover Maureen McAllister, who had just finished playing Queen Margaret to Ken Leach's King John for PACT. They did excerpts from various plays and poems, including "My Last Duchess" by Robert Browning. Ian Hughes and I did "The Macbeth Murder Mystery", as an Agatha Christie skit, which was well received, plus an N.F. Simpson playlet (theatre of the absurd). In August, I auditioned at the Academy Theatre for David Tomlinson. He put on "Song of Twilight" by Noel Coward, a three-hander with Ann Courtneidge and Melody O'Brian. I was understudying them both. Slim ladies, so had to lose weight quickly in order to fit into either of their costumes. Tim Heale was the Stage Manager and rehearsed me. David was a strange man, he relaxed by listening to cases in the Divorce Courts.

In 1974, January. Boo is potty trained except for a nappy at night, she's very good. Starts nursery school at the Teddy Bear's Creche. Hugh Rouse's ex-wife Norma is running it. She's reputed to be an alcoholic, but I don't see any sign of it. I have to take over as ASM for two shows, David doesn't treat his backstage staff very well, but Tim has become a good friend and we have long chats over a drink. His wife is Margaret Heale, another actress and a radio producer. I respect her and would never become involved with Tim.

Bill Pullen is a TV producer, mainly sports, but wants to direct drama programmes. He and Sybille have a small baby Boo's age, so we visit them and they come over to us. One evening we invite Ann Courtneidge (Jack Hulbert's niece) over to meet them, also David Friedgood and his girl friend. He was the 'SA Grand Chess Champion'. Bill is to direct a play called, "Residential" then gives Ann the lead. I play one of the residents, Mrs Humbert.

Bryan and I enter the JHB Chess Club Championships. He is very good, though I'm struggling a bit! He used to play lightening games for coffees in Port Elizabeth.

Go to see "O Lucky Man" with Malcolm McDowell. Brilliant film by Lindsay Anderson with a Buddhist philosophy. Thur 21st February – Boo's 2nd Birthday. Take packets of sweets to the creche for her party. In March – shoot several scenes for "Residential".

April 13th – Michael and Roger are both at King Edward's Public School (KES). I take them to see "The Three Musketeers". 6th May – Jane is sharing a flat with Maureen Link and they are burgled! Thur 9th May – Recorded Barsetshire Chronicles for Colin Fish.

Bryan starts working for AA Mutual Life. Wed 22nd – JHB Open Chess Championships. Boo has a cough, Yvonne baby sits. I play Lennie Aron. He's a good player, but he's a spastic, and his pieces tend to fly all over the place. Most embarrassing, I find it hard to concentrate and lose badly. I suspect he wins most of his games, as people are keen to get it over! Fri 24th – Recorded at Theatre 60, "Musical Chairs" directed by Douglas Bristow and with Illona Kazan, Stuart Brown and rugged Canadian actor Robert Beatty. I reminded him that we toured together in "Love from a Stranger," in 1954.

Tues 4th June – Radio play for Mike Silver. All the 'old guard' actors, all milling around the 'mike', no one has been told who is to do the sound effects and is most off putting! I'm used to organised recordings with Margaret and Ziona. Wed 5th – Audition at Arena Theatre with Ken Leach, for the part of the Nurse in "The Happiness Cage" for PACT. A disturbing play about lobotomy. Mon 10th – Start rehearsing the Nurse. Sat 22nd – Boo has tonsillitis; Dr Teeger gives her a jab of penicillin.

Thur 27th June – Bryan's Birthday. Record 1 episode of Barsetshire Chronicles and "Enterprise 2472", a radio play by Mike McCabe and his entry for the Italia Prize competition.
Thur 11th July – Opening night at the Alexander Theatre. I share a dressing room with Di Wilson.

She's Gordon Mulholland's ex-wife, funny, abrasive and talented, but inclined to blurt things out without regard to people's feelings. The play had a good reception, it's a marvellous cast, Hal Orlandini, Michael Meyer, Kenneth Hendel and Mike McCabe. A very distressing subject, Margaret Heale fainted. Next day, we have excellent reviews. Sat 13th – Party at Ken's house. I meet Gillian Garlick, his wife. She is blonde with fine delicate features. She played Cissie in "People Are Living

My sister Pat

There", an Athol Fugard's play about poor whites living in Braamfontein, JHB. Bill Flynn was in that production, and Yvonne Bryceland. B arranges insurance for the McCabe's and takes photos of his waif-like, red haired wife, Sue Trower.

Boo is much better, Yvonne has been babysitting her again. Tues 16th – Dubbing for Ian Walters, a German film, "The Seven Slaps". Buy Roger a denim jacket and jeans for his birthday. Sun 4th August – Visit Di at her lovely home in Parkhurst, she's laid up with a sprained ankle, hope she'll be fit for Monday night. Wed 7th – Record 4 episodes of "Personal Column" for Mike McCabe and "Ten O'Clock Tales" for Denis Folbigge at AFS Productions. Mon 12th – Opening Night in Pretoria at the State Theatre. Sat 24th – Last night of "Happiness Cage". Francois Swart gives a champagne party. Visit the McCabe's, Boo nearly chokes on a peppermint their kids gave her. Thur 29th – Leave Boo with Yvonne. Drive down to Port Elizabeth (PE) to stay with Igor and Irma von Schoultz, B's old Buddhist friends. Terrible weather, but B goes and sits on Mike's Rock in spite of the storm, supposedly meditating. (Mike was his old diving buddy, who drowned).

Tues 3rd – Drive back. He has terrible toothache. We have to book into a hotel in Bloemfontein. On Tues 10th Sept – An interview with Rosa, of the Karma Rigdol Gompa in Parkhurst. I am to be initiated as a Buddhist. Sunday – B brings back an old gnarled tree stump from God knows where, for a scratch post. Our black cat 'Mokey', gets such a fright he jumps straight over the balcony, hits the branch of a tree outside on the way down from the fourth floor. Lands on the pavement, a sorry little heap. He had to be put down. Belinda is inconsolable and B is very ashamed. I have no sewing machine, so sit up half the night sewing a long white dress for the initiation. Early next morning, no time to put on make-up or wash my hair, we all have to be at Rosa's place for the "Refuge" at six. Sue is there, radiant, her lovely glossy hair gleaming. We are to be initiated together. I don't notice she's wearing B's malla (rosary). Lecture by Rosa, I am now a Tibetan Buddhist. We go home, set up and dedicate our shrine with rice, water and flowers.

All next day I'm on a high, feel so pure and good . . .

Tues 1st October – Rosa visiting the Lama in Tibet and see her off at the airport. Sunday spend the day with the Dickman's, he treats his wife abominably, I ask him how can he equate beating his wife with the concepts of Buddhism? He just shrugs his shoulders. The next few days I record "Medical File" for June Dixon, film an advert for "Jetball", record "Ten O Clock Tales" for Denis at AFS. Belinda is tested by Dr Teeger, she's allergic to dairy products, eggs, citrus and house dust!

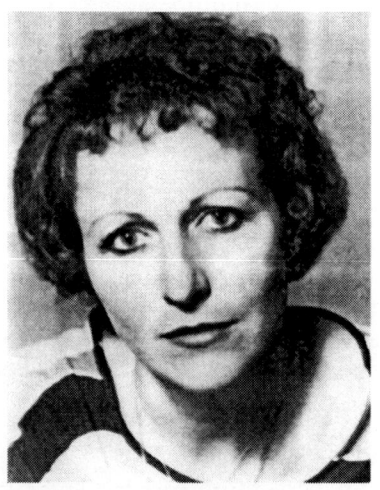

Sheila

On 28th – Meet Charles Ross, my old Guards actor friend from PARADA at the 5 star Llandrost Hotel. He says he is now an impresario in the West End! He married Liz Wallace, a beautiful Scot girl, who was in my set at RADA. He's barely changed and the thick curly blond hair is thinner with a grey tinge.

Rosa is back from Tibet. I start work at "La Lucciola", a lighting shop at Union centre. Nov 5th – Fireworks display at the McCabe's. B and Sue together in another room.11th – B comes home at 4am, says he's been meditating. Has been doing this a lot lately! Michael and Roger come over, later Heather . . . and tell her my suspicions. 16th – He finally tells me he loves Sue and they have been lovers for some time. Sun – Go to puja at the Karma Rigdol. Days and nights of weeping, eaten up with jealousy. Their relationship is an on/off affair, one minute she's called it off, then the big clinch and it starts up again. Thur 28th – Record "Kane" at AFS. She's in it. Afterwards I insist we meet to talk it over. She agrees that either they end it now or he goes away with her.

5th Dec – See Jane off at the station and give her a little ivory Buddha. She's going to UK with her boy friend, an Englishman called Roy. I didn't want her to go, but my friend Sybille made me see that it would be selfish to deny her the chance to go travelling overseas. P refused point blank to sign her passport application. In the end our Doctor, Paul Davis, signed it. Dec 7th – Audition at the Lindbergh's for "Pippin" and I sing the Granny's part, the reading goes well, Des seems agreeable, but Dawn doesn't like him being nice to me, I think she vetoed me. Bess Finney gets the part. B has resigned from the Chess club and the Karma Rigdol.

He hands in his resignation to AA Mutual Life, but Charles his boss won't hear of it. (B has sold so many policies he joined an elite sales group in New York).

Yvonne and I take Boo down to Joubert Park to see the Christmas lights. We are supposed to meet up with him, but he has a long conversation with a tramp and misses us.

Fri 27th – I find Sue's last love letter, and read B's diary. I realise how he has pulled the wool over my eyes so many times, all the 'meditating' into the small hours! I feel so humiliated. I've packed a bag with his clothes and as he comes in the door, I tell him he must go. He refuses . . . my guitar is on a hook on the wall nearby, so I hit him over the head with it, breaking it in half! Hell hath no fury like a woman scorned! He flat hands me on the side of my head and I pass out. The next day, I meet up with her husband Mike and give him any info he might need for the divorce.

In 1975 – Wed 1ˢᵗ January – Igor arrives very unexpectedly, he's now looking for a job. Thur – I go to Bernard Marks office, hoping to persuade him to give B a better deal. (They are partners in the photography studio). Bernard kisses me, there has always been a strong attraction between us, but people keep on coming into the office. I'm sorely tempted to pay B back in his own coin, but I then resist. Meet them all at lunchtime, try to persuade B to come back to the office and talk it over with Bernard. B judges me by his own behaviour, accuses me of 'screwing' Bernard. Igor tells him he's unfair, I was only trying to help. I go at 3pm to see Dr Teeger to prove there was no intercourse, but he says it's too late. (I find out later that B had had an affair with Irma in PE too). Yvonne and I collect Boo from the crèche.

When I get home he has packed his bags and hands me a letter in which he promises me he is leaving for good and they both leave. Fri 3ʳᵈ – Start temping at Fidelity Guards. Igor phones me to say B has gone to the Yemen! I assume he means that he's flown there, but in the evening, a letter is pushed under the door. He's going to <u>walk</u> to the Yemen . . . He must be mentally unbalanced. I take Boo to Yvonne at the Dorchester Hotel, so I can go and look for him. Eddie launches into a violent tirade against me, says my behaviour must have driven Bryan to this extreme. It seems he doesn't know about the weeks of deceit by my husband with Sue, a married woman with four children. Distraught, I rush out of the building determined to throw myself under the nearest car!

As I stand in the street trying to summon up enough courage, I remember my children, they don't deserve to lose their mother, because of a degenerate like Eddie, who hurls baseless accusations. I go back to my flat. Then Mike McCabe turns up. We try to make sense of the situation and decide to go and look for him together. When we open the door, Bryan is on the doorstep, unconscious. He's soaking wet, so we drag him inside and he's very heavy. Why is he wet, it hasn't been raining? His good leather jacket is ripped in several places and it looks like knife slashes. One shoe and one sock are missing? I smell his breath, he hasn't been drinking.

Jane age 18

Eventually he comes round, it seems he hitched a lift with three men. While he was asleep they dragged him out of the car and tried to drown him. His hands were held behind his back and they beat his ribs with rubber piping. God knows where they dumped him? He staggered home. At the hospital Emergency – an X-ray shows a cracked rib. I'm so grateful he's alive and have to forgive him for all the harm he's done to me. (Yet at the back of my mind, I wondered if he arranged this scenario so that I would take him back and he wouldn't have to carry out his mad plan)!

On Sat 11th January – The Saturn rocket explodes, but no harm seems to have been done to the planet. Now we (B) have decided to stay together and attempt to make a go of it, we drive around looking for a house to let. Went to see a semi in Southdale, JHB and has lovely big rooms, a big tree at the back and an ancient doll's house. They have a cockatiel, Boo loves his 'hat' feathers. We decided not to rent this house, as it's too far from work and in-laws. At night now she's terrified by a little piece of string in the bath and thinks it's an insect! Next day, we go for a walk in the Wilds with the Boyd's and take the pushchair, we picnic beside a waterfall. On the way home Zolie insists on riding in the pushchair (she's 2 years older than Boo), because she grazed her knee, then have supper with them. I've brought some filters and ground coffee. Vivian pours boiling water through the filter and it bursts open . . . We can't help laughing at the look on her face. Poor Boo has cramps in the night from the long walk and lie with her, rub the little legs until she falls asleep.

Bryan starts working for Old Mutual insurance. I change to Gerry and Vivian's new agency 'People'. He takes photos of me. Tues 28th – Talk to Raeford Daniel, critic of the Rand Daily Mail, about 'filling in', as a stringer and writing reviews of shows he can't attend. I show him some of my stories. Also meet Kate Lee and she wants info on show gossip for her page. Wed 5th February – Audition for 'The Tempest' for Brickhill Burke. Read and sing' Goddesses Iris and Ceres'. Tues 25th – The Dress rehearsal. Have been rehearsing for two weeks, Louis Burke has decided to cut my Goddesses, decides they want a dancer, not an actress. They cut out the other two actresses as well! Says they will pay for the two weeks. Anne Hamblin has just come back from overseas, so they use her instead. Mon March 10th – We have been sent comps for opening night, unwilling to go, but plain curiosity wins the day. Anne is lowered onto the stage on a flowered swing, she's too fat to walk! Much less dance! She sings our songs combined, which makes no sense? Hugh Rouse is Prospero, a bit pompous, as usual, but good casting. Ron Smerzak is brilliant as Caliban, Vic Melleney is good, George Jackson very camp.

Thu 13th – Record 'Three Part Invention' for Colin Fish. B has rejoined AA Mutual Life insurance – why does life keep repeating itself? See 'Major Barbara' with comps from Di Wilson, she's excellent. We go to see a film 'Phase 4' at a Drive-In (sit in your car and watch), a sci-fi film about giant ants. Boo is absolutely terrified, I want to go home, but Yvonne and B refuse and we have a row. I knew there would be nightmares after that. Wed 16th – Sue has phoned to say Mike has returned home and they have made love! (He was living with lovely Sandra Prinsloo in Pretoria). B is both pleased and hurt. I leave SA Breweries after 6 months of a temping assignment. Sue keeps on leaving messages on B's bleeper. He says he doesn't want to phone her back, she's becoming demanding, childlike. On Mon 28th – Record 'By Public Demand' for Ziona Bonell at AFS. On the news radio and TV – David Protter is staging a terrorist attack on the Israeli Embassy in Fox Street, JHB. At 5pm, General van den Bergh announces – they've captured Protter. B was there, of course, in his <u>spy</u> capacity.

On Sat 17th May – For some weeks now we have been rehearsing 'Streetcar Named Desire by Tennessee Williams, produced by James Roose Evans for Pieter Toerien. I play the part of Eunice, the nosy neighbour of Stella Kowalski, played by Gillian Garlick. Ann Rogers is Blanche, (I saw her in London when she replaced Julie Andrews in 'My Fair Lady'). Michael McGovern is Stanley (the part played by Marlon Brando in the film version). Michael has the reputation of being an aggressive person and suitable for that part! Anthony Fridjohn is Blanche's, very shy suitor.

Sat 1st June – Flying to Cape Town, the wheels won't come down, so have to change to another plane! Staying at the Diplomat Hotel, near the Foreshore and the Nico Malan Theatre in CT. B phones, Boo misses me and I miss her dreadfully too. We have a technical rehearsal, Ann is exhausted and has a migraine. We have to shorten the play. Tues 3rd – Opening night, play goes well. B has sent a bouquet, he phones to wish me luck, I ask to speak to Boo, but she's shy of the phone. <u>Miss You</u>

Whenever I see a little girl of three,
I think of my Boo and how I miss you.
I'm counting each day, 'till I hear you say 'Hey,
There's Mummy come home!' And I'm holding you warm.
I miss bath time and story time and singing our song.
Maybe next time, you'll come along?

Fri 6th – B says Boo is delighted with her colouring in book and T shirt with her name on it. Two shows tonight, Michael is having rows with Ann, awful atmosphere!

Sun 8th – Record "The Bringer of Bad News" for John Springett at SABC Rocklands.

Mon 9th – See Miss Brewer, a clairvoyant, in Greenpoint, CT. She reads palms, says I'm an old soul, (have had many previous lives). Says, I must beware of Coloureds . . . I don't think she means my washing! B phones, all worried, he's going back to photography, has written lots of letters to me with poems in them, says Sue is going to live with Heather, but Heather is my friend, what on earth is going on? I thought Sue and Mike were back together again . . . Tues 10th – Meet Brian Astbury at the Space theatre. We see a weird play there "Balls", two corpses speaking from their coffins, foul and lewd. Interview with Peter Curtis, who wants to know what I'm doing next year, hopeful . . . ?

Roger

Michael

B phones, says he has saved a young couple from some hoodlums and hurt his hand. Now has another new idea, starting "The Agency" for writers and actors. (Something new every time he phones!). Mon 16th – A Combi van takes us to PE (Port Elizabeth). Staying in the Summerstrand Hotel on the beach and very nice. Don helps me fix up my travelling iron. He's the ASM and very helpful. Tues 17th – Opening night at the Opera House and it's supposed to be haunted. Don is so sweet, bright dark eyes, long hair, slim, swims well and dives like an eel.

On Sun 22nd June – Staying at the Settlers Hotel in Grahamstown and sharing with Gillian, as we get on well with the same sense of humour. We open at the Rhodes Theatre. Have lunch with Gillian and Don McClennon, long talk about Buddhism and Athol Fugard. Next at the Guild Theatre in East London. We are staying in flats. Don and I are near to each other and we've grown very close . . . and become lovers. He's years younger than me, so there's no likelihood of a lasting relationship, but we are both lonely and in my case, betrayed. Between them, Bryan and Sue have made me feel so unattractive, wanting to creep into a hole and hide away. Don is so gentle and fey, it's magical to feel this way again.

Mon 7th July – Open at Lyric Theatre Durban. Staying at Golden Sands flats. Phoned Humphrey Gilbert and Bernie Jannion for any radio work. On Tuesday it's the Opening night. I tell Don the interlude is over and have decided to go back to B freely and happily, with no compulsion, Don agrees to end it, but we will always cherish a lovely experience.

Wed 9th – Meet Irma von Schoultz and go to the Art in the Park. Buy a paperweight for Don. B comes down, he's left Belinda with his mother and end up I telling him about Don. A **bad reaction!** How dare he object after all these months of lying!? Can't spend the night with him, go to Igor and Irma. Saturday night we have two shows, can hardly get through the play, my eyes are so swollen with tears. Mon 14th – B leaves, but turns back at Pietermaritzburg, too tired to go on. Another row, he leaves again.

Tues – I have an impromptu dinner at Gillian's flat. Next day a crowd of us have lunch at Greenacres. They all order fish and chips. It smells so delicious, at last I can break my vegetarian habit and eat fish for the first time in four years – have been yearning for protein! Gillian is very kind, supportive and keeps me going through this awful time.

Thur – Send off Roger's present, a sharks tooth set in silver on a silver chain, posted a card to Nan. Go to the film "Child's Play". Wed 23rd – Am told to learn the part of Blanche, I'm supposed to be her understudy, first I've heard of it! There has been another row between Ann and Mike, she's so temperamental they think she'll crack under the strain of acting with him. I know how she feels, gives her the wrong cues, as he does with me.

John Hayter and Maureen Adair come round after the show, we've acted in radio plays together (his wife used to work with me at Stuttafords, but they're now divorced).

Thur 24th – Party at Michael Tipper's. He works backstage at the Lyric. His girl friend Mae is a vast redhead lass from Lancashire with a dry sense of humour (they get married later, I thought he was gay)? I stay at the Ansonia Hotel in Pietermaritzburg. See "The Passenger" with Jack Nicholson and Maria Schneider (seen her in "Last Tango in Paris" with Marlon Brando). Phoned B at seven and eleven, no answer. Mon 28th – We open at Andre Huegenet Theatre in Hillbrow, JHB and get good reviews. There is tension between Ann and Mike, reaching to boiling point. It's wonderful to see Boo again. Heather tells me Sue and B has been sleeping together and with him in the Agency office. I spot a sharp paper knife in the CNA shop window, feeling murderous, why not and then walk up the hill and kill them both. After a while, I realise how ridiculous I am, he would overpower me.

Gillian is the one needing a shoulder to cry on now, Ken Leach has left her for Annaliesa Wieland, the little elfin Afrikaans actress. I understand too well how she feels. Fri 29th – It's my birthday, B and I have made up, Sue has left the Agency and they have both promised not to contact each other again. (I wonder how long that will last)? He says he will give me driving lessons and never does! Lots of publicity re Ann and Mike in the papers, last night he tried to strangle her with her silk scarf! She has bruises to prove it. On Saturday B comes to fetch me after the 2nd show. Mike has told the Stage Manager to raise the fire curtain, so he can show his friends round and somehow try to convince them he is innocent. Tony, (who is gay and very gentle) refuses, as it's very late. Mike punches him (he's a trained boxer). B sees this and hits Mike, we want to cheer, as the bully falls.

Sat 20th September – We see "Fortune and Men's Eyes" at the Nunnery Theatre near the University and a brilliant play, Danny Keogh, Ron Smerzack, Paul Slapolepsky and Bill Flynn are in it – the best actors in South Africa. Ron plays a raving queen. The tiny stage gives the chilling effect of a cell.

Afterwards we go to a party with them, Dai Bradley is there, he plays the young stable hand in Shaffer's "Equus" at the Huegenet Theatre.

Fri 17th October – B has become Company Manager for "The Happy Prince", at the Library Theatre, a dramatisation of Oscar Wilde's story, set to music. Rika Sennett plays the Bluebird, she sings and dances well, Graham Clarke is the Prince, Kathy Kahn a dancer. Sue McCabe is the Wardrobe Mistress! Once again they are colluding, I'm torn with jealousy, waiting outside the theatre, watching them take the huge St. Bernard out for a run in the interval each night, (he was part of the plot)! B denied anything was going on, but I was too used to the lies.

The rest of the diary for 1975 is missing!! I had finally had enough and instituted divorce proceedings with Angus (my lawyer). Moved into a house in St. Georges Street in Yeoville, JHB(owned by Mel Miller the comedian) sharing with Heather Graham. She had a small daughter Sasheen and I thought she and Boo would get on well. Heather was a very strict vegan and I had started eating meat again and discovered that living

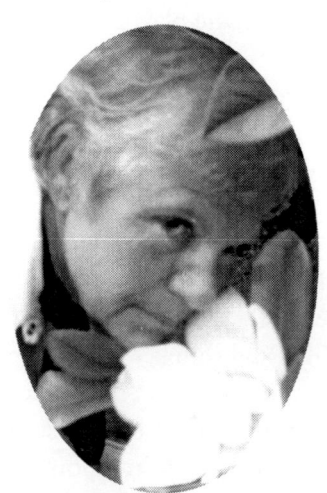

My sister Nan

with her was quite tricky. For a start she objected to my cat, Joleen, eating fish. She said it made the fridge smell . . . , so I covered up the tins with plastic, so they didn't smell! Then she said Joleen must learn to eat cream cheese . . . , no chance of that! Boo showed Sasheen how to use the potty, etc., but the nappies were forever being trailed around the house, still, that's what little toddlers do!

1976 February 21st – Boo's birthday party was not a success, Sasheen wanted to open all the presents, a tussle ensued and Heather stormed off. I tracked her down to the veggie restaurant in Hunter Street, Yeoville, JHB. We chatted and laughed it off, but she had a vile temper and as for being a Satsangi, a supposedly peaceful off – shoot of Hinduism, she should have learn't to control it. I started rehearsing "Madame de Sade", by Yukio Mishima, (who committed hari kari in public for political reasons). Janice Honeyman produced it for the Market Theatre company, Vivienne

31

Drummond was Madame de Montreuil, Jacqui Singer – Madame de Sade, Michele Maxwell, Vanessa Cooke, Sarah McNair and myself.

The Market was still in the process of changing into a Theatre. Bryan, I and many other actors had helped with the process, laying bricks and painting the walls. The Company put the play on at the Nunnery, which, though small, was adequate for our small cast. I played Charlotte, the housekeeper. The play opened to critical acclaim. Vivienne was a brilliant actress, as well as a concert pianist, but she was also a bag of nerves and a chain-smoking alcoholic . . . We were all a bit wary of her moods.

The evening of that day, I was in Court and my divorce became final, I was in my dressing room telling the others about it, when a stentorian bellow came from the stage, "Charlotte"! For the first time ever I was late for an entrance, unforgivable! I raced on babbling apologies, muttering about the Revolution! The baleful look said it all.

Radio work kept me busy during the day, playing Queen Illonya in Cameron McClure's series "Alexis of Karageorgia", with Nigel Kane playing my son. Otherwise was in three episodes of "The Dingleys". A TV series set in a bookshop in Pietermaritzburg. John Hussey played Mr Dingley, the owner, Vera Blacker his wife. Michael Irwin (who'd been my Hamlet), was my son, engaged to their daughter. Danie Smuts, a lovable Afrikaans actor, played my husband.

On the last night of the play, we needed somewhere to hold the after – party, I suggested our house, as the rooms were big enough, Heather agreed and seemed quite keen on the idea. I organise drinks and things to eat. After the show we all rock up to find Heather sitting in the middle of the cleared floor playing chess with a friend. She ignores us and I can't believe such rudeness – Barney Simon, Mannie Manim, the Directors of the Company and all the cast pretend it's quite normal, but leave fairly soon, the party is a complete flop. Of course, she and I have words the next day.

I've lost face, friend and a husband. I line up a few packets of Disprin with the full intention of ending my life. Decide to ring B on our pager asking him to meet me urgently for coffee. If he doesn't reply, I'll take them. He does reply and we meet, discover we still love each other. He was thoroughly disillusioned with Sue and having discovered that living with her was nothing like the idyllic existence he'd imagined, said she was a complete 'nutter'! We agreed to move into a flat together in Vickers, a block in Hillbrow, but did not marry again. I just missed him so much, in spite of the pain he had caused. Boo was so happy once we were together again.

On July 16th 1976 – Soweto school children rioted, Hector Pietersen, a thirteen year old was shot by the police. The kids didn't want to be taught in Afrikaans anymore. The atmosphere in Jo'burg became very tense and living in Hillbrow, the happy-go-lucky cosmopolitan Bohemian village of yore had changed. On New Years Eve, we no longer drove around watching the jollifications, whites found it wiser to stay at home instead.

On Sat, Jan 1st 1977 – Bryan finished writing "Maya" at midnight. It's a musical play about the life of Buddha. Maya was his mother and he's dedicated it to me. I'm designing costumes for it and have been to the library to research Hindu costumes from that period. Dave Wien is writing the music. Start temping at ICL, there are six switchboards and a very bitchy supervisor. Record a "Finger of Fate" at AFS. Thur 6th – My first talk on Women's Forum is broadcast. On Sun – go with Estelle Waron Nuron and the children to the Bunny Farm with Boo. Tues 11th – Phone Jack Mullen and have sent him my radio play, "The Vampire Strain". He says, I must look out for some good short stories to record for him.

Jane is on holiday here, she persuades me to have my ears pierced and we go to a jeweller in Braamfontein, he gives me a lollipop for being brave! We meet Gillian Garlick for lunch at the Zanzibar. On Wed 19th – Jane flies back to UK and I see her off, I wish she would stay here. On Thur Feb 3rd – Talk broadcast. Sat – Take Boo to a birthday party in Bedfordview, a palatial house and gardens. Amuses me that these rich wives discuss how they can save money on items like, for instance, soap powder, drive miles to find cheaper items, then buy a dozen packets . . . Fri 25th – Record "Home is the Sailor".

On Sun 27th Feb – Celebrate Boo's fifth birthday party, we have a magician, Mr Mills – a great success! She's now going to the little pre-school centre near Barnato Park.

On Fri 25th – B takes me to the Sam Haskins lecture. The grainy 35 mm. blow-ups (Cowboy Kate etc), have always been his inspiration. It's in a tent and we are deluged with rain, soaked to the skin. It's worth it, what a brilliant photographer, big and burly (like Bryan).

Roger pops in, we watch an episode of Dingleys with me in it, not too bad! On Fri April Ist – Supper with Estelle and Norrie, he dominates the conversation, very bombastic. Watch "Rich Man Poor Man". I move from 1110 to 206 Vickers. Fri 22nd April – See "Butley" by Simon Grey. Gillian Garlick and Mike McCabe are in it. (They fall in love during this production). Mon May 2nd – Collect script from Alan Nathanson. Record "The Foolish Gentlewoman" for Ziona Bonell at AFS. Sue is in it . . . Go with B to see Ian Reeves play Ice Hockey, he's very dashing! Sue leaves a message on my pager, says B has been following her again . . . Thur 5th – Left a copy of my play "Shouldn't We Complain" with Jack. Sat 7th – Audition at the Arena with Taubie Kushlick for a part in "Director of the Opera". She absolutely terrifies me! When I've sung my piece, she says sarcastically", "Are you an actress who sings, or a singer who acts . . ."? Am a bit nonplussed by this, "Um, er both." "Make up your mind"! She snarls!

Tues 10th – Boo starts at Hillbrow and Berea Nursery School for mornings only. Thur – Record "My Name is Kane" at AFS. Wed June Ist – Fitting at wardrobe for "The Watcher Sees the Game". Record "Finger of Fate" for Maggie at AFS. Thur – Shoot a Colgate Palmolive Advert. Tues 14th – Being made-up for my part in "George Fraser Collection", sitting next to Rex Garner, he comes on to me, just because we have to kiss in our scene, at the Station!?

On Fri June 24th – Heather's party in Fox Street, Turfontein, to hell & gone! A bit boring and then they started smoking pot, so we go – two taxis home. Sun 26th – See Actor's Performance of "Dirty Linen", awfully wordy play. Would hate to learn it! Mon 27th – (B's B'day). Interview with Arthur Levine for a job, as Medical Receptionist at the Florence Nightingale Nursing Home and get the job.

On Fri July 1st – Start at the Florence with lots of medical terms to learn in a hurry! A neat uniform with sideways white buttoned tops and slim navy trousers. Thank goodness it's on shifts, so I can still do radio and go to auditions, also can still collect Boo from nursery school. Days when I'm on late shift B can do it. The others are pleasant at work, also the Doctors. Mon 4th – day off and shoot Anadin advert. Have to look agonised with a blinding headache, then terribly happy and alert, playing tennis! Record 2 episodes of "The Pallisers". Record a short story. On Thur 7th – Showing of Bill Pullen's series "Jordan" with Pieter van Dissel, an attractive young Dutch actor. In this episode "Don't Shoot The Piano Player", I play the latter's widow. Mae comes over to watch.

Mon – Record several episodes of "The Pallisers" and another story for Jack Mullen. Thur 28th – Record 3 episodes of "The Man in the Mews" and a "Finger of Fate" for Maggie at AFS.

On Wed 10th Aug – Phone Angus at Videosound re meeting to discuss my idea for a TV series featuring young local heroes, eg. John Ross, for a children's programme.

Tues 16th – Record "The Day of the Tortoise" for Jack Mullen. Sun 21st Aug – Michael and Roger come over and bring a cassette to record Punch Soap Powder advert.

Wed 24th – Lunch with Angus, leave my synopsis with him. (This idea was later pinched by others and I got no credit for it)! Sat 27th – See "Kotch", good, but the name reminds me of Joleen (cat), sick throwing up a hairball!

Soon after starting work at the Florence, I was told to identify a body! The other receptionist said it was something they had all had to do – a kind of initiation. I led the Inspector from the Government Mortuary down to the basement. The morgue was in a cool room and not refrigerated, next to the kitchen. There was a terribly strong smell of disinfectant. Rows of bodies covered in sheets – with only labelled feet showing. I read the label on her big toe. This was a large white woman, two round patches of blood had come through from her nipples. She had drowned in the bath, then been revived. She was then discovered to be full of drugs. DOA (dead on arrival) at the nursing home. So, there had to be a post mortem. I fled and was very sick. Then had nightmares for several weeks! A mummified figure covered in bandages would stumble towards me . . . the bandages unwrapping to reveal a rotting corpse . . .

In Oct Thur 27th – Record last few episodes of "Man in the Mews", for Maggie and then have a little party to celebrate, (Tim Heale played the man). On Nov Fri 11th – Official opening of Belinda's new school, Roseneath. Arthur Hanna wants me to write 6 x 3 pieces on designing and making clothes for the Forces programme. Fri 23rd – Record my story "Nothing Ventured" for Jack Mullen. On Dec Mon 26th – The Dennon family visited us and a mad family, he's a journalist and she's a writer and designer. They live in absolute squalor in a little condemned house in Hillbrow near us. There is a curly-headed two year old boy and Chrysanthemum, a talented girl who's Boo's best friend at school.

On Fri 6th Jan 1978 – B photographs Nicole's wedding. I meet Sidney Duval there, the Mauritian drama critic. Wed Feb 1st – Record 6 talks on what to wear and when. I have results of pap smear, not so good! I must have a Hysterectomy, talk to Arthur Levine about having it at the Florence? Wed 15th March – Record 3 talks on Cosmetics and 3 about Zulu and Herero headdresses. Thur 20th April – Start shooting "The Gioconda Smile", a TV drama for Mike Leeston Smith. I play the Nurse. John Whitely and Di Wilson are in it.

On Thur 16th May – I'm admitted to Florence for the hyst.op. They give me a semi private room (on the house) – says Arthur and very good of him. Yvonne is looking after Boo. Two hour op with all women doctors, swapping recipes! Off work for 4 weeks.

Thur 3rd Aug – Roger comes over – it's his 18th birthday and he looks so much taller and handsome! Michael and he move into 908 Vickers on 16th. B on tour as Stage Manager for "Madame Butterfly".

On Fri Jan 26th 1979 – I fly to Cape Town to film the Extra for a soap powder advert and stay at the Holiday Inn. Have dinner at the La Perla restaurant and had delicious Lobster Thermidor, fly back on the Sunday.

Tues 30th – Record my stories "Make the Clouds Move for Me" and "The Dummy". Go to a Tribute to Breytie Breytonbach at the Market Theatre. At 75 he's a very respected actor from the old barn – storming days of SA theatre. Mon 19th Feb – Audition with Grey Hofmeyr for a part in "The Diggers", a TV series about the early gold mining days in Egoli. Sat

24th – Have Boo's 7th birthday party at Trish's. See show "Darby McGill & the Little People" and a great success.

On Thur 1st March – Sign lease for Velma Court in Claim Street, JHB. Mon 19th – Audition for "The Unvarnished Truth", Pieter Toerien's forthcoming production. Sat 24th – B & I go to the Artes Awards at the Civic. Thur 29th – I film an Old Mutual Insurance advert. Fri 30th – We moved to Velma Court. Wed 11th April – I run thru of the play. I leave the production, as was miss-cast, had to enter screaming hysterically, my voice wasn't up to it, still, never liked farce and so <u>ham</u>! This was terrible for my reputation, as an actress. The truth is, I'm exhausted from working at the Florence, looking after a small child and running around from pillar to post recording radio plays, constantly phoning for more work, plus my writing commitments! While Bryan is lording it at the Koffiehuis in the Carlton Hotel, with his table full of disciples, but earning virtually nothing!!

Roger

On Tues 24th April – Meet with Leslie Richfield to discuss the idea of joining the Monat – Hamilton Agency. Thur 26th – Party at Careways, the after school place where Boo goes to. Go to the opening night of "The Unvarnished Truth", a pretty dull evening, my replacement was not so hot (I could be biased)! Tues 8th May – Marie Bruin phoned, 5 calls for "The Diggers" in June. Yay! Am playing Marie van Tonder, the Inn Keeper's wife. Collect a script for the Bournville advert from Leslie Dektors. Interview with Percival Rubens re dubbing for Panorama films. I do a voice test on Jana Cilliers voice, (from Afrikaans to English). Thur 28th- – Record "Peal of Bells" for Sunday Theatre.

Fri 29th – B's Birthday party at Sinatra's in the Hyde Park Hotel, where we'll be putting on the Fashion Show. Dave Wein and his wife, the Yarons, Michael and Roger come, an enjoyable evening.

Tues July 3rd – Saw Roger off at Milner Park to go and do his Army Service. Very sad, he looks so thin and forlorn. Sun 8th – Roger turns up and they have rejected him, as they discovered he has a hernia, they will pay for him to have an op. Sat 14th – Boo's friend, Clinton, has a birthday party. (He is the son of one of the receptionists at the Florence). Boo is mad about him, a nice little boy. Tues 24th – The Fashion Show was a fiasco! Half the clothes are unfinished and come out in the wrong order – I announce one garment, but then another one appears! I try to carry it off with aplomb, but the last straw is, no shoes have turned up and they all have to wear bare feet or trainers! (There is a fire there a few days later, poetic justice)? On Fri 27th – Record "The Clerk's Story" for John Boulter.

Wed 1st August – 3 episodes of "You Tell the Tale". Sat 11th – "Diggers" shoot. Mon 20th – 2 episodes of "Poldark" with Nigel Kane. Tues 21st – Roger goes into the General Hospital for his hernia op and visit him after work, he's very sore! Wed visited him again with Boo and he's feeling better. Mon 27th – 1 episode "Poldark" at AFS. Dinner with Dave, discuss the music for "Maya". Thur 30th – "Digger's" shoot and it rains all day, so we just hang around. Sat 1st Sept. – Sven phones, next "Diggers" shoot is on for Sunday. Sarah agrees to relieve me then. Suddenly she refuses, for no reason. It would mean there would be no one on reception. I tried the other girls, no one could help me. I couldn't leave the place unstaffed! Had no means of letting Grey know, no phones, they were out in the bundu(sticks) . . . It was the key scene of the whole series and I was the vital witness to a crime. Grey was furious, I knew it was the end of my career, as far as he was concerned. On the Monday I give in my notice and what Sarah did was unforgivable. Arthur didn't want me to leave, but he could see I was determined.

On Wed 5th Sept – Rehearse scenes from "Hospital" all day at Milner Park Cardiac Hospital. Mon 12th – 2 episodes of "Poldark". Tues – Shoot scenes of "Hospital" and I play a clerk. Wed – record "Finger of Fate" at AFS. Sat 12th – Go to Belinda's school sports. B takes photos of various sports, including her running. Fri 28th – Record my story "The Videophone" for Jack. Mon 1st October – Phone Fempower, Medtemp, etc. for work. See John Hind at SABC and collect a copy of my play, "The Waiting Game". The subject was a hostage situation set in South Africa. They wanted me to make it Namibia, too politically sensitive here.

On Tues 9th Oct 1979 – 2 episodes "The Rendezvous. Sun 12th – Take Boo to Yeoville Swimming Pool and last Sunday took her boating on Zoo Lake, she got very sunburnt, so has to watch out and put on lots of cream. Wed 24th – Start working at the Brenthurst Clinic for Fempower temp agency for 9 months.

Mon 29th – Record 6 more talks for Arthur Hanna on the Bantu Nations – (Zulu, Tswana, Swazi, Sotho, Ndebele, Hottentots / Bushmen).

On Wed November 14th – record "Finger of Fate" at AFS. The receptionist Rosalie Waugh and I have become firm friends, she's a delightful person. Wed 19th – Go to the Brenthurst dance. I don't stay long, but just long enough to be sociable . . . Fri 21st – phone Mirella, she's now working as a PRO for Wits University Drama Department. We rehearse "Maya & Son" for two Sundays at Bryan's Studio in The Greys.

Wed 16th January 1980 – Roger is off again to the Army! Sun 3rd February – Nigel Kane Mirella, B & I go to a party at actress Christine Le Broque's flat. Tues 5th – Start a temp job at Johnston Rose's furniture shop in Braamfontein. A sour old couple, they watch my every move. Thur 6th March – Fransua Roos likes the music for "Maya". See a local TV play, "The Promentary", very good with Wendy Gilmore, Dale Cutts & Nic Ellenbogen.

On Fri 7th – Sandra Pringle, my niece, arrives from UK and the boys meet her. They find her a bit overbearing, I think she tries too hard. Sat 8th – We all go to the new LM fish restaurant. Meet up with Olga & Nigel Walker, great fun and end up at the Casablanca in Rockey Street, Yeoville. Mon 10th – Put Sandra on the train to Durban, she insists on going there on her own. Sun 23rd – I'm invited to the Preview of "The Black Hole" an exotic sci-fi film. Brilliant, everything is black, even the drinks, (liquorice). Mon 24th – I film a margarine advert at Leslie Dector Studio. Thur 27th – School breaks up and arrange for Yvonne's reliable maid Daphne to look after Boo during the holidays. Start dancing lessons with Wally Green in his Jeppe Street Studio. Very hard work, professional dancers go to him to keep fit! Fri 28th – See the Preview of "10" with Bo Dereck & Dudley Moore – very funny! Sat 29th – B takes Boo to Eastgate to see "Black Stallion".

Tues 1ˢᵗ April – Go to library to research further talks on Xhosa, Ovambo, Herero tribes.

Fri 18ᵗʰ – See "Kramer v Kramer" with Meryl Streep & Dustin Hoffman, very good, a weepy. Sat 19ᵗʰ – Dinner at Theo's with Wendy Gilmore, (B's oh – so elegant, thin Aussie client) Neville Dawson, the broadcaster, Nigel Kane and Theo's wife and we have a delicious roast pork. Fri 25ᵗʰ – Take Boo to Top Star Drive-In, see "Yanks", with Richard Gere. Sat 26ᵗʰ – Mirella's son Andrea's birthday and meet at the Alexander Theatre, then on to Act 1 for coffee. Sandra comes back from Cape Town.

On Sat 3ʳᵈ May – Have a perm at Nito's hairdressers – disastrous! They leave the solution on too long or else it's too strong, whatever the reason, when the inexperienced girl takes the curlers out of my scanty locks of hair and hair comes away too. Leaves my head covered in rows of wheat stooks . . . can't make too much fuss because Nito does it for free – B uses his salon for his models and Nito gets free publicity. I have to cover up with scarves for the next few weeks until it starts growing again. Wed 7ᵗʰ – "Finger of Fate". Tues 27ᵗʰ – Go to Ian Campbell Exposure studio for photos, take shoes and jewellery. They use one hand! Sandra must fly back today back to UK or her ticket expires, so we see her off. I hope she enjoyed her stay.

On Sat 14ᵗʰ June – phone Trish Smith, (she used to live next door to us at Vickers). Her daughter Mandy is a bad influence on Boo, she's a few years older and is always leading her into scrapes. The latest one involved them going off down to Joubert Park (home of tramps and near-do-wells), without telling me! Both begging for work as waitresses at the café (Boo is only 7). They earned tips and blew it all on ice cream! She came back after dark – I was frantic . . .

Mon 16ᵗʰ – Now known as Riot Day and always promises trouble of some sort, most whites try to stay at home. (It's the anniversary of the day, when police killed a lot of school children). I start temp work at Early Bird TV in Milner Park and difficult to get to by bus. It's a horrible place, dirty and badly-run. There's nowhere safe to put my handbag, so I stow it under the telephone table. I'm relieved at the switchboard by a sly dark girl. Bryan calls on me there with Tony Garland, a photographer friend. He wants money, a cheque, I refuse. He's always borrowing from me, but he contributes nothing to the household expenses. Since the divorce in 1976, he has only ever given me 3 months maintenance. When I come back from the half-hour lunch, the girl's boyfriend is lounging around, she tells me airily he's an ex-con! I need to go to the loo, but don't want to seem untrusting, so leave my handbag under the table. (Weeks later, I discover 2 cheques had been stolen out the back of my book, R300-00 rands was cashed at various time, the bank doesn't query an amount of up to R70-00). I never knew if it was B or the girl.

On Tues 17th – Record 3 talks on the Xhosas. Go to Joan Castleman's play, "Darker than Eden" at the huge Joubert Park Theatre. It's freezing cold. The play's not so hot either. First sight of Melanie Pilgrim one of Bud Castleman's students. He is an acolyte of B's and purports to teach drama, of which he knows zilch! Sun 22nd – B rehearses the Hairdresser's Fashion Show and leaves his lights and cameras there ready for the show the next day. The whole place burns down in the small hours, he loses everything. He isn't insured of course.

On Monday 23rd June 1980 – Phone Kenneth Hendel about work with the new Children's Theatre Tour. His lover and business partner, Colin Law, is much younger than him. Last time I met Colin he was an apprentice lighting man at the Alexander Theatre. He has a bad reputation among actors, as a manager, who doesn't pay his actors . . .

Sat 12th July – start rehearsing "Hansel & Gretel" at Colin's house. David Sherwood plays the Wicked Witch and he's very funny! Sat 9th August – Dress rehearsal. Yvonne brings Boo to see it, they seem to enjoy it. I play about 6 parts, entailing some quick changes!

Boo will be staying with her during the tour.

Sun 10th – Drive in the combi van to Durban. A cheerful trip and getting to know each other better. Colin had baked some cakes, which we all ate. We became euphoric, (later I found out they were full of pot). I sat next to Kevin, the driver, a charming young man with long curly brown hair and brown 'bedroom' eyes. Staying at the Hoffman Seaboard in West Street, Durban. Mon 11th – All go to the premiere of "Fame". Love it, come out of the cinema singing the infectious songs.

On Tues 12th – Lunch at the Tongaat Beach Hotel and have a wonderful curry lunch, (only R10 including wine). Afterwards we play around in the rock pools below the hotel. Colin has supplied us with more of his magic cake – I find myself doing somersaults, (at 48, something I would never dream of doing normally)!

Bill Smale is even funnier than I am, as he's even older and more unfit . . . we hold competitions, who can make the best shell and seaweed gardens. Later that night someone rings my room at the Hoffman Seaboard. He says he is a waiter at the Tongaat Hotel, his name is Johnny Naidoo and he has fallen in love with me! I smell a rat, the voice is familiar, but I play along. Creep along the corridor to David's room, sure enough he's busy doing his Indian waiter spiel . . . , so for the next few weeks there's a running gag about me and Johnny Naidoo!

We put on a few shows to Durban primary schools, sometimes in assembly halls, or theatres, even in very small class rooms, where we have to dispense with our sets and props, the children are wonderful audiences, hissing and booing the Wicked Witch and entering into the fun. I love doing it – we all get on so well together. Have become quite close to Kevin and ask him to a special dinner with candles, wine, incense, etc . . . he seems uneasy, says he likes me, but we can only be friends. I discover later that he is gay and brought along to pleasure Colin. Needless to say I feel a complete idiot.

The next week, I'm wandering along the beach front after an afternoon show and feeling at odds with the world, missing Boo . . . , I noticed a man is driving slowly along the road beside me. I ignore him, but he starts chatting me up. He's quite nice-looking, blond longish hair, good skin and a moustache. Says he's a Life Guard. I've seen a few of them on the beach and they are gorgeous! Never thought I'd meet one . . . and he's very persistent, parks his car and starts walking along with me. It gets a bit embarrassing, so I start answering him.

After all, why not? Bryan is in Jo'burg having affairs with a succession of women – he doesn't even pretend to be faithful anymore. This man call John, is married with two children, but says he and his wife are separated. He invites me to a party at a friend's house. Later escorts me back to Seaboard. Most of the company are in the lift. I pretend I don't know him, but he gets off at my floor and they probably noticed. In a way I'm glad, perhaps Kevin will hear of it and won't think of me as such a sad old bag. Next evening, he takes me out again – we creep over a wall in the dark, he lights a fire and cooks a braai (barbecue). We are close beside one of the Municipal pools, it's against the rules to be there, of course. It adds spice to think we might be caught. Go skinny dipping and he makes love to me in the cold water, amazing sensation!

(*My diary for the next few weeks is missing*). After the end of the tour, we were all paid, in spite of the dire warnings, so we were quite happy to sign up for the next one as this one had been such a success! The children made wonderful audiences. We went home and rehearsed "Pot Luck", which included Hansel and Gretel and various other fairy tales. It was virtually the same cast, except for Nic Collis, who was a much better cricketer than actor, he was very nice and we missed him.

One day I was walking near the 50 story Carlton Office Tower block, I'd had a row with Colin over some impossible costume changes he wanted me to make. A shifty looking African came up beside me and tried to steal the purse out of the shopping bag – cum – handbag I carried. Another one stood in front of me with his hands out ready to catch it, while a third crowded me from the back! Normally I'd have been terrified, but I was already in a flaming temper, rounded on them and shouted in my best Lady Bracknell voice "How dare you?! Go away!" This attracted the attention of passers-by and a security guard, the thieves ran away without their booty! I was considerably shaken up by this episode, but also quite proud of myself!

Colin didn't travel with us on the 2nd tour. I think Kenneth had got wind of the affair with Kevin and this time we had a different driver – France, who doubled up as the Stage Manager. A gay critic, John Mitchell, travelled with us to see what travelling in the bundu was like. Sunday October 5th – All meet up at Colin's house in Orange Grove, JHB. The combi is pretty old and frequently breaks down. Still, we manage to reach Swaziland and stay at the Swazi Inn in Mbabane. Mon 6th – Our first show is at an English School in rather a small classroom, but we have got used to adapting to small areas. The children love the show and mob us for autographs.

The afternoon venue is a nightmare! A huge covered-in Soccer Stadium. The echo from the noisy kids is so loud, we can't hear each other at all . . . they won't shut up, so we have to play the whole thing in mime! John Mitchell can't believe the conditions we have to work in. Thur 16th – Go on to Kingwilliamstown, then on to Grahamstown, where the 1820 Settlers started out. Fri 17th – Leave for Umtata, on the way we see a car with a coffin sticking out of the boot. The roads in the Transkei are terrible and various animals wander along or graze at the side of the road and it's worst at night too, of course. We stay at the Umtata Holiday Inn and later go down to the disco. A very dirty drunk African hits on me and I can't shake him off. Thank God, other members of the cast surround me and spirit me off before a scene erupts. Tues 21st – We have been working our way up the coast and are now back in Durban. All stay at our old haunt the Seaboard. Somewhere along this tour the old combi packs up and France has to hire another one and sign for it. Later Colin refused to pay for the hire (what a nasty piece of work)! Otherwise it was a fun tour and we all were paid in full.

After one show in the Transkei, we went back to the combi, full of the joys of spring . . . David, as the wicked witch had been booed satisfactorily and had been mobbed for his autograph. A whole lot of cleaners dressed in identical mob cap, aprons and long skirts were sweeping the parking lot. The whole cast started singing and dancing to the music of "Fame" – even dancing on the roof of the combi. The cleaners joined in with us, dancing and singing. The wonderful exuberance of Africa is symbolised for me in this joyful memory!

Thur 1st January 1981 – (*Bryan has left for good and is now living with Barbara Scoggings.*) Spend the day at Emmarentia Dam with Jane, Michael, Roger, Boo and Jade, her best friend and her mother . . . Jane drops a huge watermelon in a stream and it bursts open – what a mess! Anyway, we have a wonderful braai!

My Mother

Saturday 3ʳᵈ January 1981 – Go to the library to get out books about Voice Production, as am a bit rusty. Have agreed to teach Drama and Voice at Amanda Wildman's Drama School for teenagers and adults. Also directing "Huis Close" with a class.

In the evening, go with Jane and the boys to Le Chaim, a sort of underground cellar haunt in the Jewish Hotel. Hear good jazz and a brilliant singer. Sun 4ᵗʰ – B has been and packed up the rest of his stuff. Thur 22ⁿᵈ – A bill arrives at the flat, they want payment for the announcement of Bryan and Barbara's engagement! Phone her flat to speak to B, she answers, I slam the phone down, before I say something I would almost certainly regret.

Sunday February 1st – Michael and I go with Estelle and her new lover, Bill, to a Braai at the Kensington Club. (*Norrie had died of a CVA some months before. He had escorted me home after dining with them. When he got home he collapsed and died . . . I always felt guilty, somehow*). Mon 2ⁿᵈ – Bill and Estelle have had a row. He phones me, in a strange mood, stroppy, teasing . . . he says he wants to visit me tomorrow, asks if I have a double bed? I don't know how to react to this, am a bit frightened, try to humour him. He is a Texas oil man, looks a bit like Jason Robards. I suspect he could be violent. Tues 3ʳᵈ – If Bill really intends to visit me, I don't want to see him. Michael and Roger are living with me at the moment, Michael has tickets to go and see "Cold Stone Jug" at the Market Theatre. Am glad of a legitimate excuse to avoid Bill, I leave a note on the door pleading a prior engagement. The play was very good about Charles Herman Bosman's stay in prison, when accused of murder (he was acquitted). Wed 4ᵗʰ – I phone Estelle, she says how much she misses Norrie. No mention of Bill's call. She says they had a row and I decide not to mention his call to me, so as to avoid stirring the mix!

Bill has phoned twice. On my answering the second call he owns up. It was a cruel trick, they were testing my loyalty to Estelle . . . She was listening on the phone extension in their bedroom. It's just as well my instincts about him were right. Our friendship is over, I won't have any more to do with her. He was jealous of our closeness, I had warned her against letting him move in with her. He wants to dominate her completely with no room for any other friends. I'm not sorry, I was worried about Lenora's influence on Boo. I found out later that when she went over to play, they would secretly peer into Estelle's bedroom and watch the pair of them making love . . . , surely the adults could have been more discreet?! Fri 6th – Boo staying with me this weekend. On Sunday Jane moves in as well – what an amazing and wonderful thing – all my children staying with me under one roof! They are very supportive at this time – God knows I need it.

On Friday March 13th – My students at JAPTA put on a performance of "Huis Clos", not at all bad! Sun 15th – House warming braai at Jane's little rented semi in Yeoville. She's made it look very nice and doing it on a shoestring! The boys, Boo and her best friend Debbie Ash and Mike Keir. He gives

Michael

us a lift home. Tues 17th – Phoned Rosalie at AFS. She's getting divorced, her husband has been having an affair with his secretary (she's half his age), poor thing is quite distraught.

Thur 19th – Neil, Jane's erstwhile English boyfriend has unexpectedly appeared from UK. They had broken up before she left . . . So as not to seem churlish and not knowing what to do with Tony, her current South African boyfriend and has handed him over to me! Tony is a bit puzzled by this change of partners. I'm not complaining, he's very attractive, longish blond hair, moustache and beard, is a photographer in his forties. Fortunately we get on very well. Fri 27th – Get Boo's stuff ready for Scripture Union Camp. Daphne takes her to Roseneath to catch the bus and Bryan is there to see her off. In the evening go with Tony to see "Lennon" at the Chelsea, Jane and Neil come with us. Meet up with Colin Shamley, the folk singer, B and I knew in the Troubadour days, later meeting up again at the Buddhist Gompa. He asks us back to his flat, listen to Lenny Bruce recordings. Neil is a keen guitarist, mad about Oasis. Sat 28th – Boo comes back early from camp, vomiting and sick with tonsillitis.

Saturday 7th May – Spend a lovely weekend at the Drower – Copley's in Irene near Pretoria. They pick us up and Boo brings her friend Debbie. They ride on a pony twice, then swim in the pool. I meet Madge Wallace, a charming statuesque woman, who was a model and started one of the first and foremost model agencies in Jo'burg. Also Barbara's mother, a vague person, who is rumoured to be an alki . . . Barbara is very attractive and vivacious, (when B had to learn to ride as an extra in the TV series "The Settlers", she gave him quite a few lessons) . . . the next day Neil and Jane join us and take us all back home.

Wed 19th – See German Mary, the clairvoyant at the Carlton Centre. She's very good, has been extremely accurate in the past, she reads my Tarot cards and tells me one of my husbands is likely to die before long, he must watch his diet and life style . . . It must be Bryan, he's always said he would die when he was forty . . . , but how can I tell him? He's no longer with me. She says my mother is ill and might not get better, and I must try to visit my family in UK. I have some money saved up from a couple of film adverts and shall start to make plans and take Boo with me, show her how beautiful and historical England is and why I would never take on SA citizenship and lose my English passport.

Sunday 24th May – Bryan has Boo this weekend, Jane & Neil take me to the Lion Park for the day, the lions are somnolent, she says Neil nags her & not happy. Tues 26th – Dr Davis says Boo's tonsils are infected and makes an appointment for her to see Dr Wolfowitz, the specialist. Thur 28th – Lock is not working on our front door, Rocky the cat goes missing, Boo goes out and finds him, but I can't open the front door to let them in, the bolt is stuck. I phone Neil and he comes and fixes it. We go to Olga's flat, she seems quite normal today. (She's been acting strangely lately, has a kind of religious mania, hung up on Mother Mary and insists on saving presents to put in a kist for her)!

Saturday 13th June – Plans are afoot to fly to UK. Julian Richfield, my new agent from Monat Hamilton, brings over a cheque for R1,350-00. (Proceeds from film adverts). Bless his cotton socks! Go with Jane to a posh 2nd hand clothes shop in Craighall and buy an off-white leather coat, plus various gifts for the family in UK. Go to Olga's in the evening, see "The Dollmaker" with Jane Fonda. In one scene, her child is choking, she performs a tracheotomy on the child's throat – I could never do that. Sun 14th – Braai at Jane & Neil's, Jimmy Thompson, Mary Anne & Mike Keir. He's very cut up, his mother died earlier in the week.

Pop into Yvonne's flat and meet Kay (Cajik) Cazimierz. He insists on walking Boo & I back to the flat. He is Polish, unhappily married, has nice blue eyes and a lovely curly mouth. Reminds me of my old singing teacher (Ali Arletovich) in Durban. Wed 16th – Gives me a lift to the shoot of "Westgate" at the Chamber of Mines Hospital.

Thur 18th – Dancing at Wally Green's Studio. Coffee with Kay at the Café`d'Italie.

Wed 24th – Boo sees Dr Wolfowitz again, she's better (hooray)!

Thursday July 2nd – Olga and I are both looking for work and go to Drake Personnel and Michael Tipper, Mae's gay ex husband works there too. Mon 6th – start at Permanent Life in Kine Centre. Boo & I watch Carl Sagan's beautiful programme about the stars, "Cosmos". Thur 9th – it's end of school term. Collect traveller's cheques and air tickets to UK, unusually dear because of the Royal Wedding. Take Boo to see "The Adventures of Basher" with Jeremy Crutchley, at the Alex theatre, he's very good, she enjoys it.

Wed 15th – Fly to UK today. Recorded the last episode of "Freedom Trip" at AFS. Michael (my son) meets me back at the flat, takes us to the airport. Kay is there to see us off. Iberian Airlines, comfortable seats and the food is good. Boo is nervous at first, then settles down well and says she loves flying! Stop at Nairobi Airport, but not allowed off the plane, because it comes from South Africa and sanctions. Smooth flight, not much turbulence over the Sahara and next stop Madrid. We wanted a cup of Spanish tea, but they demanded pesetas and we only had Rands. My niece Catherine meets us at Heathrow, as she works there for Emirates Airlines.

She helps us with our baggage and then has to go back to her office. We were booked to stay at Cranley Gardens in Kensington, but they are full up, so we are transferred to the Henry V11 in Leinster Terrace, not so nice and the rooms very big and dark. London is overflowing with wedding tourists. Friday 17th – Catherine meets us in her car at Hatton Cross, we drive down to Nan's house in Broadstone, Dorset. We stop off for a drink at the Old Mill pub and sit out of doors in the sunshine, so Boo can be with us.

Sat 18th – Visit Jane's godmother Freda Evans at her lovely old house in Cranbourne, wander round her beautiful garden, then sip a sherry and reminisce about the days, when I was a pupil at St Nicholas School in Hexham, where her husband was Headmaster.

Sunday 19th – We are staying with Nan and Colin in their bungalow. They are very kind, but she is still her old bossy self, the "Army wife" and Colin is amiable. They listen to my stories of living in South Africa for while, as Boo plays with the little boy next door. They are keen to get back to watching a golf programme, so I subside. We all go to the Golf Club for a very nice lunch.

Monday 20th – Stay with Mummy at the Shaftsbury Rest Home near Bournemouth. We have to tip toe around . . . , poor Boo gets into trouble with the old ladies for playing with a tennis ball in the driveway, she's only nine after all and very quiet. I take her into Bournemouth by bus. We try to swim at the shingle beach, but it's cold and rainy. Mummy and I are not getting on very well, as I have to defend Boo from the prying residents. Tues 21st – Still raining, another row with Mama! Sat 25th – Colin comes to take us back to Broadstone. We have made up our row, but she says awful things about the rest of the family, especially Pat, who is ill with some mysterious ailment. Still, I may never see her again.

Jane and Neil

Sunday – Nan takes us to Corfe Castle, almost all in ruins, but most atmospheric – King John shut up Maud and her infant son there, starved them to death. There must be quite a few ghosts – Boo is enchanted, says she <u>loves </u>castles! We go on a boat, to the Isle of Purbeck. Mon 27th – Ferry ride round Poole Harbour, which Boo enjoys. She gets up to mischief with her little friend from next door, they throw ripe cherries at each other and a few of them hit the walls of Nan's caravan, which is parked in the garden. Of course, they have to clean it up! (*Jane and Neil married secretly at Port St John's today*). Tues 28th – Train from Poole via Southampton then back to Waterloo and back at Cranley Gardens. Boo isn't very well, so we watch the fireworks on the TV in our room. Eat in the restaurant in the Basement, a sort of franchise place, rather like Mike's Kitchen in Jo'burg. Boo has her first shrimp cocktail, adores it!

Wednesday 29th July 1981 – The Royal Wedding day! We had planned to queue in the Mall and cheer like mad, but Boo just isn't well enough, such a disappointment, we might as well have stayed in Jo'burg . . . So we watched it all on a rather small TV. Lady Di looks so fresh and lovely in her flouncy taffeta dress and Charles very good looking. They kiss on the balcony, quite restrained on his part, I thought. At least we hear the original broadcast, (as in SA they heard Colin Fish paraphrasing it). Watched them boarding the honeymoon train, drink a toast and share a small bottle of champagne.

In the afternoon she seems better, so we walk to Hyde Park. Watch the ducks on the Round Pond, see the statue of Peter Pan. Watch "The Sound of Music on TV" in the evening. Next day go round the Tower of London. This is more like it! She's very intrigued by the smallness of the suits of armour and the tiny winding steps in the Princes' Tower. I tell her the sad story of how the little princes were murdered and we shudder at the execution block, where Anne Boleyn was beheaded. The Crown Jewels are not available, being cleaned or something? On the way back, I spot our old pub, the Anglesey Arms, we sit outside and I have a draught beer like old times, when Peter and I were newlyweds. Strange the things that stay in one's memory . . . it was the haunt of darts playing taxi drivers, one had a most curious under arm delivery, but was very accurate. There were two lesbians, one was very good looking and fascinated me. They sported a pair of Afghan hounds, unusual breeds.

Friday 31st – Pack up and entrain at Charing Cross, en route for my sister Pat's house in Deal. Her husband, Mike Hill meets us. I thought they lived in Lord Nelson's house, but Mike tells us it belonged to his aide, Lieutenant Parker (he says Nelson never owned a house, which seems strange, where did his wife live)? Pat is cheerful, but almost totally bedridden. Her lovely blonde hair mostly grey now and she's only fifty two. We both cry and hug each other, after a wait of nineteen years. She says I look the same as ever! Bless her (I do use a brown rinse on my hair which helps)! She and Boo get on well together. Mike is an angel, does everything for her, thank goodness she has someone who is so devoted. Her daughters, Sally Montague-Brooks and sister Fran, her husband Nick Morgan and their red-haired baby, Rosie, are staying there as well. Fran looks like a plumpish Charlotte Rampling and very attractive. Sally is very tall with piercing blue eyes.

Boo and I are staying at a neighbour's house up the road. I'm in an attic with three old wooden dolls in Regency dress standing upright on a shelf. One has a Napoleonic uniform. They have fierce black eyes that stare at me. When I turn the light out, the curtainless windows allow a stream of moonlight to flare along the floor, sparking angry flashes from their eyes. I can't bear it and go to the other room to share Boo's narrow bed!

Saturday 1st August – We wander round Deal, a lovely old fishing port and go on a trip in the lifeboat, to Boo's delight. I have long chats with Pat – so much time to re-capture, it would take days. She stays upstairs in her room. I want to be with her, but she tires easily, and one has to be sociable . . . Mike is very amusing and a wonderful cook. We watch "The Lost World" and Alan Price in "Fundamental Frolics". Later, Sally comes back with us to the other house and helps me find another place for the creepy dolls . . . I sleep much better. Sun 2nd – All go for drinks to the "Zetland Arms", the children and I sit outside. Back to Pat and Mike's for delicious roast lamb and say goodbye to her, (for the last time). Take the train back to Charing Cross with Sally.

Mon 3rd – Phone various managements and theatrical agencies to sound out the possibilities of work, if I return to England for good. Not a very encouraging response . . . Take the ferry to Greenwich, hoping to visit the Observatory, but it's closed on Mondays! Go onto the Cutty Sark, what tiny little cabins. My old sweetheart, Dik, from Ridley Hall is running a restaurant. He's hardly changed, put on a little weight. His lover Susan is short, fat and helps run "Dik's". We have a very nice meal and Boo gets on well with her daughter Clare.

In the evening, Terry Bayler, my old boyfriend from RADA comes to the Cranley Gardens Hotel. We sit a little self – consciously in the lounge sipping a sherry. He's still a fine looking man. Slim, greying, but rather sad. He's a Roman Catholic and going through a painful divorce. Works as a stand-up comedian . . . , can't quite imagine it. Still, it's lovely to see him again.

51

Tues 4th – (School should start today). Visit Madame Tussaud's, she insists on going through the Chamber of Horrors, all those executed aristo's . . . awful, but she takes them in her stride, hope she doesn't have nightmares (she does)! On to the Planetarium – wonderful! She's enthralled . . . Walk to Regent's Park, it's so hot, we both lie on the grass and relax for a while. It's been a frenetic pace since we returned to London, trying to fit in as much as possible. We see the film "Airplane", very funny, especially when the two Buddhist monks in their orange robes relax by floating above their seats in the lotus position! Wed 5th – Boo slept badly of course, bad dreams . . . she's overwrought and homesick and we're both so hot, the hotel room is like an oven. Why did I bring so many warm clothes? Have a quiet morning and meet Jane's friend, Jill and her two daughters at Dino's in the Piccadilly Hotel. She offers to look after Boo so I can go out. Meet up with my old friend Gordon Price for a drink in Hampstead. He's balder and quite wizened, now with his fourth wife. He remembers working in an Insurance office with Jane, when she first arrived in UK.

Thursday 6th August – Go to Trafalgar Square to feed the pigeons, they perch all over us. On the way to see the Changing of the Guard, we meet a man with three monkeys, all dressed up in bright knitted jerseys and caps, I take a photo of her festooned with them! She is duly impressed by the smart uniforms and precision marching. We walk halfway round the National Portrait Gallery, but our feet are so sore, we have to rest. After lunch go to the matinee of "Evita", with Elaine Paige as Eva, and Jonathan Price as Peron at the Prince of Wales Theatre. Our seats are up in the Circle, so we have a bird's eye view of the soldiers dancing in formation. It was a bit above Boo's head, but I thought it was wonderful and have always been fascinated by Eva's story. "Don't Cry for Me Argentina", was very moving. Mummy phones to say Jane is married! Why not wait till we get back? Can't understand it.

Fri 7th – Fly from Heathrow and luckily we are not overweight. Boo loved watching the sun shining on the clouds. It's a good flight and she wasn't as nervous, as on the outward trip. Sat – Met at Jan Smuts Airport by a whole crowd – Yvonne, Kay, Jane, Neil and Michael. It's great to be back. Jane explains why they married, while I was away – to save expense and the usual furore . . . the real reason is, she's pregnant. Not a good augury for the future of the marriage . . . I don't like Neil very much, he's an intellectual snob. Still, I hide my feelings, but it's a bit sad. Wed 12th – Phone my new agent, Yvonne Lavine, all the radio producers and Vanessa Barling re replacing Ros Chapman, as Madame Salieri in Pieter Toerien's production of "Amadeus" by Peter Shaffer. It is a smash hit.

Sat 15th – Record a demo tape of accents and dialects for Studio 80. Mon 17th – Buy Obex slimming pills. While I was away, Michael and Roger looked in my wardrobe and found my pills. Cooked them in a psychedelic birthday cake for Roger's birthday . . . Apparently the whole kitchen was awash with coloured icing! Collect the script of "Amadeus". See Mary, the clairvoyant and later in the year, there will be a new man in my life, Pisces or Taurus, through work or somewhere near water? Thur 20th – Record three episodes of "The Bride of Enderby" for Mike McCabe. Sun 23rd – Audition for a new TV presenter at SABC. I have a mock-interview with Stephen Grenfell, as Charles Dickens, it was quite fun. He is very fat, mandarin-like. The auto cue was indistinct, difficult to read. Thur 27th – Record two episodes of The Bride. Start work at AFS while Rosalie is on leave.

Opening night – Richard Haines is magnificent, as Salieri, we all crowd in the wings during his big speech! As well as Madame S, I play all sorts of other characters, adding to the period atmosphere. After show party at Mairi Cameron's flat. David the lighting man sees me home.

Sunday 29th – My birthday and Boo gives me – 18 presents! Jane and Neil give a lovely writing case, Yvonne an iron. I take cake and Baby Chams to the theatre. Sun 30th – Go to the opening of a new restaurant, "Tiberius" with a group from the show.

September 1st – Start doing reception at AFS again, this time indefinitely. Mae and Allen come to my flat, give it an Indian themed make-over. Now I have a bed sitting room, Boo has a nice big bedroom and her old room is now the spare . . . Fri 2nd – Record 2 episodes of "Crisis Call" for Brian O'Shaughnessy at Gerrie van Wyk's Auckland Park Studio. Fri 4th – We have a night off and go to see "Pigs in Passion" at the Market Theatre. Helena Kriel and Kevin Smith in a highly sexual drama, he is a very attractive coloured actor.

Thur10th – Extraordinary Red Letter day – it <u>snows,</u> up to 4 inches, first time in living memory! Boo's school announce an unofficial holiday, the children, in their thin cotton uniforms throw snowballs, make snowmen, get soaking wet, Boo has a cold after this, but what fun they had! The traffic came to a stop, people throwing snowballs, (some with stones in them)! Everyone smiling and in disbelief. Fri 18th – Party at my place after the show, 20 people come, George Jackson, Bert Raphael and Michael Manoim the last to leave, Nick, Olga's boyfriend, passes out and has to sleep it off in the spare room. Thank goodness for Yvonne's baby sitting!

Wed 23rd – Record a "Finger of Fate". See Bryan and Barbara together at the studio, gives me quite a shock (last month's maintenance cheque never came). He has other things on his mind. It's a Benefit Night for Unmarried Mothers at the Alhambra and Pieter Toerien is really putting the boat out! There are drinks and snacks for the audience in the foyer.

Friday 2nd Oct – Record 2 episodes of "The Spoilers "by Bagley. We have a terrible rain storm, Ian Crewe lets me go home early.

Friday 9th – Yvonne and Boo have gone to Durban to celebrate B's engagement party, most of her relatives live there. Sat 10th – Paul Kruger's Day, all the shops are closed.

Sun 11th – Go over to Neil and Jane's for a braai. Boo is with me all day, call in at Mae's in the evening. Mon 12th – No show today, go to see "Adapt or Die" by Pieter Dirk Uys with Neil and Jane. See Richard Haines, Ralph Lawson, and Terry Norton (who plays Mozart's wife Constanza).

Friday 16th October – Jane phones to say our Michael has phoned his father, Peter Blandy from London, he enjoyed his sea trip aboard the Greek cargo ship and is fine. Such a relief to hear he's OK. I see Mary the clairvoyant again. She says I will meet an earth sign, Taurus or Capricorn, through work … will marry again and be successful in work and love. Michael has had problems, but will win through? Roger will be a success. Jane might have twins!

Mon 19th – We rehearse with Michael Atkinson in the part of Salieri. He's unsure of words and moves. Michelle Bestbier, who plays the singer and shares my dressing room, gives me a lift home and we pop in to have coffee with Terry Norton. Tues 20th – Opening performance with Michael, he's very good, only fluffs a little (but isn't a patch on Richard). Sat 24th – Jane,

Boo and I spend the afternoon with Gillian Garlick, (who is now married to Mike McCabe and very happy). Boo plays with Abigail (Ken Leach's daughter). Mirella goes to see our play with Ian Grey, the Drama Critic. They enjoy it and then we all go to Rumours and Etoile afterwards.

Sun 25th – Richard Haines's Farewell Party, as he's going to do a show in London. (Jane has taken Boo with her to the Magaliesburg Mountains). Everyone who is anyone is there! His house is most attractive, mostly pale greens and blues and shares it with Jimmy White. The latter has been on a carrot diet, his skin is bright orange! Yvonne Lavine's husband, Tony, gives me a lift home. Sat 31st – Bryan and Barbara marry in St. George's Church, Yeoville. Boo is a bridesmaid in pink and Ben Kruger, the best man.

Friday November 5th – After the show, Mirella and I go to Rumours. I bump into a man on the way to the bar. He apologises in Swahili and I reply likewise. We stare at each other . . . I invite him to join us. His name is David. He's a strange mixture of Turkish and Greek. Dark skinned with beautiful big dark long-lashed eyes, black curly hair, a body Michel Angelo would have loved to sculpt. He lived in Kenya recently, so the language comes naturally to him. He promises to come to our show. Thur 12th – David comes round after the show . . . I'd given up expecting to see him again. He has a profile like an Assyrian bas-relief, a proud nose and mouth nice teeth, gorgeous – and he's a Capricorn! Fri 13th – Do a photo shoot for Mike Robinson, a pre-menopause pill advert, have to pose in before and after attitudes, my tennis dress is a tight fit these days. After the show, we go to Rumours with David and Mandy Wildman. His surname is impossible to pronounce.

Saturday November 14th – David picks me up after the show and stays over . . . , he is the most incredible lover! So sensitive . . . , next day we go to a braai at Neil and Jane's. Pop in at his house in Jules Street, Malvern on the way home. A real bachelor's pad. He's built himself the most incredible bed up on stilts! Works at his Greek brother's plastics factory, nearby. I discover he's fourteen years younger than me. Well, Bryan was twelve younger and that worked (at least for seven years). The age difference doesn't seem to bother him. Fri 20th – Party at Noeleen Leslie's, David comes with me. Bryan and Barbara are there and so we leave early. Sun 29th – Roger comes back from the army, serving on the border, looking bronzed and much taller.

Monday December 7th – See Mary, tell her the prediction about meeting a Capricorn has come true. Says Jane will have a fair-haired boy in February, (he's born on March 3rd, near enough and fair headed). David is sensitive (true) and has a bad temper, no sign of that so far, he's incredibly laid-back. Fri 11th – Party at Georgina's model agency in Commissioner Street, JHB (she's my agent). All the models are there – Nelly is going overseas, another is having a breast implant and hear all the gossip! David has to go to his brother's (Taki) Xmas party and then picks me up afterwards. Sun 13th – We have a lovely long lie-in. David and I go to Neil and Jane's new rented house in Birnam, Athol Oaklands. I christen their small splash pool and Jane's best friend, Maureen Link is there with her mother, she's pregnant too – Jane is getting pretty big! When we get home, make love on the floor nearby the dimly lit Xmas tree lights.

Fri 18th – Left my keys in the flat, spend the night in David's house. Boo is staying with her father. Hear Roger is back from the Army for good, great news! Sat 19th – Get spare keys cut, David is moving in with me Boo and David get on well, he has a lovely humorous way with her, calls her "Muff", short for muffin, I suppose. Maybe it's a Turkish endearment? Go to Jane's and play with Boo in the pool. Roger is there. We leave early and go to Mirella's for dinner and bring presents and a bottle. Boo doesn't like her son Andrea very much, there's something a bit sly about him.

Thur 31st – 2 shows. A whole lot of us see the New Year in at my flat. Great noise outside, cars being rocked, bottles thrown down from the flats above Kotze Street, Hillbrow, quite a vicious feeling in the air – we always used to walk out and about on New Year's Eve, but not any more, it's too dangerous. We lean on the balcony and watch the fireworks . . . a very drunk African woman, almost naked, runs screaming up and down the road.

Monday January 4th 1982 – Boo auditions for a breakfast cereal and has to bounce on a trampoline . . . not quite her thing! I go to the Flymo audition at Videosound.

Fri 8th – After show drive to a party at the Drower – Copley's in Irene. She's outrageous as usual, flirting like mad. Her mother and father seem nice. Meet Eric Brummer, the State Pathologist, he's white-haired and very drunk. Peter dancing around after swimming clad only in a towel. Sun 10th – Horrifying news! Barbara's mother drowned in their pool, suicide is suspected . . . an eerie feeling, we were talking to her on Friday, she seemed perfectly happy, balanced. Family braai at Jane's, Dick and Liz Blandy with their child Bronwen, Roger, David and the Strangs.

Thur 14th – Terrible gales in UK, hundreds of oak trees blown down. Hope Michael, Nan and Colin are all right. Embarrassing mix-ups with complementary tickets, Roger and his girl friend are turned away by our stupid Stage Manager! Mon 18th – Boo is bilious after staying with B, spends the day with Yvonne. Go to Kathy and Steffan's for drinks. He is a bit-part actor in the show, (his father was a Director of AA Assurance, when B worked for them and did so well).

Wed 20th – Lunch with Rosalie, hear B has had a heart attack, is in ICU at the Gen. Send him a pot plant and a note to say I love him, I still do, in spite of everything . . . I think being married to a girl 12 years younger, plus eating unsuitable rich food and too much coffee and cigarettes has brought this on. He did have warnings of angina, when we were married, but I managed to persuade him to cut down on the things that harmed him. He's discharged a few days later.

Sat 23rd – Last performance of "Amadeus, quite sad, but there's no party.

Tues 26th – See a marvellous play at the Market Theatre," 1789", about the French Revolution. The audience is in the middle of the room and the actors perform all round the edges! It's theatre in the round, but inverted! Very stirring in a Brechtian style.

Fri 29th – David and I drive to Maduma Boma, a private Game Lodge near Hoedspruit. It's a lovely place, with its own private pool. Servants are mainly invisible, only come in the morning to make beds and wash-up and at dusk make up the braai. We've brought our own provisions. It's the day of George and Louisa's wedding, Boo is going with Jane & Neil. We can relax, play chess, skinny dip, see lots of wild life, beautiful birds and make love . . . We had booked this ages ago and sent our deposit, so I didn't want to lose it.

Tuesday February 9th – Ask at the OK bazaars shop for a house model job, they say I'm not fat enough – their main clothing market is aimed at plump women – Yay!

David and I have a long talk, he's not pulling his weight, especially financially . . . , he spends the night at his place, for a change. Wed 10th – Phone Nic Ellenbogen, will read my play when Mannie Manim has finished reading it. (The Waiting Game) I think? See "Krapp's Last Tape" at the Market, very good. Fri 12th – See Shelagh Holliday, she's rehearsing Viv Drummond's part in Ron Harwood's play "The Dresser", Sadly Viv is on the booze again. I see it in the evening, with her in the part. He based this play on his stint with Donald Wolfit at the Lyric, Hammersmith.

Thur 18th – Walking across Claim Street, on my way to work and I notice an outsize puppet on the pavement near a private nursing home. Going closer, see it's the body of an old woman. Can only tell the sex by the pitifully exposed pubic area, her nightdress is bunched up under her, she's almost completely bald except for a few long white wisps, her skin is yellow. Her skull is cracked, blood has run onto the pavement. I'm frozen with horror and pity – how did she land in the street like this, did she fall out of a window? Go into the home and ask reception if they know what is lying outside? They are unnaturally calm and say they will deal with it . . . the poor soul had cancer and was having chemotherapy. The women carry on with their office work, as if this was a normal occurrence, but they do thank me for letting them know. Dazed by this callousness, I back out. She's still lying there . . . passers – by pretend not to see her and sidle by the spot. I pull her clothes down to hide her sex. Go on to work, but am so distracted and I lose my purse somewhere.

Sat 20th – Boo's birthday party, Hire "Outland", bit above their heads but the kids seem to enjoy it. Tues March 2nd – Shoot the Empisal advert at Budget Rentacor House. At Jane's house, I lose one contact lens in the washbasin, they call a plumber! Eventually I find it all dried up on the side. The photographer says lenses makes the eyes look dull, so I take the other one out. Wed 3rd – Further shots at Panorama Studios. At 3 pm Jane's baby boy is born at the new General Hospital. He is Alistair Lloyd Routledge, six and a half lbs.

He's gorgeous, with bright eyes and fair hair. Jane has such narrow hips, she had have a caesarean. Sat 6th – Uniewinkels fashion show at Witbank. Allowed to visit Jane and baby at the Gen. Thur 11th – Helena Kriel is working at AFS for me. Audition with George Canes for "The Oaktree Gang", a children's programme. Fri 12th – show at Krugersdorp. The old tannies (ladies) love me, because I'm not skinny like the other models, I get a special round of applause!

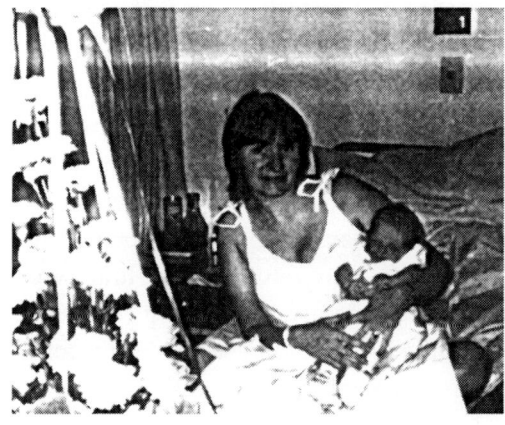

Jane with new born Alistair 1982

On Wednesday 31st March – Shoot the Wimpy advert. I play a spinsterish woman in a feathered veiled hat sitting in a Wimpy café. Two little boys are playing games with paper darts and one lodged in my hat, to my annoyance! That's it! Only paid R206, but it was fun to make. Thur 1st April – Roger gives me money to pay off Michael's debt. Hear he has moved to a hotel in London. Thur 16th – Boo in great pain from a swollen left ear and so take her to Dr Wolfowitz, he lances it. Ken Baker gives me comps to see him in "Inherit the Wind" at Wits Great Hall and go with Ann Courtneidge, an excellent show. Sat 17th – Boo feeling much better and is with B. David and I go to see "Madame Butterfly" at the Market. This is the original play, which was the base for the opera. Jeremy Crutchley plays Madame B and simply marvellous. Richard Haines directed it. Sun 18th – It's very cold and go to Jane's, Alistair is focussing well, eyes now a hazel colour, his hair still fair. Fri 23rd – Boo has check-up with Dr W.

Wed May 5th – Record 2 episodes of "You Tell the Tale" for Denis Folbigge. Maggie Heale gives us comps and take Boo to a matinee of the ballet "La Fille Mal Gardee". She is entranced and loves the amusing clog dance by the (male) Grandmother, clever ribbon swirling by village girls. Sun 9th – it's Mother's Day. Roger gives me a lovely hand-made lace tablecloth, Boo, a Miss Piggy figure for my printer's tray. Spend the day at Jane's. Alistair is really bonny now. Wed 16th – Sharpville Anniversary. Not too much trouble, just some stone throwing, trains delayed and police out in force in Soweto.

Thur 24th – Police go to the factory arrest David and take him to John Vorster Square. He's charged with illegal entry into South Africa! Apparently he had no passport, so borrowed his other brother Peter's passport to get in. How stupid! Peter lives in England. Fri 25th – Wait one and a half hours to see David. A very abrupt Afrikaans Warrant Officer treats me like I am a criminal. When I see him, he's in a dirty cell and has to talk to me through the bars . . . , he's very upset, of course, afraid I'll desert him, tell him I still love him though deploring his actions. He's worried about his possessions, house, car, cameras, etc . . . Sat 26th – Harold, David's friend from work, helps me pack up things from his house and take them to my flat. Sat 3rd June – Take David spare clothes and toiletries. I can only see him for five minutes. He says it's very cold and has no blanket. Gives me a loving letter written round the edges of his old diary, they refuse to give him paper. He thinks his brother might be able to organise bail, if he gives them a guarantee. Same awful treatment by the Warrant Officer, I feel sorry for all the other relatives of prisoners, waiting there.

On Sunday 1st August – All go to Dick Blandy's farm, Michael arrived from UK last Wednesday, will be back working with Barker McCormac his old firm. The children have a lovely time, ride on the old horse and play tennis. Their red setter is called Edward, such an un-doggy name!

On Wednesday 25th August – Go to the first night of "Romeo & Juliet" at the Market threatre with Drummond Marais and Sarah. It's raunchy, bawdy, but there's no poetry, romance. Juliet is Vanessa Cooke, disappointing, she's usually so good. Sat 28th – my 50th B'day Dinner at the Lichee Inn, Jane, Boo, Michael, Roger and David. Eat far too much, but great fun! Sun 29th – Braai at Jane's house in Birnam. George Kerr says his immortal line "how does it feel to be old"? Flummoxed I say, "I don't know, but I'll let you know when I am". Rose, one of the guests, offers to take my picture of Mary Queen of Scots to be framed in her shop.

Saturday September 4th – School Fete. Boo isn't well, has a cough, so stays with B and Barbara. I have promised to run the make-up stall and don't want to let them down. It's hot and hard work. Do about 50 Dracula and

David, Sheila, Jane, Belinda (Boo), Roger,
Michael and Yvonne at Lichee Inn

Frankenstein faces! (Make R75). Tues 7ᵗʰ – All day call for Dairy Maid Hostess ice cream advert. I'm the Hostess, looking glam in a Margaret Thatcherish way! At 21 Rockridge Road, Parktown. Beautiful old house. The main hall has been used for many posh adverts. Michelle Maxwell's brother Michael plays the cad (She is on tour in a tribute band to the Andrews Sisters).

Sun 19ᵗʰ – Go with Jane & Drummond to visit Michael and Roger, they've moved into a two-storied ivy clad house in Observatory. Meet their marvellous new dog, Fonz, he's an Alsatian/labrador with one lop-sided ear and a constant smile! A brilliant football player . . . They have a swimming pool, very dirty, though. Sat 25ᵗʰ – Party at Mae's for Brian and Allen, her two gay friends. Drummond turns up in freakish Art Deco make-up with his new man, Cecil Holloway, tall, dark (married with kids, like Drummond) both out of the closet, living together.

Monday 11ᵗʰ October – Start working at the "Incredible Machine" in Tony Factor's Centre. This machine takes photos and prints them out on T shirts or on plastic oblongs which have a mount, like a normal photo frame. Make some of Yvonne, Boo and myself.

Tues 12ᵗʰ – Record a theatre play," Shall We Join the Ladies"?

Sat 13th November – Roger's Fashion Show at Halfway House. He looks good on the catwalk – a natural! Friday December 3rd – David comes with me to Dublin Motors, we collect my very own little yellow Beatle! Cost R1600 and is roadworthy . . . now all I have to do is learn to drive it! Sat – first driving lesson with David at Sandton. Drummond is in Brickhill-Burke's "Mame", gives us comps. He's very good, but it's too long. On Sun 5th – 2nd driving lesson at Norwood Hyperama Parking area with Roger this time.

On Friday 10th December – Row with Sharon of the Incredible Machine and give me 3 weeks notice. Take Boo to the audition at SABC to play the part of Jane Bagby in the children's series "River Horse Lake". Collect the script of Simon Grey's "Man in a Sidecar". I have moved into Jane's house, while they are in Cape Town.

Saturday January 1st 1983 – Have sacked Dolly the servant and phoned Polly Street for another servant. Dolly was awful, dirty and she lied to me. When Olga started having an affair with Roger, she took some pearls from her mother and hid them under his mattress. (He was staying with me at the time, but knew nothing of her religious mania, she was a most attractive woman). Her mother went to the police and they came to the flat looking for them, while I was at work. Dolly told them the pearls were not there. Later I looked under his mattress, found them and gave them back to Mrs Caroto. The pearls actually belonged to her, but her mother had locked them away, because of her increasingly irrational behaviour. It's a peculiar story.

She went to Bloemfontein to do the make-up on a photo shoot. At her hotel she cut up the curtains and bedspreads in her room . . . , said she was making outfits for her and Jesus to wear at their wedding! When she came back, she told me she had found blood on her panties and said it was Jesus's Blood. Being Belinda's godmother, she sometimes took her out . . . , now I was really concerned, especially when she told me that the last time Olga had done so, she had said that if Boo held her hand and they stepped over the balcony of her 6th floor flat, Jesus would hold them both up in the air! (I recalled the rumour that her father had attacked her mother, when Olga was six and had been confined to Sterkfontein Asylum ever since)! I meet up with Olga, have to tell her never to contact me or my children ever again, I can't take the risk that she might involve her in some mad scheme. It's a horrible thing to have to do, she was my best friend for years!

Wed 19th January – 2nd rehearsal of "Man in a Sidecar", directed by Peter Goldsmid at Honeydew. It's a lovely thatched roof house done up to look very English, with fake roses attached to a lot of the local plants and authentic antique furniture inside. I play the baby Jonathan's nanny. Dorothy Ann Gould, Drummond Marais and Andre Jacobs share this house in a complex drama.

On Friday February 12th – have 5th driving lesson in Loveday Street. Bob went white when a big truck came barging out of a side street and would have hit us side on, but I managed to swerve just in time . . . , thought I did quite well, but he was quite shaken. He has a theory that the worst drivers he's had to teach have been, either – vegetarians, actors, writers or artists – not much hope for me then!

Sat 13th – Arthur Hall was on today's shoot, he's usually such a dear, he plays the doctor. Lynne's baby was in the scene and was supposed to cry a lot, Peter made him do it (maybe pinched him)? She became distraught, said they'd better record the crying now, as she wasn't going to let them do it again. The continuity girl became hysterical, chucked the sound 'cans' down and fled round to the back of the house. She's just had a miscarriage and subsequently divorced. We are all upset by this, but Arthur says "I can't concentrate with all this noise"! He's right of course, but what an insensitive remark . . .

TV Play
"Man in a Sidecar"
1983

with Director
Peter Goldsmid

Sun 14th – David and I have a serious talk. Since he was released (after his brother paid a guarantee), he has been very morose. He works all day at the factory, most of the night renovating his house, when I do see him he's like a zombie. I suggest he moves back into his house, so he can oversee the alcoholic handyman and his assistants . . . he sends most of his money to his mother in Turkey and the rest on his house, I can't afford to keep him. Without sexual attraction, we have very little in common. He plays a lot of squash, doesn't read much and there's the age difference.

Sat Feb 19th – Boo's 11th Birthday party and take her and her friends to see "The Devil and Max Devlin", have a tea party afterwards. Sun 27th – Braai at Jane's, George and David work on my car, timing, plugs, etc. Someone leaves a bag of cookies near the pool, I feel peckish and eat a couple . . . rather a strange taste. Half an hour later, I'm talking to Louisa and have the strangest feeling, it's as thought the top of my head has shifted sideways, as though a boiled egg has had the top sliced off, I'm perfectly normal otherwise, not giggly or talking nonsense. Feel incredibly sleepy and lie down on the sofa. Jane said she couldn't wake me up. I surface later in the evening without ill effects and shamefacedly admit I'd eaten the cookies. She says "Silly Mummy". Feel like her child.

Thursday March 10th – We shoot the last scene at the house in "Man in a Sidecar", Jonathan is so sweet, as he watches Andre blowing soap bubbles. Fri – Shoot another scene in a busy street, I talk to Dorothy Ann, but the background noise is so loud, Peter says we'll have to dub that scene. Sat 12th – It's the Wrap party, Boo staying with Helen Edgar. Drummond and Andre don't come, but in spite of that, we dance a lot and have a great time! Sun – Helen brings Boo back from Durban, she's very sunburnt from windsurfing. I go on the Dr Atkins Diet.

Mon 21st – Weigh myself and have lost 2 kgs! Read through at the Arena Theatre for "Night of the Iguana" by Tennessee Williams. Tues 22nd – Plot Act 1. Must get a record of German marching songs. I play Frau Fahrenkopf, Norman Coombes is my husband, Karin Jerg, a pretty Danish – born girl, my daughter, Frank Dankert is my son. The part of Maxine Faulks, the hotel manager, played by Annabel Linder. Eric Flynn is Shannon, the ex-priest (a part originally played by Richard Burton in the film). He's very attractive and charming. Sandra Duncan is the spinster travelling with her grandfather Anthony James, a famous poet. Fri 25th – Lovely birthday party for Karin at no 58 and only got home at 2am. Tues 29th – Another driving lesson. Jane phones, she's very upset with Neil, has found out he lied about his age, his birth date, he's only 29, she thought he was years older, I don't see that it's such a big deal, but she wants a divorce . . .

Friday April 1st – Boo with me today, and with Bryan for the rest of the holiday. We are staying at Jane's house, they are at Dick Blandy's farm in North Transvaal. Sat 2nd – Coffee with Mirella, her brief liaison with Chris, the Rhodesian Satsangi, has not softened her rock-hard personality, she's fed up with Nigel Kane, as usual. Letter from Mummy, her writing is barely readable, and her mind seems to wander halfway through writing a sentence. She's moving into a Rest Home in Broadstone, near Nan and Colin. At least she'll be looked after there. Sun 3rd – David arrives home after 11pm. I've told him to go back and live in his own house.

Wed 20th May – When I woke up this morning there was no sign of Rocky, our cat. When I get back from work I find him lying stiff behind Boo's bed. Froth on his mouth, might have had a stroke or a fit? He'd always been a peculiar cat – once he jumped on Jane's back and bit her on the neck for no reason. My girl said she thought he was sleeping . . . David and I drive around with him in a shoebox, find a recently dug spot near a park and bury him there. Boo doesn't know yet, she'll be terribly upset. Final Dress Rehearsal with an audience. Thur 21st – Open at Pretoria State Theatre, all goes off without a hitch, good audience. Sandy Duncan is wonderful! Thur 28th – I'm driving with David and someone bumps into my rear, I get whiplash. The man stops, he's been drinking, we exchange details. I go to the Rand Clinic for an XRay.

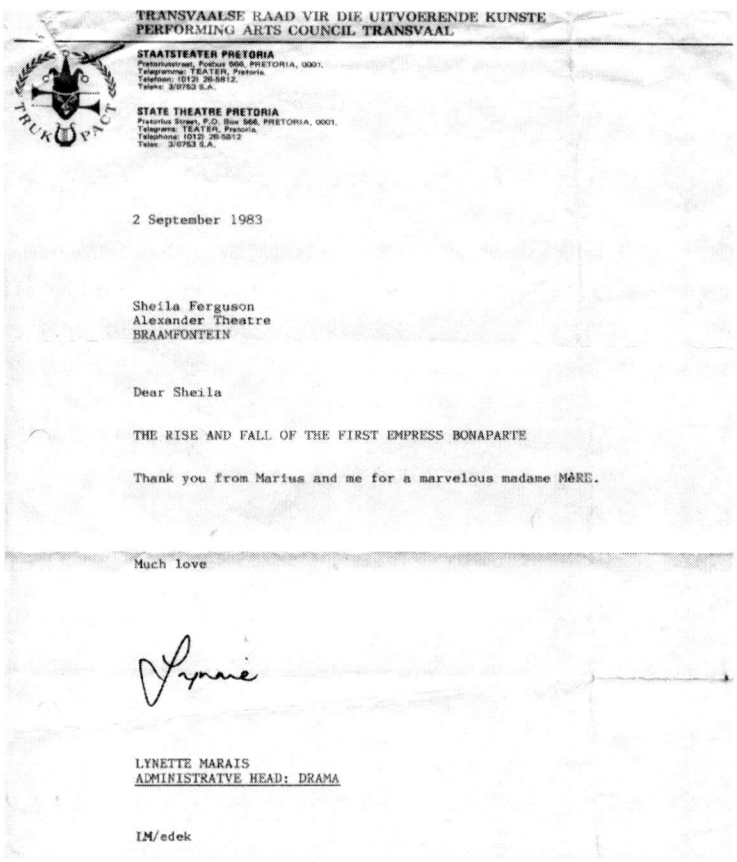

TRANSVAALSE RAAD VIR DIE UITVOERENDE KUNSTE
PERFORMING ARTS COUNCIL TRANSVAAL

STAATSTEATER PRETORIA
Pretoriusstraat, Posbus 566, PRETORIA, 0001.
Telegramme: TEATER, Pretoria.
Telefoon: (012) 28.5812.
Teleks: 3/0763 S.A.

STATE THEATRE PRETORIA
Pretorius Street, P.O. Box 566, PRETORIA, 0001.
Telegrams: TEATER, Pretoria.
Telephone: (012) 28-5812
Telex: 3/0763 S.A.

2 September 1983

Sheila Ferguson
Alexander Theatre
BRAAMFONTEIN

Dear Sheila

THE RISE AND FALL OF THE FIRST EMPRESS BONAPARTE

Thank you from Marius and me for a marvelous madame MÈRE.

Much love

[signature] Lynne

LYNETTE MARAIS
ADMINISTRATVE HEAD: DRAMA

LM/edek

Letter from Performing Arts

On Tuesday 24th May – Our accountant Dan Ermann comes over to collect our Income Tax forms. Have lunch with Coleen and Iain Winter-Smith. After the show we all go to Annabel Linder's tastefully furnished town house. Watch Laurence Olivier's film, "A Life", it's very good. She is an amusing person, our dressing rooms rock with laughter!

Wed 25th – Bryan is coming back from Los Angeles, (he took my play with him to show producers). Fri 27th – Theresa Iglich has been taking me to and from the shows, I give her a torch mirror. Go for drinks after the show at the Alex Bar, meet Ronnie Wallace and Brian Bailes. Sat 28th – Last night of Iguana – party at the Arena. I'm sad it's over, they were a nice crowd. Kevin Smith is there, he's now Karin's boyfriend.

Thursday 2nd June – Take Mae and Boo to see the "Amdram Overflow Show" by Pieter Dirk Uys and is very funny. David is late picking us up, another row. Fri 3rd – More arguments, told him to leave at the end of the month, or I'll go to my solicitor . . . Sat 4th – I take Boo ice skating. Carol Ann Kelleher visits, a very pretty girl, she was in Iguana with me. I sleep on the couch again, put a sheet over the window, shading the bright hall light, (David is still there, but I refuse to share the bed).

Sunday 11th – Trish Downing (who was in Amadeus) and Patrick Willis get married in a garden, lovely wedding. She looks radiant! We give her a set of white plates. (Same as the ones David has been flogging to the Africans in the market). I wear a shimmer Indian gauzy dress, a bit garish . . . meet tall dark musician Malcolm Munro, he's studying at Wits, a fascinating man.

Friday 24th – See Mary the clairvoyant. Says I will meet the right man next year, possibly in Cape Town. Michael will get a job later in the year, Roger will be OK eventually, David <u>will</u> leave, but not yet. I must persevere with the driving lessons.

Monday 27th – Start rehearsals for "The Rise and Fall of the First Empress Josephine" by Pieter Dirk Uys. Wed 29th – Audition at Videosound for I&J. Thur 30th – Mirella & I go to the first night of "Everyman", Bruce Millar is good and sings very well. Party afterwards and then go on to No. 58. Sit next to a party of lesbians – they assume Mirella and I are the same . . . , we play along & pretend to be gay.

Thursday July 22nd – Combi leaves for rehearsals at the State Theatre Pretoria. Fri 23rd – See "Comedy of Errors" at the Wits theatre with Drummond. Meet Malcolm Munro again. Wed 27th – Phone Kelly Girl for next week's temp job. Collect re-modelled fur coat from Derber's. A soft squirrel, which was David's mother's – now a short jacket.

The Final Dress Rehearsal with an audience. My costume is really lavish, crimson and purple, ermine-trimmed, with a train. Wear a curly black wig (it's a bit itchy) and a diamond tiara. It's based on the portrait of Napoleon's mother, 'Madame Mere', as she was known. Ron Smerzak is very good as Napoleon, even looks like him, but much taller and sexier! Jacqui Singer is excellent as Josephine. Thur 28th – Opening night. Appreciative audience and later a party in the Cellar, Pieter seems happy with our performance.

On Monday 8th August – Go to see 'Agnes of God' at the Andre Huegenet with Christine le Brocq (she's in the play with me). It's very good, though a bit melodramatic. Pauline Bailey is good as the Mother Superior, but Lena Ferugia is totally miscast, as the innocent Nun, she's far too worldly-wise. Wed 10th – dress rehearsal for the Jo'burg opening at the Alex Theatre. When I got home, there was a telegram from Nan. Mummy died in Poole Hospital on the 8th. Thur 11th – Opening night and I'm in a state of shock, dazed with grief . . . . , there's no point in trying to fly to UK, they've probably had the funeral already. Besides, I have no money and have no understudy. 'The show must go on', that awful cliché`. Jane, Neil, George and Louisa all come to the show, there is a party afterwards, but I go straight home. Thank God we made up our quarrel with Mum before I left UK. Fri 12th – I phone Nan, get the details of how it happened. She was in hospital having oxygen for her asthma and she just slipped away, I hope painlessly. At least she didn't have to suffer a long painful illness, as so many old people do.

Sat 13th – I get a good write-up in the Rand Daily Mail. Yvonne and Boo to see the play, they enjoyed it, Boo goes around afterwards collecting autographs from everyone. Mon 15th – Mummy is cremated today. Sun 21st – I'm in bed with a cold. David and I snuggle up, have made up again, he is very sweet, Boo loves him, he makes her laugh. She doesn't really remember my Mother, so feels no sense of loss. Mon 22nd – Malcolm phones, we have a long conversation. I like him very much, but my infatuation has simmered down, what is left is more lasting. He's incredibly dedicated to his music. Post a letter to Nan, enclosing a poem to my mother. Tues 23rd – Malcolm popped in after the show, David was waiting to take me home, was grumpy and wouldn't come with us for coffee. Malcolm says he wants to keep things platonic, which is fine by me.

Wed 24th – Post letter to Barclays in Broadstone with a signature for Indemnity, so Nan can draw Mummy's money. See "Die Spinner" with Gys de Villiers at the Alex theatre lunchtime show. A brilliant solo performance, he's a young draftee going to the border, trying to cope with the horrors of war. Sun 28th – Spend the day at Dick's farm with family and friends. I take a nice cake. Mon 29th – Record 3 episode of "Dick Francis". Tues

30th – General Pact audition with Lynette Marais and Marius Weyers. Have to do some Afrikaans, miss out a bit . . . , I suspect they found my Afrikaans hilarious, but were kind enough to hide it!

Friday September 2nd – Do a "Finger of Fate". Bump into Ben the Rabbi at the Claim St lights – I met him in Annabel's dressing room. He's a so-called New Wave Unorthodox rabbi and a very sexy man. We have a long talk over coffee at the Café` Wien. His Synagogue is in the huge house, where he also lives, apparently the congregation paid for it, seems a peculiar situation. Sat 3rd – Last night of the show and a bit sad. Mae and David join us at the after-party. Sun 4th – Boo and her friend Michelle swim at Jane's, it's sunny but the water is freezing! Alistair is getting so big and strong!

Monday 5th September – Supposed to work at Jeff Janks, but had a strong premonition not to go there. There have been so many robberies of shops and offices in that area of Orange Grove, in addition, no buses turned up, maybe there was a strike . . . Go to Kelly Girl to apologise to Tamara, (she's a tall skinny girl with a deep husky voice, not sure she is a woman, but later she marries a man, who owns shoe shops, so I was wrong). She sends me to another company. Fri 23rd – Record 1 episode of "Martin and Son" for Mike Silver.

Sun 25th – Go with Jane to Swartkops, a beautiful place near a strong flowing river. Alistair has a lovely time splashing with Boo and her friend Michelle.

Mon 26th – Work at Alcan. Have lunch with Maggie Heale in her 9th floor office at Wits. Delicious 'coq au vin'! Ask Walter at AFS if he would be interested in an adaptation of either a Dorothy Dunnett historical novel, or perhaps a Stephen Donaldson science fiction epic? Fri 30th – See Richard Haines in 'The Real Thing' – excellent!

Saturday 1st October – I draw R 170 to lend Roger, so he can buy material for his new clothing factory 'Alternative Apparel'. He makes me a nice denim jacket. Wed 19th – Help Pat Parr-Burman with the SARRAL music royalty returns at AFS. Walter wants me to go back to working there, but Kelly Girl won't release me. He's read my play 'Tokoloshe' and wants me to write a radio adaptation and he will submit it to Springbok.

Thur 20th – Phone Louis at Sonovision re writing an episode of 'Squad Cars'. He says no drugs, prostitutes, or friendships between members of the Police Force! Go to the library to get hold of old newspaper reports of court cases, view them on micro-fische and will get Colin Fish or Dave Gooden to vet them.

Sat 22nd – See 'Heat and Dust' with Mae. India in the old days of the Raj, brilliant!

It's Drummond's birthday party. The Theme is 'Putting On the Ritz'. I wear a black saucer-shaped Forties style velvet hat with a veil, a slim black wool lace dress, quite effective, sporting a long black and silver cigarette holder. Drummond is resplendent in blond wig, silver bow tie, white fur waistcoat, white shirt and see-through pants! Lit candles are stuck on rocks in the garden. He serves delicious beef stroganoff.

Tues 26th – Audition with Georgina for Pyotts Biscuits. Go to Rumours, meet Anthony Laxton, brother of guitarist Julian, a very attractive man, wearing a very funky white fringed leather jacket! Sat 29th – Champagne breakfast at Georgina's lovely home, everything is yellow and white. Family day at Boo's school, a Fancy Dress competition, she goes as a Gypsy. Sun 30th – Exhibition of Japanese Art at Joubert Park Gallery. Go with Mae, Stewart and Boo. Exquisite kimonos, origami, ikebana, but we were too late for the Tea Ceremony.

On Friday December 1st – Sonovision accept my script of 'Squad Cars'. I record the TV showing of 'Man In A Sidecar'. Fri 9th – At a party at Georgina's at lunchtime. Drink too much on an empty stomach. Take Boo to' Florian's' for supper in the evening. She asks me about Fergus's death. This had never been mentioned in front of her, but something I said must have made her curious, opening up the agonising memories.

(In Kenya in 1957, Peter and I had been invited to a dinner party at the house of our new manager. The ayah was off sick, we had no one to leave the children with, so we put Jane and Fergus to bed on a mattress, which fitted into the back of the Volkswagen beetle. She was 18 months old, he was 11 months. Peter had to park the car on a down ward slope, as his battery was flat. There was an extensive rockery round the house, we were out of earshot – Peter went out to check on them, but heard nothing, so assumed all was well.

Fergus suffocated, lodged head down in the cushions behind the seats. Jane was fast asleep. This horrific accident was the end of our marriage to all intents and purposes! Though we had to carry on for Jane's sake . . . , the full story is in my memoir 'Beyond White Mischief').

Sunday 11th – At Jane's all day. Move a heavy cupboard from Yvonne's to our flat. David arrives with two adorable kittens, Persian crosses, one is brownish tabby, the other grey. We call them Yin and Yang! He said, he had heard a strange squeaking at the back of his van, stopped to look in the engine, nothing wrong. Drove around some more, then chanced to look in the open back and in a corner found the kittens . . . , so we had to adopt them both, Boo was ecstatic, of course! Thur 15th – Receive my letter of appointment from Protea Labs. to do reception/switchboard. Fri 16th – Luncheon at Mike Silver's in Central Avenue. In the afternoon Reg Habib, the sound engineer and Susie Gehr, a charming young actress friend of mine get married. The reception is at the Courier Restaurant in Rosebank.

Sun18th – Mirella is engaged to Brian, a nineteen year old! Have been to see their flat (R400). Lunch with Mae and her sister Pat, she drinks a lot, but not this time, lovely lunch, turkey and all the trimmings, ice cream cake, and watch videos.

Sun 25th – With Jane and Neil and I make brandy butter. They give me a small brass Buddha and Boo and Ali get so many presents! Debbie Ash arrives with her spoilt child, Nicky. We took our new kittens with us and they were much admired and behaved very well.

Mon 26th – Party at Mae's in the evening, candles everywhere. We take smoked salmon and wine. Mae provided her delicious home made pate`, blue cheese, biscuits etc . . . , meet Glen, a Bryan look-alike, who talks up a storm. Also Anita, an elderly artist, slim and elegant with lovely white hair all dressed all in white. Boo has been staying in Pietermaritzburg for 4 days, she had a wonderful time, swimming on both the North and South Coasts. They all went with Roger, Debbie Ash and Nicky.

Sat 31ˢᵗ Dec – At Jane's and George and Louisa come over, plus Mae and Yvonne, it isn't as noisy as usual for New Year's, but some car rocking in Pretoria Street, Hillbrow.

Sunday January 1ˢᵗ 1984 – David has finally moved out, but we are still on friendly terms. One of the problems was that I couldn't afford him . . . , no maintenance was coming in, but I didn't have the heart to prosecute Bryan. I knew David was making money flogging the plates, plus the money he made working in the factory. He said he could live on R50 per month, to which I replied, "So could I, if I lived on a park bench"!

The last straw was when I engaged a new servant from Polly St Employment. She went looking in drawers and found R700, which he had hidden below his underwear. She took most of it, only leaving enough to deceive him . . . , he came back in the evening, found most of it gone and accused me of taking it! Reason prevailed, when next morning she failed to appear. He apologise, I said that I would never go into his personal belongings and he should put his money in the bank!

Sun 8ᵗʰ – David's birthday and we go with Jane to Buttons Riding School. Boo has a ride on a fat, slow pony called Applejack and has a wonderful time! Alistair paddles in the pool. In the evening we watch a very good programme on Margot Fonteyn. Trish and Patrick Willis come round for some vegetarian pot luck. Mon 9ᵗʰ – Someone phones, says his name is David, (not my David). He has an American accent . . . , I ask him where he knew me from. He says the wedding – like a fool I say, "Oh, it must be Susie's wedding".

I ask him, who gave him my phone number? Of course, he says Susie . . . , I can't remember if I gave it to her, haven't seen her for years. He's very amorous, says he likes my mouth. Eventually he persuades me to agree to meet him on Saturday morning at the Café̀ de Paris.

Sat 14ᵗʰ – Sit waiting in the Café̀ de Paris for an unknown American, wearing a red carnation! Feeling very foolish, after a while I begin to wonder if in fact it was an obscene call . . . , if so, I hate the idea that he knows my number. See "Gorky Park "at Mae's, William Hurt is very good. Sat 28ᵗʰ – Meet Kay, my old Polish friend for coffee at the Café. Elsie

Human comes to me for a Voice lesson, (she has a very guttural Afrikaans accent), which she is anxious to soften.

Monday February 13th – Kenneth Hendel phones, he is now a Senior SABC radio producer, he wants to record 'Tokoloshe', but needs me to put in more sound FX and suitable music at the beginning. Sat 18th – Boo's 12th Birthday party held at Bryan's new Studio. She and her friends see "Staying Alive" in the viewing theatre, very posh she says, her cake is shaped like the caterpillar in Alice in Wonderland!

Mon 20th – Watch Kenneth direct his play in D2 studio and have lunch with him in the Executive Dining Room. Roast beef and all the trimmings! We reminisce about the Children's Theatre tours, he laughs, when I tell him about my crush on the gay driver. He gives me a list of pointers for radio plays writing.

On Tuesday 21st February – Boo takes meringue mice with her to school for her class party. Have given her R50 of new clothes, R20 gift voucher from CNA, a duck mascot, and a steel coil that jumps down stairs! David is coming over to watch 'Dallas'.

Wed 22nd – Clive Buckley picks me up to go to the 'Speed Chess Tournament'. Meet a lot of the old crew, I knew four years ago. I'm soundly beaten and with one draw. Hans Kirsch gives me a lift home. He knew me, when I lived next door to him in Lake Success.

He used to come to my Fancy Dress parties – he's balding now, but still has a muscular body.

Sat 25th – David comes to watch TV. We hear an awful car crash outside – I expect him to rush down to see if he can help, but he says he doesn't want to get involved . . . , one thing about Bryan, he would always help people in trouble. I go down, but luckily no-one's badly injured. Sun 26th – Dull cloudy day, change the sitting room around, so I can type in comfort and have got to the final break-down for 'Tokoloshe'.

Thur March 1st – Record a 'Finger of Fate', talk to Walter about writing the series. Kerry Arnell is there, we get on well. Go and have lunch at the

'Three Sisters', a nice Greek restaurant in Hillbrow, I try moussaka for the first time. Fri 2nd – Take Boo and Michelle to see 'Brainstorm', with Natalie Wood, it's similar to Space Odyssey. Sat 3rd – Michelle stays over, they both go Ice Skating. Afterwards on to Jane's for Alistair's birthday party, he's given a tent . . . and is stung by a bee – big fuss!

Fri 9th – Out with Ronnie and his Chess Lebanese cohorts . . . , drinks at the Llandrost Hotel, then on to a Chinese Hawaian meal! Sat 10th – Prawns at Lisboa Antigua with Ronnie et al . . . Sun 11th – Manage to type some more pages, but then Boo & I go out with Ronnie and family to Alberto Chicago . . . Boo is in good form! Seem to have eaten the most exotic food lately . . . Since I met Ronnie at the Chess club! Sat 17th – See Mary, I will meet the man this year, a businessman, older than me, (not Ronnie). Sun 18th – Go with Jane & Neil to Dick Blandy's farm.

Thursday April 5th – Record a one hour play for Colin Fish. It's "Sonar", a weird ghostly play about whales by Capetonian actress Mollie Thompson, with Michael Richard. It's the best radio part, I have ever played, so moving. A mother with twin sons, one of them feels he is kin to the whales and is lured by their calls . . . Fri 20th – Steve comes over, he works with me at Protea. Sun 22nd – Ring Karin, go to see her in "Out of the Blue", a feminist play. She and gorgeous Kevin, (who now has dreadlocks), Carolyn Barkhuizen, and Gys de Villiers all come to tea. They share a Commune in Rosebank. We go to a midnight show of "Woodstock" in Hillbrow. Mon 23rd – Spend the day with Jane, give them Easter eggs. The last braai at Athol Oaklands, before they move to Weltevreden Road, Northcliff.

On Tuesday 24th April – See 'Torch Song Trilogy' at the Market theatre and go with Karin, Kevin and Carolyn. Danny Keogh and Wilson Dunster are very good, as the gay French couple, especially that they are both quite straight! I think the third act is too long though.

Fri 27th – Have my exit interview with Protea Labs in Sandton. Have had transport problems, there are no buses, the combi never waits even if one is only a couple of minutes late, then have to take a taxi . . . otherwise, I enjoyed working there. David gives me a lift to the airport to say goodbye to Jane and Alistair, they are going on holiday to UK.

Tuesday May 1st – Phone Ken Hendel re my play, he's sick. Thur 3rd – Phone Vic Mackeson re ditto, he hasn't read it yet, he's going on a course, ring him back in a month. Fri 8th – Take Boo to see 'Footloose 'with Kevin Bacon and it's great fun, brilliant dancing! Wed 9th – Last day at Protea and take cakes. Go for drinks with Bev, Tommy and Steve. Thu 10th – First day at Freight Services (usual job, reception /switchboard with some typing). Meet Peter Duck, the manager and Valda Lombard. Steve comes over in the evening. Sat 19th – Go out to Steve's commune, nice people dance a lot, super evening! Stay over with him. Sun 20th – Yvonne's birthday, give her a double fitted sheet. Michael has dislocated his shoulder, poor chap! Wed 23rd – Advertise my Beetle for sale in the Star newspaper. I'm a useless driver, didn't pass my licence and the only one's driving her are Roger and Michael, they are getting either speeding or parking fines . . . , which I have to pay, as it's in my name! Steve comes to dinner to meet Boo. I make lamb stew and trifle. He is married, but separated and misses his two children very much.

Friday June 1st – Opening night of 'Brother's of the Head', at the Arena, a very strange play about Siamese twins. Martin le Maitre plays both twins and Karin Jerg, the love interest. Excellent show, go with Steve and Boo. Sun 3rd – Braai at George and Louisa's. The whole crew there – Jane and Ali have returned from UK, Neil, Michael, Roger, Steve, Boo, Dick and Liz and their family. Mon 11th – Darryl Joseph, a coloured guy from Solar Force, where Roger worked, arranges to take the car and pay it off over 3 months.

Thur 21st – (Pat my sister dies, my darling kindred spirit. Thank God I went over and saw her there in '81 . . . she's only 54). Fri 22nd – Boo stays with Bryan. Steve comes over and takes me to a Ghosts and Monsters Party with Neil and Jane, I go as a witch, Steve as a highwaymen. I nearly choke on the CO_2 fumes, part of the spooky FX. When we get back, Mike Hill phones, tells me Pat died yesterday, she contracted 'flu, then developed pneumonia and died peacefully in her sleep. Sat 23rd – Mae visits in the evening, tries to comfort me. Sun 24th – Go to St Mary's Cathedral in the morning, to pray for Pat. Spend the rest of the day with Steve at his commune. When I get back home there is a 4th obscene call from 'David'. I tell him I've been to the police about his calls, put the phone down . . . , all I need on top of the anguish over Pat.

On Wednesday 18th July – Steve, Anne, John and I all go to the Mongolian Stir-Fry. It's all the rage, little restaurants springing up all over town. Sat 21st – Boo is with Bryan. Visit Steve's cousins, Ian and Dot in Bryanston. Meet his sister Mona. Sun 22nd – Begin to type 'Suspense' play. Bryan phones. He's lost his copy of 'The Dreamer', which was titled 'Maya'), wants to borrow my copy and send it to America. (I never get it back)! He tells me about his new literary agency with Ken Marshall. Always a new scheme!

Sun 29th – David comes over, takes his two small Persian carpets and a lamp. Steve and I have a lovely day at Ian and Dot's. Come back to find Ying had wee'd all over my double bed. Wash out all the bedding, dry it and put it back on. She does it again! I catch her in the act, so Yang is in the clear! Phone David and tell him to collect her toute-suite. He takes her to his brother's home, their kids will love her to bits.

Mon 30th – Boo is very upset that Ying has gone.

Monday August 5th – Take Boo and Michelle to see 'The Natural' with Robert Redford at Kine Centre. Have appointment with Jannie, Roger's old boss at Solar Force, to collect R450, a third of the amount he owes, pleads poverty and only gives me R100!!

Sat 11th – Go with Steve to the Wits 2 day Writer's Symposium. On Sunday, bump into Wim and Rosa, my old guru from the Tibetan gompa . . . , she has abjured Buddhism and gone back to her original beliefs, now a Roman Catholic! We have a delicious Elizabethan – style meal with people throwing bread at each other, gnawing on huge chops and swigging tankards of ale! Some have to pay forfeits for imaginary crimes . . . all very silly and indigestible! Did they really carry on like that? Go on to see 'McCready at the Wits Theatre with Frank Barrie doing a one-man show, excellent.

Wed 15th – Steve takes me out to dinner at Golden City, Chinese food. Afterwards we discuss our relationship. He feels he has too much stress, too many problems connected with his divorce and not being able to see the children often, so as to be able to concentrate on us. I'm very sad, as so fond of him.

Have an appointment with Mrs Quinn, Headmistress of Parktown Girls High, a very good school. Get Boo's certificates ready, her Book of Life, medical reports, etc. It goes well, I think. She has pink rabbitty eyes, a twitchy nose, quite pleasant though. We won't know the result until November. Sun 19th – Write 'He Who Laughs' all day – finish 2nd draft. Am very stiff, but have a good sense of achievement.

Mon 20th – Ring Vic M, 'Tokoloshe', is scheduled to be recorded in the New Year, Kenneth will re-write it in correct radio format. See Walter at AFS, show him 'He Who Laughs', it will be produced soon. He gives me a copy of 'Suspense'. Mon 27th – it's my 1st Aerobics session with Shane Smith in Fox Street. Great fun. Wed 29th – Take cakes to work. Valda Lombard has queued up early in the morning to get tickets for the Queen concert in Sun City, gives me two for my birthday, how wonderful! Boo is mad about Queen, she will be so excited!

Wed 29th Aug – (contd . . .) There's been another obscene call and Boo answered it. He said, "I want to f**k your p**y". She freaks out, phones me at work. She says there have been others, but she was too ashamed to tell me! As if it was her fault!? This is the last straw! I leave work early and go to the police and demand they change my phone number. It's done within 24 hours. Please God, he doesn't find out the new number . . . I'm convinced it's someone we know and how does he know her name, when she'll be at home? There's a dinner party in the evening at my flat, the last thing I feel like hosting, but Boo and have to put a brave face on it. Rose from the frame shop takes my Mary Queen of Scots picture to get a new frame. She gives me a lovely set of matching silver cruets. Michael, Roger, Jane, Neil and Alistair, George and Louisa, Yvonne and her bullfighter friend Mario are there and Boo, of course. We have chicken a la king.

Thur 30th – Record a 'Finger of Fate'. Boo goes off to stay with Bryan and Barbara for a few weeks or until the dust settles, so to speak. She's so upset about the call, doesn't want to stay in the flat on her own in case he comes round, he told her he knows where she lives . . . I wish I could find him and punish him somehow! The accent changes, wonder if it's an actor, or even if it is the one I was supposed to meet at the Café de Paris? If so, it's my stupid fault for falling for his act . . . am unwilling to give my number to anyone now, even my family. Fri 31ˢᵗ – Sign a contract for a year with Shane Smith, I really enjoy aerobics. Phone Jannie re the money he owes me for the car.

Saturday September 1ˢᵗ – Go with Mirella to see the band 'E'void' at the Chelsea. A good band, but it's very smoky and overcrowded. They wear freaky make-up and way out clothes, copy 'Kiss'. Sun 2ⁿᵈ – Finish re-write of half hour Suspence play, 'He who Laughs' based loosely on an experience Pat had in the Scottish Highlands, when she and a party of students were helping a farmer with the harvest. I had written to her to check details, but it upset her to remember it.

Mon 3ʳᵈ – There's an explosion in Loveday Street, a very built-up industrial area and it's some kind of mine. The political atmosphere is becoming increasingly violent. Take the script in to Walter. Go to Traffic Dept, transfer car into Jannie's name, then on to him give him the papers, he hands me two post-dated cheques and hope they don't bounce! Phew – at last!

Thur 6ᵗʰ – Another explosion, this time it's a limpet mine at the Supreme Court. No one is hurt, but the nearby roads are all cordoned off, I think the Nats are getting rattled.

Sat 8ᵗʰ – Have a spaghetti supper at Mirella's and then we go on to Rumours. Meet two raffish looking characters, Viktor and Leo in tight-fitting biker's leather's. Viktor has wild black hair and Dali-esque pointy moustaches and Leo is tall with blue bloodshot eyes. Leo gives me a lift home.

Wednesday September 12ᵗʰ – I phone Bev at Protea. She says Steve isn't involved with anyone, as far as she knows . . . I really miss him. She puts me through to him. He's living a hermit's life and has had a huge bill from the lawyers, poor chap! My Michael comes over to collect his driving summons. Rose brings my portrait and it looks marvellous, a dull gilt period frame and non-reflective glass. Fri 14ᵗʰ – a Farewell Cocktail Party for Neville Organ (the Silver Fox), our MD and a pity he's leaving, he's very dynamic.

Sat 15ᵗʰ – Boo is with me, she bakes a lovely chocolate cake! Sun 16ᵗʰ – We go Ten Pin Bowling at Ponte (a tall completely circular building) with Leo and his son. He's separated from his wife and afterwards have a nice meal at his flat, roast lamb. Mon 17ᵗʰ – Take Yang to be spayed. More summonses arrive for Roger, (my car, of course) I'll be so glad when it is finally in Jannie's name.

Tues 18th – James gives me a lift home from work, he's dark, thick-set, but very charming with a marvellous sense of humour. Collect Yang and she's fine. Thur 20th – I beat James in three games of chess! He gets amorous at the door, but I side-step him, Steve is coming to dinner. Fri 28th – Boo is with Bryan. Take Yang to have her stitch out. Work in the School Hall in the evening, sorting things out for the Fete`. Next day again do lots of scary make-ups and sell food. Sun 30th – A quiet day cutting out patterns. Boo and I go for a walk in Pieter Roos Park. When we get back a strange man calls, I think maybe it's Leo, but it isn't, slam the phone down quickly, there's the sound of a cockatiel chirping in the background, have become terrified that it's 'David' again!

Wednesday October 10th – Mirella, Andrea her son, Ross Coburn (James Coburn the film star's son) Boo and I drive to Sun City to see 'Queen'. Hardly any groups have dared to come out to South Africa, because of the boycotts, so this is a rare pleasure! Also we are so lucky, because Freddie Mercury has laryngitis and cancelled all the other shows except this one. (It must have been the onset of AIDS). I have awful 'flu, but can't bear to disappoint Boo, she is mad about Queen! Mirella and I swop our tickets with the children, so they get a good view, the rest of us stand in the pit . . . the volume of noise is horrendous, but it's a wonderful concert and Freddie is magnificent!

Mirella knows the band members, as she organised their gigs in Italy. Afterwards we go backstage and meet them, Roger May is so friendly. Freddie is incommunicado and is with the doctor. Boo gets all their autographs, she proudly wears her Queen T shirt!

Monday 29th – Bryan dies of a heart attack brought on by a violent mugging. He went to Sun City the week before, supposed to have won a lot of money. Came back to Jo'burg by bus and as he walked to his car he was set upon by three Blacks. One hit him on the back of his head with a cricket bat and he was pistol whipped by the other two. The next week he had a massive heart attack in the night. Barbara took him to the Gen. He had a second attack, they cut him open and tried to massage his heart, but it was useless.

He said to her, 'I hope I didn't let everyone down.' He was only forty. This is the second death of a family member this year, oh what a terrible year. Boo is coping wonderfully well, his mother distraught, her servant Daphne fainted clean away, when she heard the news.

Friday November 2nd – Bryan is privately cremated at Doves. His Memorial Service held at Barbara's family's house. A very good speech by Ben Kruger's father. Boo and Yvonne cry, I have cried myself out. Michael and Roger give us moral support. Lots of our friends there, Tony Garland, Julia, Bud Castleman and Joan. Barbara and her family all sit together in another room, giving me sour looks . . . I hear them saying, why was I there? My God ! Belinda is his only child, I'm her mother! Where else would I be?

Sun 4th – Cathy Pringle, (Nan's daughter, arrives at Jan Smuts. David gives us a lift home. She's very nice, much blonder than before, but I recognised her jolly round face!

Steve joins us, we have a super braai at George and Louisa's. Sun 11th – Viktor phones, Boo and I go out with him and his daughter to the Tivoli Pizzeria in Rosebank. Back to his house in Honeydew, where the children swim in a big rainwater tank.

Tues 13th – Lunch at Wits with Maggie, discuss my adapting 'Humbug' (based on 'Scrooge') for AFS. Wed 14th – Try to find Boo's Insurance Policy from her dad, nowhere to be found, then discover it had lapsed anyway . . .

Sat 17th – Skating cancelled, Boo not up to it, she stays with Yvonne. I go with Drummond to the IDEM Writer's Awards at the Johannesburg Country Club, lovely lawns. Meet lots of my old acting and writing friends. Mirella's fiancée takes me to the Piccadilly Cinema in Yeoville to see 'Siddhartha', beautifully directed film about Buddha's early life by Conrad Took.

It remands me of the good old days, when Bryan and I were still madly in love – at least I was and would rather remember him that way. It's so hard to believe he's really gone . . . , what happened to him is typical of the increased violence in this country. Many of our friends have been attacked lately, especially in Hillbrow. There have been increasingly violent riots.

Belinda was chased by some Africans on her way to school. Now she has to be escorted by an adult. Mirella wants to go back to Italy for good.

Tues 20th – At last some good news, a letter from Parktown Girls High. Boo has been accepted, one of only two girls from Roseneath School! It's a real feather in her cap! We dance a jig for joy! Steve phones, he is a free man at last. Divorce is final!

Fri 23rd – Give Michael an antique map he wants . . . Jane is in Somerset West, will get her present at Christmas, when we go to stay with them. Sat – spend most of the day with Steve.

Saturday December 1st – Freight Services Dance at Tiffany's in Braamfontein. Steve wears a tuxedo, I'm in a halter-necked black silk jersey dress and it's enjoyable. Mon 3rd – Boo sees Dr Sevel, she's just come back from Veldt School, hurt her back falling from a rope suspended over a pond, says it's just bruised. Wed 5th – Roseneath breaks up, she's sorry to have to say goodbye to her friends. Tues 11th – Lunch out with all the girls from the office. Phone Erica Rogers re an audition for a film advert, she's just started a new agency.

Friday 21st December – David, Boo and I set off for Cape Town in his car. We leave at 5 pm, so he has to take pills to keep him awake and he drives non-stop. At Stellenbosch, we argue about the best way to Jane's house in Somerset West and eventually find it. A lovely house with a large garden and many fruit trees. No wonder she loves it here, is plumper, which is good and Ali is well and becoming a 'holy terror'! Sat 22nd – Neil says he loves Cape Town and will show me round – I only know the streets near the Nico Malan Theatre and the Foreshore. I listen to the recording of 'Humbug', the play I adapted from Dickens for Maggie. David goes to the bottle store for something and doesn't come back for three days! Sun 23rd – We drive round the Signal Hill on the side of the Table Mountain. What gorgeous scenery! Go for a long walk in the Nature Reserve, marvellous proteas, heather, Namaqualand daisies of yellow and orange, succulent vagies(sun worshipping succulent plants that open in the day) in pinky colours.

Mon 24th – Buy last minute Christmas presents, paddle at Gordon's Bay in the Strand, but it's very windy, Al is naughty! Watch a video in the evening, 'Rollerball'.

Tues 25th – Wonder of wonders, David pitches up. Said he met a friend and went to stay with him, never thought of letting us know! We have a lovely dinner with all the trimmings! Al very excited by his presents . . . I give Boo a Swatch watch, (all the rage then). Give Jane a pressure cooker, an ornamental condiment set and a soap set.

Wed 26th – Go to Paarl Rock, it's huge and smooth. Have to hang onto a chain to climb up it, slide down on my buttom, Boo and David manage it all right. Have a cold lunch at a picnic spot nearby, Al makes friends with the other kids, he's a gregarious little chap.

Thur 27th – Go into Cape Town with Neil. Shop at the Flea Market, buy hair clips, a pisces pendant for Boo. Walk through the Gardens, no sign of the friendly little grey squirrels that used to come right up to you. Have lunch at Forrester's Arms, outside in the sun, it's a bit like the Sunnyside Hotel in Jo'burg. Sat 29th – Michael and his friends pitch up, leave their washing for Jane to do, then slope off. Boo and I go up Table Mountain, wait three hours to get on the cable car. Worth it though, what a splendid view! Sun 30th – It's very hot. Have a braai at a lovely picnic spot near the banks of a river below the Mountain. Mon 31st – David has gone missing again . . . Jane, Neil and I toast the New Year with champagne.

Tuesday 1st January 1985 – Resolve to lose weight – as usual (gave up smoking completely in '81). Have a braai at a spot near Somerset West and we swim in a tidal pool, along with jellyfish and crabs, look for pretty shells with Boo and Al. She uses a snorkel for the first time. Wed 2nd – Go to the Strand, lovely waves, we surf (more or less)! Al wades in quite deep. Half an hour trip round the Hout Bay to past the Seal Island and what a disgusting smell! They are very tame and there are so many of them they keep slithering off the Island . . . Boo is in ecstasies though! Then on to the 'World of Birds' and all so tame, flying free in a large enclosure, parrots in every tree, plus monkeys and squirrels. Fri 4th – It's cool at last, Roger turns up and been hitching for two days. We have to leave, unfortunately. David turns up, in a bad mood. Set off at midnight, arrive home at 3am. He drops us outside our block. Had to get the watchman to help us with our baggage, as not a good place to be alone in the street at that time!

Tuesday 8th January – Want to move out of Velma Court, Claim Street, as far too much traffic these days. Look at various flats, book one at Helderberg, but Boo says she has too many enemies in that block, so had to cancel it?! We finish marking her new uniforms.

Wed 9th – She starts at Parktown Girls and I escort her to the bus at Majestic Towers. Take two Summonses for the car to Jannie at Inner Sleeve, his driver has been getting the fines, but I get the Summonses and have to go to Court to explain . . . Thur 10th – Boo has blisters from the new school shoes. Last free day of my holiday and sunbathe in the Park.

Fri 18th – Dinner with Steve at Gatrille & Son. Superb cooking, I have pan-fried trout, he has ham, veal & venison pie. Sat 19th – Boo is with the Yugoslav caretaker's children, Beba and Gouron at their house. Visit Inge at her flat in Reynard Hall. She's Swedish, intelligent, I like her very much. Sun 20th – Walk with Boo to Mirella's flat in Yeoville, sit and chat, she cooks beef olives for lunch. Wed 23rd – Inge comes to supper.

Sun 27th – Script Writers Association Meeting in Parkwood. Tues 29th – Inge is knocked down by a car in her lunch hour. Mae's back has given in (she's terribly overweight), now Steve's car has broken down! Wed 30th – Freight services Social Evening. Steve says he's coming over at 8, I asked him not to . . . knowing the Social might run on . . . Clive, who works with me, gives me a lift home, but he's very drunk. I manage to get rid of him, but then Steve arrives almost immediately and Clive comes back and starts banging on my door . . . uh oh – Steve is not impressed!

Friday 1st February – Belated Christmas party at Georgina's. Sat 2nd – Boo goes skating.

Fri 15th – Clive gives me a lift home with Newton Mdombo, one of Manica's clients from Lusaka. He's staying at the Diplomat Hotel, he's not impressed, says it's a bit 'crummy'. Boo goes to her first Disco Dance at Parktown Boys High, comes back by 11.30. (A relief)! Sat 16th – She's skating and I fetch her (it's in a sleazy part of town), there's no bus, we walk home from Carlton Centre, quite a fair walk.

Sun 17th – Walk to Yeoville Swimming Pool, bump into Clive and his small son. Go on to Mirella's house, meet Fernanda, an extrovert South American actress.

Sun 24th – Boo with Yvonne for the day. Mirella picks me up, go to lunch at the Clay Oven. Fernanda and Juan Palomo, a Chilian guitar player are singing there.

Later Mirella phones up, distraught, her live-in lover, Brian has bashed her up – it's the middle of the night, I get a taxi and go there, thank goodness Boo stayed over with Yvonne. Brian is out of his skull on drugs and booze, she's horribly battered and bruised!

Juan is still therand gives me a lift home. I hope that is the last we will see of Brian!

Wed 27th – Mr Patton's Farewell party ands we give him a clock.

Thursday March 14th – My stove blows up, a great blue flame – the whole building is plunged into darkness! Sun 17th – Go to Atlas Air to play Action Cricket. Meet Clive's wife Wendy and kids. Yay! My Michael has a new job, Import/Export, R3,000 pm and a company car! Great!

Sunday March 24th – Saftu (Actors) Meeting. Talk to Michael Brunner, Arthur Hall, Theresa Iglich (who was with me in Night of the Iguana). There's a cheese and wine party promoting an Insurance Scheme for Actors. Tues 26th – Have lunch at the Piaf restaurant with Clive, patch up our row, friends again, but he must stop getting so drunk, also stay purely platonic . . . Sat 30th – Jane, Alistair and Fonz, (the Alsatian) arrive on a flying visit. They are back from Somerset West and now living in Adderley Street, Randburg and have a pool and large avocado tree at the back!

Saturday 6th April – Braai at Jane's. George and Louisa, their children, Boo, John and Eddie from next door and their girlfriends, two broad Lancashire lasses! Tues 9th – Do a Staff Training film with Clive Scott and Ann Stradi for Stuttafords in Sandton, directed by Roberta Durrant and Uwe, her photographer husband. Tues 30th – Boo sees Dr Sevel, he takes out 4 teeth, she's very brave!

Thursday 9th May – Audition at Heyns Films with Cedric Sundstrom. Read script of "Samantha's Men" (thought it was awful). Rennies have amalgamated with Freight Services, there is a party to introduce everybody. Now there are two people for each job . . . very awkward, the latter feel insecure now. Sun 19th – Arthur takes me out to lunch at the Porterhouse and I have nice prawns. We go on to Mae's Exhibition at Greenside. View Hein van der Walt's paintings, huge imitation African style, strident colours . . . drink too much red wine. Sat 25th – Parktown Girls Fete. I book Nigel Kane to open it, (at least I can do another actor a good turn, although he's only paid R150). I run the Tape Derby Tote – hard work! Sun 26th – I'm moving into Mae's old flat, she's gone to another floor. Arthur comes round with Chinese takeaways – bless him!

Tuesday 11th June – Opening night of Arthur's play "Chekov in Yalta", Mae comes, we have drinks with him afterwards. Wed 12th – Have moved to Rennie House in Braamfontein. I'm one of 6 switchboard operators . . . the supervisor is an evil gauleiter! Tues 18th – Opening night of PACT production "Uncle Vanya". Arthur is in it, join him at the after-party. Thur 20th – Do an Ad for Georgina for a Medical Directory. Sat 22nd – Boo goes skating. Thur 27th – Last day of school, Boo stays with her friend Beba. I stay at Jane's, as they are away. Arthur comes round.

Wednesday July 3rd – Neil picks me up, I stay the night with them. George and Louisa come over, I learn to do macramé! Sat 6th – Supper with Mirella, then on to Rumours, meet Malcolm Chalmers and Billy McGinley, a Scottish drummer. Sun 7th – Go to the opening of Rugantino's Restaurant in Illovo. Wonderful party! Meet Hymie Brest of EAG Engineering. Afterwards go to the opening of an Art Exhibition in Fox Street.

Mon 8th – Boo is off caravanning with her best friend at school, Bronwen, a Springbok swimmer.

Saturday 12th July – Supper with Mirella at her flat then on to Rumours. Meet Billy the drummer and Julius Eichbam, editor of the magazine 'Opera'.

Sun 13ᵗʰ – Mirella, her son and Boo all go to the Field and Study Centre at Parkmore for the day, in aid of SANCA. Have a Barbecue, there's a Hula Hoop Competition, Electric Bull Riding! See Coleen Harvey and Iain Winter Smith, my mates from Children's Theatre. Mon 14ᵗʰ – Bad news, hear Neil is out of a job, Michelangelo have gone bankrupt . . . Billy comes to supper, we help Boo with her project, 'The Seasons'. She's making rigid foam cut-outs of Greek Gods and Goddesses, painting them in poster colours, highlighted with silver and gold. Hang them from wire coat hangers, at different levels to form mobiles. Discuss arranging an Olde Tyme Music Hall evening? Watch 'Dynasty' and 'Cosby'.

Tues 16ᵗʰ – Her brace breaks, go to Dr Hurwitz. Wed 17ᵗʰ – Billy looks a bit like Dr Livingstone the Scots explorer with his side whiskers! Takes me to see 'Rambo 2', very violent, not my sort of film, but he is a sweet gentle person, I like him very much, his birthday is the same day, as Bryan. Thur 18ᵗʰ – Boo's lost her Swatch watch, phone Allen & Isaacs re claim. Her friend Michelle stays over. Billy comes over to watch the broadcast of his Jazz Concert. Roger is coming by train from Durban tomorrow.

Sat 10ᵗʰ August – There has been very bad rioting and burning of cars for weeks now. I'm in bed with 'flu. My back and left hip is very sore from washing our clothes in the bath, have had no girl, she hasn't been and can't let me know what's wrong, as she has no phone in Soweto. Mon 12ᵗʰ – At last have received the form for Boo to apply to become a British Citizen. She has a South African passport, but the whole world seems to hate white South Africans, because of Apartheid and because of the way the Government is treating the Africans, it's worse than it's ever been. She refuses point blank to become a British Citizen. I'll keep the form for later, when she may change her mind.

Thur 15ᵗʰ – Record Tuesday Theatre 'Shot in the Dark' for Maggie Heale. I'm back at work after the flu. P.W Botha announces his Referendum . . . I can't vote, as am a Brit. Let's hope this brings huge changes . . . the trouble is, that only Afrikaners can vote so, they will support his Separate Development policy! A friend of Leo's, Jan, phones and takes me to his duplex in Sandton. Beautiful place, tastefully decorated, shaggy blond carpets. It begins well, he's a brilliant cook, but then we start discussing politics . . . , turns out he's a violently dogmatic Boer, says he would like to put all the African Olympic trainees in a field and shoot them! First I assumed he must be joking, but then I realise he means it. My liberal thinking makes him see red. Thank goodness, I manage to persuade him to drop me back home, before he gets too aggressive. Hope I never see him again!

Boo has gone to another Parktown Boys Disco. Says she vomited at one stage (there is no alcohol allowed at these do's)? Still she enjoyed herself, danced with three boys!

Wed 21st – Jan phones, all apologies, says he'd had too much to drink. That's no excuse!

Friday August 23rd – Have been to Dr Davis about my back, have sacroiliitis, caused by washing heavy towels in the bath and playing swing tennis at Jane's! Yasha Katz from AA Mutual Life brings me forms for life insurance to sign, so that if anything happens to me, Boo will be cared for. She's with Yvonne.

I go to see Mae's new home in Robert's Avenue in Kensington. She's made it look beautiful . . . there's a large conservatory with big bay windows and potted trees, another sitting room indoors and a huge kitchen – her bedroom is a pink dream! Her best friend Geoff, the gay hairdresser, gives me a lift home.

Tues 27th – Go out for a drink with Clive, he wants to resume our relationship. I'm unsure, he is a married man. Sat 31st – Combined birthday party at Jane's for Roger and I. Alistair Prescott and his wife Val are there, she's 69, very slim with glamorous long blonde hair . . . and their son Craig. Also Roger's new girl friend Amelia, she's Afrikaans, with reddish – blonde pre-Raphaelite hair, does cartoon animations. Mae gives me macram`e pot holders, Roger a book on pot plants. On the way home, we have coffee at the Gazebo in the Sandton Sun. It's like a giant birdcage – huge domed ceilings with balconies and see – through lifts. Gilt, chandeliers, a heady atmosphere! I have pecan pie – delicious, Boo has cheesecake.

Sunday 1st September – Boo with me, quiet cold rainy day, so work with her on a project. Wash clothes and vacuum. Yvonne comes over, not very well – is depressed over a workmate's early death and it reminds her of

Bryan, she'll never get over that. She gives me some money towards Belinda's school fees. Sun 8th – Spend the day at Dick and Liz's farm, it's sunny, lots of kids there! Wed 11th – Jan phones, wants to be friends, tell him never to phone or try to see me again. Sat 14th – Get my new Trust card and learn how to use it in the ATM.

Tuesday October 1st – Go to Magistrates Court. Explain that I had sold my car, but it was still in my name 3 months later, as Jannie hadn't finished paying me for it . . . they quash the parking fines his salesman had incurred, but still fine me for Contempt of Court!

Thur 3rd – Boo phones me from school, she got 60 % for Maths!

Sat 5th – Roger is staying at a farm commune. He's organised a Rock Concert with ten bands. Jane takes Michelle, Boo and I there. Lovely day, great music, food and drink organised by Maxime's. There's a big rainwater tank, we swim in it with lots of skinny dippers! We visit Guy Roger's (Penny's son) cottage. A thatched roof, very attractive, but with a huge spider on the ceiling! Dick and Liz Blandy arrive. I give her the earrings she wanted. Jane and I are making ceramic jewellery and she bakes them in the oven, make a bit of pin money this way. Get back late, drop Michelle off home.

Mon 7th – Boo on holiday for a week, goes to stay with her friend Beba.

Sat 19th – Clive comes over early. We go shopping for glass to mend the balcony door, (which he broke) and putty. He's no handyman, makes heavy weather of it! Wed 30th – Lift home with Clive. David phones, what a surprise! Clive comes back late, banging on my door, I get a fright, break my little toe on a chair, rushing to open the door. He's drunk, of course.

Friday November 1st – Jenni Fletcher and I from Renfreight help to raise money for 'Operation Hunger' by manning the phones at Sandton – great fun! Sat 16th – Rosalie gives me a lift to the Idem Awards. Sat 23rd – Jane and Michael's birthdays. He's overseas, give Jane a cut-glass vase. Sun 24th – Jane takes Boo, Ali and I to the Renfreight Christmas Party at Santarama. Sheila Smith and I helped to organise it. Quite fun, but some people bought some very expensive gifts for their children, others very cheap ones . . . Our Entertainment Committee had agreed to stipulate, no gifts over the value of R20, so that when gifts were handed out by Father Xmas there would be no embarrassing disparity in quality . . . , but people always have to show off. Any how the magician was good, but the little gift food packs pretty awful! Ali was very impressed by Father Xmas, (he's only three). Go on the Dromedaris paddle boat and the toy train.

Wednesday December 4th – See 'Pigs in Passion' at the Market Theatre, with Kevin Smith (Karin's boyfriend) and Helena Kriel, very sexual play. Chat to Kevin in the bar afterwards, Helena ignores me, bitch! Sat 14th – Dick Blandy picks Boo and I up. Arrive at his new farm at 4.30. It's near Pietersburg in the Northern Transvaal, a beautiful place, but the previous owners left it in a very run-down state. Heather, Kenny and Shanna their baby are already there, they are going to manage the property for him. We walk down to the dam and that night we sleep in Dick's bedroom with the kids, he sleeps in the lounge on the sofa. There's a bat in our room, gives me the horrors! The ceiling is broken on one corner of ceiling, it must live in the attic.

Sun 15th – Jane, Neil and Ali arrive. We all go for a walk past the plantations of granadillas and kiwi fruit. At night there's no TV . . . , we talk until the small hours.

Mon 16th – Misty, windy and cool, so go for a drive round the rain forest, see wonderful ferns and a beautiful waterfall. Have lunch at the Baragwaneth Hotel. Boo and Ali go for a walk in the valley below Hotel. It turns very misty, and we think they are lost, but they turn up, thank God! They had been playing in the garden. We all play cards in the evening at the farm.

Wed 18th – Drive to the Kruger Nattional Game Park, entering at Palaborwa Gate. Drive to Letaba, Olifants and Shingwedzi Camps. Stay the night at Shingwedzi. See hippos, impala, elephants, giraffes, and zebras! There are little meerkats standing looking at us at the side of the road, Ali and Boo are enthralled! The list is endless, as squirrels, buffalo, waterbuck, kudu, nyala, lizards, eagles, buzzards, kites, marabou storks and hornbills appear, as we drive slowly along. Neil is a great authority on fauna, birds mainly, otherwise we wouldn't know the names of all the different kinds of buck. What a relief to get to the camp and make a braai. Jane, Boo and I sleep in the bungalow, Neil and Ali sleep in their Igloo tent. Thu 19th – Boo up early and see crocodiles, herons, giant tortoises. Spot a grey-headed kingfisher, which Neil says, is rare. See a huge goliath heron and three cheetahs near Punda Maria, a much older camp up north near Zimbabwe border. Exit at Pafuri Gate and then drive through Venda, very poor little huts, just like Bophuthatswana. Sat 21st – Drive through Hendrik Verwoerd Tunnel to Moeketsi. Back to the farm with brown bathwater and bats, spiders and mosquitos. Boo and I leave with Dick and his kids (I pay him for the petrol). What a fantastic trip!

Sunday December 22nd (contd . . .) We have an uneventful trip home and Dick is so tired, his wife Liz, drives us home. We enjoyed the Kruger Park very much, but glad to get back to relative civilization, especially hot clean water! Mon 23rd – Run around doing last minute Christmas shopping. Take Boo to see "The Meaning of Life", by Monty Python. What a horrible film – a grossly fat man eats so much in a restaurant his stomach explodes, all over the other diners! Tues 24th – Clive takes me out to lunch at Toty's in the Carlton Centre. I buy Boo white lace mittens and ditto stockings at Garlick's – weird but it's what she wants . . . he insists on buying me a pair of black lace panties! Wed 25th – Take Yang with us to Jane's and rains all day. Roger brings Emilia We have delicious American turkey.

Fri 27th – Clive phones at 10, says Wendy has found out about us and wants to meet for lunch at the Sunnyside Park Hotel to discuss the situation. Horrors! Wendy and I are too upset to eat, but he scoffs away at a huge plate of mutton curry, as if nothing had happened! It seems he caved in easily when she questioned him – told her all about me.

When I think of how I endured days of Gestapo-like interrogation from Peter and never gave him the man's name (the reason for my abortion in Durban . . .) and eventually left my children and my home because of it! All it took now to divulge our affair was one session! It's quite a relief to know it's finally in the open. We both agree not to see each other again, but I know he won't leave me alone. I'll probably have to find another job, we'll still keep bumping into each other . . . I won't miss the sex, but will miss the fun we sometimes had. Roger comes over to fix my tape deck and record player.

Thursday January 2nd 1986 – Back at work at Renfreight. Sun 5th – Go to Neil and Jane's, they are quarrelling, as usual. Wed 8th – School starts, I'm dieting again.

Sat 11ᵗʰ – A wonderful Concert in Ellis Park, 75,000 people. No rows, no rioting or bombs, everyone very friendly, great music! Roger, Emilia, Elise, Chris, Boo and I.

Sun 12ᵗʰ – Recovering from too much sun and alcohol! Visit Mae for champagne and orange juice. Something worth celebrating – we've both lost a kilo. Fri 17ᵗʰ – Go to Jaff and Co to try on clothes for in-house modelling. Model uniforms for the UBS.

Fri 31ˢᵗ – Supper with Rosalie at her attractive little house in Hunter Street, Yeoville.

Tues 4ᵗʰ Feb – Parktown Girls PTA meeting. Robert Joseph phones. Wonders never cease, he's taking Rosalie out! Gives me Brian Sloan's number. We had met at Robert's party and got on famously, waxing nostalgic over the old days at RAPS.

Sat 22nd – Celebrate Boo's birthday at Jane's, Neil is away fishing. Go to Roger's band's Farewell Gig with him, at a warehouse in town. Very smokey and noisy.

Wed 26ᵗʰ – He's flying to Vienna, we all see him off.

Mon 10ᵗʰ March – At last, a letter, he arrived safely in UK after many adventures . . . is staying with Michael. Wed 26ᵗʰ – Term ends, she's off to Durban with Michelle. Thur 27ᵗʰ – See "Out of Africa" with Meryl Streep and Robert Redford, wonderful music, softly evocative settings, makes me long to go back there(Charles Dance would have been better, Robert miscast).

Sunday 4ᵗʰ April – Neil takes us to see the gold smelting process at Gold Reef City – fascinating! Mon 19ᵗʰ – Give a pint of blood for the first time at Renfreight, felt drowsy for two hours afterwards. Tues 20ᵗʰ – Yvonne's birthday and give her flowers and nice soap. Fri 23ʳᵈ – Boo goes to a Youth Church Meeting. Sat 24ᵗʰ – Stir-Fry at Dick & Liz's farm, meet Bobby, even Boo thinks he is gorgeous! Watch Rugby, the Springboks win.

Mon 26ᵗʰ – AA Mutual Insurance, Bryan's old firm crashes. Have had to let Allen & Isaac's insurance of flat and belongings lapse . . . Wed

28th – Jonathan Taylor, one of Bryan's old mates wants a copy of the libretto of 'The Dreamer', but I lent him my copy to take to America, never got it back.

Tuesday 10th June – Roger phones from UK, he says he's fine. Boo is busy swotting for exams. I'm in the process of obtaining forms so she can become a British citizen. Go to Pretoria with Neil to collect her passport. Bump into Bill Pullen, he's divorced from Sybille, now in UK with Alexandra. Sun 13th – Go to Jane's, give Ali the sweater I knitted, he's a bright little boy, had a very good school report . . . Boo got 62% average for her exams. Wed 23rd – Watch another Royal Wedding – Sarah and Andy and she looks really bonny.

Saturday 2nd August – Wendy and Clive turn up to discuss things . . . weirder and weirder, she wants us to resume the affair! She is now having an affair with the barmen of their local bowling club, says Clive has been absolutely miserable since I stopped seeing him. What next? He takes Boo and I to visit his house and meet his son Michael, officially!

Sat 16th – Clive takes me out to 252 Jeppe Street and there's a band and we dance. He wiggles his bottom in a lascivious way, horrid. Sat 23rd – Science Expo, Boo exhibits a mock-up of Hillbrow Streets, complete with the Tower and winking traffic light (she did have some help from a neighbour of Yvonne's, but it's still a marvellous effort!) I answer an advert selling a twin-tub washing machine, Jane takes me there and I buy it for R100! Nothing wrong with it, works like a charm, now hope my back will get better.

Sat 30th – Weekend at Rustenburg celebrating my birthday, stay at Hunter's Rest with Clive. Gamble at Sun City, win, lose and win again, great fun! Lovely food at the hotel.

Wednesday 3rd September – Red letter day, Dr Hurwitz removes Boo's braces, now she has lovely white straight teeth! Wed 10th – See '9 and a Half' with Mickey Rourke and Kim Basinger, very erotic . . . Sun 21st – Clive takes Boo, Dallas, and I to Melville Koppies and the Botanic gardens (Dallas is an attractive boy, who lives in our block). Sat 27th – A windy day at the Races, the Gold Cup. I wear black and white with a big hat, uh oh ! Nearly lose it.

Patrick Macnab, a Director of Renfreight sees C and I and asks us up to the Stewards Box, but the usher won't let us go up there, as C wasn't wearing top hat and tails . . . we don't back any winners!

Thursday October 9th – Go to Durban for the weekend, with Clive and Boo. Stay at the Gloucester Hotel, a real dump! A big flat with 2 bedrooms and a lounge, but sleazy and smells of cockroaches and dirty bed linen. Visit the Aquarium and then go on to Margate. The waves are rough, but Boo and I swim. I'm knocked over, get up, down again – can't get my breath. She pulls me up, saves my life! She's a strong swimmer and a strong girl (like her father), thank goodness for that! Sat 11th – Off to Umhlanga Rocks, have a lovely day lying in the sun. In the evening, walk all over Durban looking for a Disco for youngsters, no luck, turned away from the Palm Beach Hotel. Boo gets the sulks, no pleasing her. On Sunday make the long drive back to Jo'burg.

Monday 13th – She's back at school. At work I move to the 11th floor Rennie House, once again on reception and switchboard. Sat 18th – C comes over, he's embarrassingly drunk, tell him to go. Next day he phones pleading to be forgiven, I tell him we'll be platonic friends only, can't take his common behaviour! Mon 20th – Samora Machel, the President of Mocambique, dies in an air crash near our border, foul play is suspected.

Fri 24th – Eddie Parnell (who has been divorced by his second wife, the Welsh champion Darts player), has returned to SA. He has advanced lung cancer (caused by painting the walls of a room with the windows closed and by years of smoking). Soft – hearted Yvonne has taken him back and he has lost half his lungs in a recent op.

Sat 25th – Our rent has gone up again, too much for this poky dilapidated flat and must get out. Fri 31st – We look at the flat at the top of Mae's house in Kensington. Agree to take it, sign the lease with the Martin's and give notice to JH Isaacs. We will be sharing with Caren. She'll have the big bedroom, Boo and I the two smaller ones. There's a lounge and a veranda running around the outside of the house. A long uncarpeted passage – will have to do it up later, otherwise I visualise Mae's reaction, when we go galumphing along it!

Wednesday 5th November – Clive takes me to see 'Loot' with Mike McCabe, Jimmy Borthwick and Michael Richard. Go backstage, chat to Mike, his step-daughter Abigail Leach is at Parktown with Boo. Sat 15th – Go to Gold Reef City with C and Boo, watch the band 'Cinema'. She smiles at us both, nodding our heads in time to the music!

Mon 17th – Phone Miss Schutz, headmistress of Jeppe Girls School about Boo transferring from Parktown, then ditto Parktown's Mrs Quinn.

Sat 29th – C borrows a truck & we load my furniture on it – with Jane's help. It's raining and he has no rear view mirror – tricky! People on the street help us unload in Kensington. We are now at 58A Roberts Avenue.

Monday 1st December – Buy uniform at the school 2nd hand shop, transfer account to Trust Bank in Eastgate. Tues 2nd – Big row with Caren – what a super bitch! She wanted me to unpack, but I had to go to the Opening of the Memorial Brass Plaques being laid on the street in front of the Market Theatre with Yvonne and Boo, it's the only memorial Bryan has with his name on it, since he was cremated. It's not a good start to our shared stay! She knows I'll help her later.

Mon 1st December (contd) – In the evening join Mae for a drink, Caren also, an uneasy peace prevails . . . , she has some odd habits, especially re cooking . . . and doesn't wash her own dishes and we are her skivvies now? Wed 10th – Renfreight's Christmas Party on 7th Executive floor, then the Dance on Friday. Sat 20th – C takes me to Charlie C's club in Louis Botha Avenue, very rowdy, singing, lots of standing on the tables, not my scene at all, but he loves it, he's drunk of course. Get him to take me home, usual row.

Wed 24th – Christmas Eve party at Mae's, all the old gays from way back Andy and Joey and their baby Anastasia – what a spoilt child! Thur 25th – Spend the day with Neil and Jane, the children have fun in the pool, (was this the time Boo dived in and rescued Ali, who'd fallen in the deep end)? Fri – Watch the Aussies play the Spring Boks at cricket at the Wanderers club and a very good game.

Monday 5th January 1987 – Back at work. No Xmas cards from Michael or Roger?

Tues 6th – Letter from Nan, saying Sally Brooks (Pat's daughter), had a 2lb 5oz baby boy (Adam). Her father, Clive Exton, the writer (previously Montague Brooks), meets Mike Hill, her stepfather at the hospital for the first time.

Wed 7th – Boo starts her first term at Jeppe School. Thur 9th – Zia, Rosalie, Mae, Marylix, and Robert Joseph come to dinner and a wonderful evening! Sun 11th – Boo and I go for a long exploratory walk and end up at Rhodes Park Swimming Pool. Thur 22nd – She goes off to Veld School. Mon 26th – C takes me to RAPS at the Rosebank Scout Hall – What a weary bunch of people are assembled, with little enthusiasm and less talent! So different from our vibrant group in the late 60's, Robert tries to drum up some action.

Fri 30th – Back from Veld School, she's stiff, aching and with a sore throat! Hooray, the telephone is installed. Sat 31st – C takes me to 'Front Page', the newspaper – themed restaurant, the menu in sepia format and delicious food.

Monday 16th February – RAPS play reading – 'Dr Knock' a weird existentialist play. Stuart Helps is the doc, Alberto the Patient, Sue the Nurse. Sat 21st – Caren is away! Yay!

Boo's birthday party and quite successful, end up playing charades in the garden. Of course, Mae complains about the noise . . . Jane and Louisa, her two children, school friends from both schools, C and his son (Some weeks later Jane confides that C tried to molest her and Louisa, used suggestive language – when he's drunk he becomes an animal)! Sun 22nd – C takes me to the Progressive Party's Garden Party for people who've helped with the election, it's held at Douglas and Pam Gibson's beautiful home and garden. Tues 24th – Do clerical work at the Progressive party HQ (we are trying to bring in universal voting rights – Helen Suzman is our Rep in Parliament).

Monday 9th March – Robert decides to do my play, 'The Waiting Game'. Wed 11th – Help at Progressive HQ. Birthday party for Lourdes Valadas, a large taciturn Portuguese lady. I've moved from Rennie House to Manica

House down the street. They deal mainly with Mocambique Forwarding. I'm now Trevor Styles's secretary, plus switchboard. Afterwards go on to Harry's Grill with C, Jill Gabler and John Trowell. On to Trattoria Romana restaurant.

Saturday 21st March – See 'Children of a Lesser God' about a deaf actress, Marlee Matlin and with John Hur, excellent film. Thur 26th – Caren's party and a very peculiar crowd . . . , odd watching her lesbian friends trying to interact with her verkrampte (bigoted) Afrikaans father! Sat 28th – Georgie's birthday. Big row with C, Jane has just told me about his sexual overtures during Boo's party. Mon 30th – Alberto gives me a lift to RAPS, He reads Paul – maybe I'll end up directing this epic!

Wednesday 1st April – No C of course, but manage to get a lift to the PFP meeting.

Sat 11th – Boo goes with Georgie and family to stay at Uvongo on the coast. Yvonne's ex husband, Eddie Parnell dies of Lung Cancer in the hospice. He was living with her for the last few weeks, full of pain, out of his mind with morphine . . . he was trying to cut the roses out of her carpet and thought they were real . . . ended up at a bus stop in his pyjamas. For all his faults he was a courageous person, the way he defended poor tenants against the rapacious landlord Chaim Wainer. Wed 15th – His funeral at Tom Kight's Funeral Parlour and I wrote a poem for him but no chance to read it out – Gave it to Yvonne to put in the open coffin. I couldn't bear to look in. His ex wife Mary and her snooty daughter turned up, draped in purple (they ignored him when he was so ill). The crows were gathering now in case there were pickings.

Thur 16th – We've been burgled! Got home from work to find our TV lying near the front door – Caren's tapes, her HiFi, a valuable ring stolen, they must have been disturbed before they could finish our side, but poor Mae has been cleaned out, this old house is so easy to break into. Wed 22nd – Boo back from Uvongo, school starts today. Caren and I are definitely not sharing anymore and give her notice.

Thursday 7th May – Boo and I go to the school play, 'The Prime of Miss Jean Brodie'.

Sun 10th – Caren finds a huge rat in the kitchen – such drama, but I can't help laughing, as the current top hit is the reggae song, 'There's a rat in the kitchen'! Mon 11th – RAPS, Decide to do Paul Slapolepsky's play instead of mine, easier and with a small cast. Wed 20th – Yvonne's birthday, give her two pressed flower paintings.

Monday 1st June – Hold the RAPS 'At home 'at my house. Show a video of 'Blithe Spirit'. A hilarious evening, about 15 people came. My old friend from the 60's is there, Humphry Ward. We were both married to other people at the time, but are now free . . . he has illustrious forbears, Julian and Aldous Huxley, Mrs Humphry Ward, the Victorian novelist. Wed 3rd – See 'Noel and Gertie', at the Alhambra (about Noel Coward and Gertrude Lawrence), with Humphry.

Mon 8th – He takes me to 'Bones' in Rosebank for a drink. Wed 10th – Lose diamond ring when taking off gloves to get change for the bus. Fri 12th – Boo going out to a party, but it's so cold! Post insurance claim form for ring. Fri 19th – See 'The 4th Protocol' with Pierce Brosnan and very good (go with C after he begged & pleaded, but agreed to go only as a friend)!

Saturday June 20th – Last night of RAPS School Festival at the Wits theatre. Lovely to see all the old faces, Shelagh Ray, Arthur Coombes, the Cowaps and Ian Kennedy. 'Offending the Audience' won the Award – (but there were better entries). This last consisted of teenagers being very rude to the audience, it seemed to be unscripted and rather unpleasant! Fri 26th – Boo is out till very late, am worried sick . . . Georgie's mother is supposed to give them a lift home from the Disco.

Saturday 4th July – Caren has finally left and she didn't pay her servant, but took my watering can! Left her dining room table, sideboard and said she'd collect them later. I see 'Blue Velvet with H, very erotic film with Dennis Hopper, William Dafoe and Isabella Rossellini (Ingrid Bergmann's daughter).

Sat 5th – Jane helps me move the furniture around, a heavy door falls on my head – with no noticeable effect! Thur 9th – End of term, Boo with Yvonne.

Sat 11th – I find Dorothy Labuschagne, a young white woman asleep in our garden, when I come back from shopping. She seems dazed, drugged, doesn't know how she got there . . . I feel sorry for her, help her into the house, give her food, treat her kindly, she helps with the dishes. Tells me she's lost track of her parents. I think she's Afrikaans, speaks English with difficulty and she sleeps in our spare bed.

Mon 13th – Get her smartened up, give her some of my clothes and a handbag. Take her to Kelly Girl, they give her forms to fill in, so as to apply for temp work. I carry on to Manica. When I get home in the evening there's no sign of her. Ring up Kelly Girl. She never filled in the forms, when I left she walked out. Now I feel guilty, maybe she was illiterate and I embarrassed her by taking her to get a job . . . that was one explanation, the other being that she was a criminal type and I was well rid of her. When I told Boo what happened, she thought I was stupid to have taken her in.

Tues 14th – American Swiss have a ring exactly the same as the one I lost and will get a buying order from the insurers. Wed 15th – Boo is at the Disco till 1am. I get so anxious and worried . . . Have a big row with Mae about noise and says we make too much noise. I say it's her guilty conscience that stops her sleeping, because she refused to listen to my side of things over the Caren affair. Fri 24th – See 'The Outside Edge' with Sandra Duncan, very good! Clive takes me, but is very drunk and snores during the play. We have a big argument. On the way home after he drops me, he drives into a ditch, gets stuck, has to call a pick-up truck to pull him out. I tell him to stay away from me until he's been to AA and got cured! Tues 28th – Phone Mae, go for a drink, explain re lack of carpets and unintentional noise and we make up again.

Thursday 20th August – Costa from RAPS has a theatre group, principally Africans. They put on a show at Athlone School. Boo and Georgie come, but they got bored and wander off. The shebeen (African pub) scene is very funny and they should work it up into something longer.

Saturday 22nd August – Georgina's Fashion Show,' The Big Scene' in the Camellia Room at the Sandton Sun and paid R125. Boo's friends

"Boo"

98

come over, stay the night, next day Sandra and Boo get up early to run in the Company Relay. Sun 29th – Take Boo to see 'Guys and Dolls' at the Wits Theatre. It's semi-professional, pretty good. Marilyx and Joseph Gerassi, not bad, Lana Green plays the Salvation Army girl. Drinks at the Wits bar and then on to a party at Marilyx and Robert's house.

Wednesday 2nd September – Another fashion show for Georgina at the Benoni Country Club and they love it! Tues 15th – Karin Jerg has started working for Renfreight and meet her for lunch at Juicy Lucy. Thur 17th – Jessie Mackenzie coming to see my half of the house. I'm looking round for somewhere else, because of Mae! Mon 21st – Karin confirms that it was our agent Yvonne Lavine, who shot herself. She had bowel cancer and was in great pain. How awful for Tony and the children. Mon 28th – RAPS AGM, as they are closing down, because of not enough support, selling off their assets. I don't go and send apologies.

Wednesday 14th October – See 'Othello' at the Market Theatre with Costa. John Kani plays Othello, but he's a mis-cast and also mis-directed, just because he's black – it doesn't make him right for the part. He should be the strong conquering General, but with a weak Othello the whole balance of the play goes awry. Richard Haines is Iago and is magnificent. Sat 17th – Rehearse 'Blithe Spirit 'with Liz. Sun 18th – Audition for 'Grease' at Athlone School, Boo has to sing and dance, but she's terribly nervous and shy. Wed 21st – Do our little excerpt for Costa's group, I play Madame Arcati. His 'shebeen' scene goes down well.

Thursday 5th November – Give R350 deposit for no 15 Sanview to Mrs Strauss, the fat wheezy caretaker. It's a flat block in Roberts Avenue, opposite the Marymount Hospital where Boo was born in Kensington. A two-bedroomed fla, very convenient for the bus and shops. It's serviced with big clean sunny rooms. Sat 7th – Humph takes me out to the 'Front Page' for dinner, have duckling with orange sauce, yum! We toast with Nederberg Riesling wine. Really enjoy his company! Boo only comes back from Disco at 1 am. Shudder to think what she does till then. Sun 8th – Scads of people tramp through the house with a view to rent. Mon 16th – Our group meets at Damian's flat. It's a sinister place, lit only by candles. He's small, dark, elf-like, appears to be under satanic influences . . . Fri 20th – H and I out to dine at the 'Grub Store' in Norwood, it's a jolly place and nice music.

Sun 29ᵗʰ – Renfreight Christmas party and a great success, Ali loves it! Mon 30ᵗʰ – Read through 'Grease', I'm playing the Headmistress.

Thursday 3ʳᵈ December – End of school term. 'Shipwreckers' party at the Braamfontein Hotel. The drinks are over priced and leave early. Tues 8ᵗʰ – Roger arrives from UK with his girlfriend, Belinda Duncan, a very pleasant pretty blonde girl. Fri 11ᵗʰ – Anglo American Office Dinner party with H. He works for them in the Architectural Dept. He dances quite well, nice evening. Wed 16ᵗʰ – Roger Belinda, Boo and I go to Gold Reef City. Sat 19ᵗʰ – See 'Glass Menagerie' with H. Mon 28ᵗʰ – Move into Sanview an love the flat!

On Thursday 31ˢᵗ December – H and I go to All Night Al's restaurant and then on to Neil and Jane's for New Year's party with various friends. Boo is staying with Yvonne. Next day she phones, Boo was out all night, turns up at 11 am . . . She's getting to be quite a handful!

Wednesday January 6ᵗʰ 1988 – Meet Angus re getting Mrs Martin to cough up the deposit. He'll write her a letter. Sat 9ᵗʰ – Boo is sick. Sun 17ᵗʰ – Rehearsal of 'Grease'. The sets are very colourful. Sat 23ʳᵈ – Georgie's parents, Maureen and Ian Sutherland come to dinner. He's a skinny laconic Geordie, she's a really lovely charming woman. He speaks his mind, no matter what! We have chicken curry and H brings wine. Fri 11ᵗʰ – Belinda Duncan's Farewell Party, she's going back to UK. She's a nice girl, adores Roger, but he says she's neurotic . . . Sat 30ᵗʰ – See film 'Dirty Dancing'

Alistair

with Patrick Swayze, terrific, I love it, but H doesn't.

Wednesday 3ʳᵈ February – PTA meeting and go with Maureen. Sun 7ᵗʰ – 'Grease' moves into Wits Theatre. H gives me a lift home. Mon 8ᵗʰ – Argument with Jo Gerassi, the producer and tell him I'm leaving the show, because he chucked out Charles, who was acting and singing the 'Danny' part well. Jo is going to play the part himself! Order a taxi and leave. Next day Jo phones and says he will cancel the whole production, if

I quit – I feel sorry for all the other people who worked so hard, so agree to carry on. Thur 11th – Do an audition for 'Surprise Rice' at Glenhove Road. Receive a cheque for R300.64 from Mrs Martin. It certainly pays to have a lawyer! Mon 15th – Opening Night and it goes well, we have a good audience. Jo's isn't a patch on Charles's performance, but he certainly looks the part, with his dark Latino colouring.

Sun 21st – Boo's birthday, she's 16. Braai at Jane's. H and Yvonne there. Mon 22nd – Arrange for her to get her British passport. Tues 23rd – Full House and 25 turned away!!!

Wed 24th – Boo has a sore throat and stays at home. Sat 27th – Last night of 'Grease', nice party afterwards. We stay the night at H's sister's house in Parktown. He's house sitting while they are overseas.

Tuesday 1st March – First free night and watch film 'North and South'with Patrick Swayze. Wed 3rd – Manica SA move over to Freight Base, I stay in Braamfontein. Sat 5th – Al's birthday party, he's six. Sun 6th – H away on a hiking tour with Tom and Rita. Do huge wash and make a cake. Fri 11th – Very bad floods on Mozambique area. See 'The Last Emperor' Bernard Bertolucci's masterpiece with H. Tues 15th – Boo off school and has a temp 39.5. Ask doc to visit, but doesn't come, so take her to him, she has quinsy, a mild form of diphtheria, prescribes anti-biotics and bed rest. Fri 18th – She's been off school all week. Sat 19th – Visit Evelyn Raath, late of Renfreight and meet her brother Bob. His wife died of cancer recently, he loved her very much. Drove his car into a tree trying to commit suicide, but survived. He has dead eyes. She wants me to go out with him. I'm sure he will try again soon. Besides, H and I are going strong.

Sunday 20th March – Go to a braai with H, Boo visits her boyfriend, Sean. Wed 23rd – Take her to see Dr Wolfowitz – ENT re her throat. Sat 26th – Jeppe Girl's MA Dance. She looks stunning in a strapless black and silver net and lace dress and it makes the most of her assets, a good bust and shoulders, yet hiding pump hips and thighs. Sean escorts her and she said she enjoyed herself. Stays over with Georgie's parents.

Friday 1st April – Good Friday. Lovely day at Gold Reef City with H. Sat 2nd – Meet his ancient uncle and aunt in Irene, near Pretoria. Wed

6th – Founders day. Tea with the McDonald's, his old friends. George is a bombastic prig! Interrogates me about my family connections, Douglas Pringle (Nan's brother-in-law,) etc., very military minded. His wife is petite, dainty, sews beautiful altar cloths. George reads books at Tape Aids for the Blind. Wed 13th – Boo goes into the Princess Nursing Home for a tonsillectomy. Next day she's very yellow and woozy. Sean visits and she tries to hide her face under the bedclothes! Poor dear! Fri 15th – She leaves hospital and I'm working, so she goes to stay with Yvonne to recuperate. Tues 19th – See Angus about making a Will. Fri 22nd – See 'Hope and Glory' with H, a John Boorman film about the Blitz. Wonderful, very well acted – brings back my memories of being bombed (in the North East of England).

Wed 27th – She's back at school. Fri 29th – Go with H and Boo to see 'Sarcophagus', an excellent play with Maggie Heale is in it, Jeremy Crutchley gives a superb performance, as a radiation victim.

Monday 6th June – We decide to drop our entry 'Losers', for the Amfest and concentrate on 'Winners' with Damian and Liz. Fri 24th – Boo staying with Georgie.

Saturday 2nd July – RAPS Festival, see 'Woza Albert' with H. Sat 9th – Go to JHB Art Gallery. See 'Ramaquatsi', a very strange documentary about the workers in a gold mine in South America. Film shots of mud-soaked men with baskets of stones on their backs, all struggling up and down a huge hole, as big as the Kimberley Diamond Mine hole. Some of them fall off the ladders and die, suffocated by the mud. Totally horrific conditions, but poverty is so bad, they are forced into it just to feed their families.

Tues 19th – Michael phones from UK, is going to send me money to buy a lounge suite – bless him! Sat 23rd – Amfest. Not a very good crit of 'Winners', they said Liz was too old, true, but that did not negate her acting ability . . . Damian was good, but Martin was hopeless, (thank God we cut out 'Losers' in which he played the lead)!

Mon 25th – Take Boo to get ID card and passport. Buy a dusty pink 4 piece lounge suite at the OK R999. Sat 30th – See 'The Unbearable Lightness of Being' with H. Become a devoted fan of Daniel Day Lewis (son of the poet C Day Lewis). Send birthday cards to Roger (still in the UK) and Nan.

Friday 5th August – Wonderful weekend in Swaziland! Stay at the Mountain Inn and play on the one-armed bandit gambling machines, lose money but have fun! Buy some greenish re-cycled glass animals from the Ngwenya factory. The local children collect up discarded coke bottles and bring them to the factory. Products are influenced by excellent Danish simple designs. We visit Sue and Andre on the way back. H is very sleepy, stop near the Sappi paper pulp factory and a most vile smell ever, orange sodium spotlights outlining belching reddish fumes. Dante's Inferno.

Thursday 11th August – Belinda's JA Course starts at the Wits Business School in Parktown. It's for High School leavers – How to Run Your Own Business. Her group make car sun blinds and paint individual designs on them. Georgie is with her and they both seem really interested. Fri 19th – Collect her passport. Phone Tape Aids for the Blind, want to start recording for them.

Friday 2nd September – Fly to George in the Cape. It's a weekend arranged by Mienie of SA Airways, awarded to the secretaries, who have booked the most flights with SAA.

(We sent many oil rig workers from Malaysia to Richard's Bay oil drilling site). Stay at the Knysna Hotel – wonderful food, especially the locally fished out oysters! We all have drinks at a pub on the end of a jetty in the lagoon. Huge yard tankards of beer, which we all share, while a steel band serenades us from a boat alongside! I share a room with another secretary. Sat 3rd – Delicious lunch at the Mossel Bay Hotel, then on to the Kango Caves. Absolutely awe-inspiring with the huge caverns are well lit, showing the Bushman wall paintings, stalagmites & stalactites. Some of the party dare to go down a claustrophobic tiny tunnel, but not me! Next we go to Outshoorn to visit an ostrich farm. Tiny little black jockeys balance on saddles and race each other. We are offered the chance to ride one – Valda Lombard does and falls of straightaway! Spend the night at the Game Lodge, share with Fay again. I decline the offer of ostrich or kudu steaks.

Sun 4th – Back to George, to catch the plane back to Jo'burg, but are delayed by bad weather. I don't mind, would love to stay on, what a fantastic week-end! H meets the plane.

Wed 7th – Start with Tape Aids after work, at Happiness House in Braamfontein. Starting to read 'Samsara'. I'm in a two-man booth, on the other side of the glass, a controller records and checks there are no unnecessary noises (Coughs, etc). Sat 10th – Go with H to see 'White Mischief, 'about the so-called Happy Valley in the Aberdares in 1940's in Kenya. Expatriates and remittance men led a decadent lifestyle of drink, drugs and casual sex. Charles Dance plays the 'Earl of Erroll', who was shot by the jealous husband of Greta Scacchi, Jock Delvers Broughton, played by Joss Acland. By the time I lived there in the mid-Fifties, there were not more of them that had survived . . . It's so moving to see that glorious place again, the most marvellous landscape, Mount Kenya towering in the background.

Wed 14th – H goes overseas, he's going to back-pack, staying at Youth Hostels. I would have thought he was a bit long in the tooth for that, but he has no qualms about it! He says it's his last chance to go to UK . . . Tues 27th – A Party to celebrate Tape Aids's move to Waverley, Colin Fish's wife Liz is ther and Jonathan Taylor.

Saturday 15th October – H is back in one piece! Meal at the Grub Store, see 'Little Dorrit' at the Norwood cinema, very good! Fri 21st – Interview with Miss Shutz, Boo is not allowed to leave and come back later. Go to 'Flight' at the Market, Gys de Villiers with a hairpiece. A parallel to the Jewish flight from Israel, but set in Rhodesia (Zimbabwe) and very good.

Tuesday 25th October – Interview with Dr Du Toit, the school psychologist and Boo is with me. He says she is a gifted child, could leave school and go to work, but come back later. Miss Shutz says she cannot – we are at cross purposes. She will have to take her exams and go on to Higher Grade, even if she fails (she had bunked so much, had missed so many lessons, that she was afraid she would never pass any exams! I never knew she was bunking until the end of term. I was horrified, but not very surprised, she was so rebellious)!

Sat 29th – H is on a walking tour with Tom and his mates. I visit Mae at her new semi, off Jules Street in Malvern, not far from David's house. She's made it look nice in her usual style . . . like a pink birthday cake!

Friday 2ⁿᵈ December – Meeting with Neville Venter, our new Director. Sat 17ᵗʰ – Go to Neil and Jane's to house – sit for them and they leave for Knysna. Their alarm goes off and won't stop, the neighbours gather round the gates complaining. H comes over to help – eventually we get it turned off! Sat 31ˢᵗ – New Years's Party at Stephanie and JP's house. A lovely effect as we arrive, candles alight all the way up their long drive.

Wednesday January 4ᵗʰ 1989 – Start work again. Record at Tape Aids. Fri 6ᵗʰ – Go with Boo and Yvonne to start her new account at the Trust Bank. Sat 21ˢᵗ – H moves into a flat at the Seftel's house. Wed 25ᵗʰ – See 'Cocktail' with Tom Cruise and Bryan Brown with C and think I must have had a row with H. Sat 28ᵗʰ – See 'A Fish called Wanda' very funny film with Michael Palin and John Cleese with C. Tues 31ˢᵗ – Sheila Smith's farewell drinks. (So many people are leaving, too many people for each job since the two companies amalgamated). Go with H to 'Saturday Night at the Clair de Lune' at the Leonard Rayne Theatre, Bill Flynn plays a short order cook and excellent. We have a long talk afterwards – he thinks he <u>does</u> love me?

Saturday April 1ˢᵗ – H takes me to Jameson's in Commissioner Street, where the punk band, the 'Dyslexics' are playing. They are Michael's friends, thought they might know where he was, as I haven't heard from him for ages and I don't have a phone number.

Men are not very good at keeping touch with their Mum's! No one seems to have a clue . . . Mon 3ʳᵈ – Sometime this week H asks me to marry him (after I told him C had proposed)! I talk to Belinda about it, which one should I choose, if any? She is amazingly mature and considered in her answer. Says Humphry is more compatible with me, our tastes are similar and Clive drinks too much and becomes embarrassing . . . (When did my rebel become so wise)? She doesn't really get on with H, but it's still early days, the mutual dislike only intensifies later. Tues 23ʳᵈ – I tell H I will marry him and now I have to let C know my decision. We watch a local production of 'A Midsummer Night's dream on the box. He moves in with me the following week.

Friday 9ᵗʰ June – See lawyer re an Ante Nuptial Contract. Wed 14ᵗʰ – Interview with the Rev Campbell of the School of Truth. Wedding date booked for 5ᵗʰ August. (He's Interdenominational).

Sunday 18th August – Visit H's Uncle Reg and Aunt Millie in Pretoria. He's very frail, but won't leave his musty old house, full of ancient relics and junk! Ants everywhere and even running out of the sugar. Millie lives in a Masonic Haven, a very nice little flat-let, but she acts as a hostess for Reg. We have tea and stale biscuits. Wed 21st – See 'Pathfinder', a weird Finnish film and go with Boo and Georgie. Fri 23rd – Look for an engagement ring at a friend's house. She is crippled and sells jewellery from home to earn extra money. A charming woman and spot a lovely gold ring, inlaid with pearls and turquoises, beautifully chased, circa 1850, it's quite unique! Tues 27th – Tape Aids party, opening of the new venue, a large house in Waverley, the party is in a marquee in the parking lot area. Good food and wine in abundance, meet up with many old actor friends.

Thur 29th – Have lunch with Evelyn Raath. She's very sad, her brother Bob committed suicide not long after he met me … (nothing to do with me). He missed his wife so much and he gassed himself in his car. I knew he would do something, as you could see it in his eyes. I remembered a girl I had worked with at Freight Services. Things started to go missing, rings, money. She was found out and dismissed, but in the mitigation afterwards we were told about her distressing life. Her father had committed suicide and he was a martial arts junkie, tried to perform Hari Kari on himself, but botched the disembowelling …, some how managed to hang himself …, she was very young, when she found him. No wonder she was so dysfunctional.

Monday 3rd – July – H is learning to monitor my reading at Tape Aids. He manages the mechanics, but is inclined to nod off. Fri 14th – Today have been retrenched. Have been expecting it for a while, ever since they found out I was going to be married. Carlos Marques, my boss showed me the letter, says he's sorry I'm leaving. Go to Glynis's house, she's going to organise the flowers in the Chapel and my bouquet. I show her my dress, a harlequin pattern in purpley colours, blue shoes and pillbox hat with tiny veil.

Saturday 22nd – H takes Boo, Georgie and I to the Eric Clapton Concert in Swaziland.

(He's not allowed to perform in SA because of the boycott). We plan to meet Roger there, as he's helping with the sound backstage. We drive to Bad Plas, stay overnight in rondavels. Queue at the Swazi border for 6 hours! But a very entertaining trip. H wears my 'Spy meets Spy' (from the cartoon) black big-brimmed hat, a feather stuck in the band. Performs his exercises in the middle of the road . . . the girls chat – up all the likely lads waiting in cars all along the road in the huge snake-like queue. H has a set-to with the German tour guide woman, when he refuses to get out of the way to let her bus through. She throws oranges at us, as we drive away. Eventually get there at 9pm! Missed most of it, but we did see Joan Armatrading sing 3 songs. Most disappointing, no panache, wore a sober navy suit. Brenda Fassie was supposed to have gone on earlier, but she had a row with the organisers. (A well-known Jo'burg singer and a girl friend of King Mswati, is also a junkie). At last Eric comes on in a baggy pink suit, wows us for three hours! We never did get to meet up with Roger. Slept in the car and well rested. Have breakfast at the Royal Swazi Inn.

H now becoming increasingly eccentric, went and sat cross-legged on the floor in the corner of the dining room, thought he was being 'hip'!?

Thursday 3rd August – Roger appears at last from Swaziland, in time for his birthday and my wedding. **Saturday 5th August 1989** – We are married in the School of Truth Chapel at 10.30. It is a simple service. My family and many old friends, including Zia Garfield, Maggie Heale are there and Mae at the church only. The reception is held in Gillian's lovely garden in Parktown. An Indian chef, who did catering at Rennie House organises the food, which is excellent and plentiful. We have fine weather, so the buffet is set out on trestles in front of the house, and the champagne is flowing! Stuart helps us out, our old friend from RAPS gives a speech. Many of H's friends from Anglo American also are there. Sadly Mae didn't come, as H refused to let her bring a 'gay' friend. I had to tell her to come alone, it was nasty to have to say it, but he felt his sister and her 'posh' connections and would be outraged – the prejudice in SA was strong, especially because of the AIDS epidemic . . . I try to look soignée but a plump woman never does! H wears a pale grey suit, off set by his florid face. Roger and Boo distinguish themselves by pinching a bottle of champagne as a prank, but Gillian is furious. Pretty mean, as there is plenty of booze, she is being the 'Roedean Headmistress'.

The honeymoon is at 'Sparkling Waters' in Rustenburg. The first thing we do on arrival, after unpacking, is to go for a walk. H jumps happily over a small stream, expecting me to follow him unaided. I slip in the mud, have the wrong shoes on and sprained my ankle, he's walked on without a glance. I have to call him to help me up. Back at the hotel they have no walking stick, so I have to make do with a heavy pick handle! Also attacked by mosquito's in the night and in pain from the sprain. Glad to get back home.

In 1989 a great scandal erupted – Winnie Mandela's followers, known as the 'Comrades' had been causing a lot of trouble in Soweto, bullying and bossing people and into all kinds of subversion. A little boy of 14 called Stompie Sipei was one of them, it was said that he had 'grassed' to the police and had been what they called a 'sell-out'. Apparently this was not true, but the suspicion was enough, Winnie must have acted much as King Henry 11 did in the medieval era, when he said to four knights, 'Will no one rid me of this rebellious priest' resulting in the death of St Thomas a` Becket, which he regretted for the rest of his life. Perhaps she just 'turned a blind eye'. No one really knows what happened, except that the poor young boy was killed by the Comrades. In Nelson Mandela's book, 'Long Walk to Freedom' his mention of the case says, she 'showed poor judgement', but that he wholly supported her. 'She had been alone for almost 27 years, isolated and inclined to drink too much.

Wedding Photo   *Humphry & Sheila Ward*

Wed 9th – PTA Meeting and find out Boo has been bunking again . . .
Wed 16th – Lunch with Roger, find out what Michael's been up to. Thur
24th – Farewell lunch at the Wanderers Club organised by my boss Trevor
Stiles, very nice meal. Fri 25th – Interview with Jacqui Hogan and the
American manager of the 'Wits Business School' and re a job. Have dinner
with H's landlords and the Seftel's – Orthodox Jews. He warned me, but
I found it hard to keep a straight face, when he put his napkin on his
head – the father has a yomaka on <u>his</u> head, that's what they do at dinner
on a Friday.

Friday 1st September – Start work at the Wits Business School in Parktown.
I'm a receptionist and giving advice on the different courses, organising
catering for the many cocktail parties, booking lecture rooms and
answering switchboard queries with Sharon Meyersohn. Our overall boss
is the fearsome Jacqui! It's a very interesting job, but hard to get to from
Roberts Avenue, two buses. H refuses to give me a lift.

Fri 8th – H goes to Zimbabwe with Tom, Rita and the rest of his crowd. I'm
a bit hurt that he chooses to go off just after we married . . . Sat 9th – He
phones from Chipisi, wherever that is? Let Tape Aids know no recording
for two weeks, as H is my monitor. Sun 24th – He's back, but has lost his
cheque book.

Sunday 1st October – A Braai at Jane's in Adderley Street, Randburg. It's H's
birthday tomorrow, give him a good leather wallet. Mon 23rd – H's daughter
Sarah arrives from UK. Fri 3rd November – See 'Dead Poet's Society' with
Robin Williams, best thing he's ever done. Sat 11th – Also 'Scandal' about
the Profumo case and pretty good.

Monday 25th December – Celebrate at Jane's, Boxing Day at David and
Gillian John's. Drive down to Umhloti on the North Natal coast and stay
in a flat belonging to John Ford (one of the lecturers at WBS at only R50
per day). A lovely flat with the balcony facing the sea view. It's a belated
kind of honeymoon. Wed 27th – His son Jason turns up with a friend.
Fortunately there are spare beds! We walk down 300 steps to swim in the
tidal pool. Drive to Umhlanga Rocks Hotel. Sun 31st – Walk along the
Marine Parade in Durban, bump into Tom and his friends. Thousands of
Africans everywhere and in an exultant mood, this is the first time they

have been allowed to go on the whites-only beaches. They swamp us, bumping, pushing . . . the mood turns ugly and go back to the flat.

Tuesday 2ⁿᵈ January 1990 – Drive back to Jo'burg. Wed 3ʳᵈ – Back working at WBS, Resume Tape Aids in the evening. Stop off at the Radium Café in Melville, a bit rough and ready, but surprisingly good food!

Friday February 2ⁿᵈ – F.W. De Klerk's momentous speech. Opens up the possibility of real Democracy and fair play for all races! What a brave man!

Sun 11ᵗʰ – Extraordinary, Nelson Mandela is released at last! Mon 12ᵗʰ – See 'The Belle of Amherst' a one woman play about Emily Dickinson. Vanessa Cooke just didn't have the repressed passion needed to bring this to life. I love her poetry, so much I was bound to be disappointed. Sat 17ᵗʰ – H is on a walking tour with Tom and cohorts in the North East Transvaal. He's stung by a wasp, seems he's allergic to it, says his leg is very swollen. Tues 20ᵗʰ – He's back, none the worse for his adventure. See 'Curl Up and Dye' a very funny play about a hairdresser written by Pam Sue Grant. Val Drummond Bell is in it, I knew her years ago at Stuttafords. Wed 21ˢᵗ – Boo's birthday, take her out for a meal at the Porterhouse. Give her Doc Marten's boots (it's what she wanted!) and a bedside clock. It's the deadline for applying for Damelin's Correspondence Course (she enters it, I pay and she flunks the course).

Saturday 24ᵗʰ February – Succumbing to her entreaties, we allow her to have a party on her own, without our supervision. H and I go over to Jane's. There are complaints from the other tenants the next day, mainly about the noise . . . a glass is left in the lift door is broken by one of her guests . . . this does not endear her to H.

Saturday March 3ʳᵈ – Ali's 8ᵗʰ birthday, H has arranged for us to go away to Nelspruit, to stay with Sue and Andre for their wedding party. All their friends combine to give them a microwave. At the Bundu Inn for dinner and very primitive conditions at their farm, mosquito's have a field day! Next day we swim and have a braai near the waterfalls.

On Thur 8ᵗʰ – See 'Rapid Eye Movements' at the Wits Downstairs Theatre, directed by Maggie Heale, good. Sat 10ᵗʰ – 'Shirley Valentine', with Tom

Conti as the Italian waiter, hilarious! Wed 14th – Record Tape Aids, afterwards dine at Pessera in Corlett Drive, with Eileen the head of Tape Aids. Fri 16th – A Gala Night at Franklin Players, they present 'Stepping Out', a musical about middle aged women learning to tap dance, fun, must think about joining them?

Sat 24th – We have a new house in Windsor East, 7 Eldorado Place, (purchase bond arranged by my old company). H is busy painting it – A nice little garden, lovely big sitting room in farm house style and a duplex with three bedrooms. Sun 25th – H's son Jason helps to move some furniture. He's a nice boy, cheerful, red head. His other son Arnold is an architect in UK. I clean and line cupboards and drawers. Put up net curtains in the sitting room. There's a pool in the complex and an attractive garden area where children and pets can play safely. Fri 30th – Move to the house with Boo and Yang. Open account at Trust Bank, Cresta. I like Cresta shopping centre, plenty of shops and within walking distance if H is away. Boo has her own bedroom, already covered with heavy metal and punk posters. H hates them, lots of friction between them, mainly about the loud music . . .

Monday April 2nd – I'm on leave. Wed 4th – Van Zyl Slabbert gives a talk at the WBS Breakfast at the Sunnyside Park Hotel. He's a luminary of the PFP. What an intelligent charismatic man! Sat 14th – 'My Left Foot' Daniel Day Lewis gives a fantastic performance and a gifted paraplegic. He spent a month in a wheel chair getting into the feel of the character!

Saturday May 12th – 'La Lectrice' (The Reader) very good erotic film. Sun 13th – Roger comes over, suggests Boo shares his house in Yeoville, (he knows about the dissension).

We arrange to give him R350 pm, plus R50 pocket money for Boo.

Mon 14th – I arrange to see a marriage counsellor at FAMSA, but H isn't keen and says it isn't necessary . . .

June 3rd June – Belinda moves out, plus crockery, pots & pans, linen, etc. to Roger's house in Becker Street. Thur 14th – Dinner at David and Gillian's, say goodbye to Chris, her eldest son, as going back home to Australia.

Thursday July 12th – Farewell drinks at the Business School and I enjoyed working there, but the difficult bus problems just got too much for me. Janice Hunt visits us, I like her very much – tell her she must meet Roger, so they can get married and I'll have her as my daughter-in-law! Her sister Greta is another matter, one of the Anglo crowd, she used to go out with H. Thinks she owns him . . . a tall moody Dane like her namesake.

Audition with Terrance Shank offers me a part in 'Inherit the Wind' for PACT.

Fri 13th – Leave WBS – good day for it! Visit Rennie House and Manica in Ameshoff Street, to see my old friends. Go to see Boo (I miss her) and give her, her SA Passport.

See 'A Chorus of Disapproval' with Janice, a very funny film about a repertory company, clever use of both sides of the stage with Jeremy Irons, Prunella Scales and Anthony Hopkins.

Mon 16th – Start a new job with Spedag, a Swiss/SA forwarding company similar to Renfreight. H objects to me working, says I've 'cost him a year of his life', because he will only be able to take leave next year? Sometimes wonder what kind of logic he's using? Sun 22nd Sun 29th – Read through '84 Charing X Road' at Eris Malan's house, (niece of General Malan) for Franklin Players. I'm to play the American Actress, H has a non-speaking part in the shop scene, (he sleeps through it).

Sunday August 5th – Our 1st wedding anniversary. Go to Roger's birthday braai.

Tues 14th – H is behaving oddly again and seems to be drinking more, especially late at night . . . , the dogs next door were barking, he broke the padlock on their gate. He did make them stop, but that's not the point. He's very anti Boo (Belinda), she has a very bad cough and cold, I gave her Medinite and she stayed over. In the morning, he made tea for us both, but not for her! I gave her mine and made more for myself. He's annoyed because she was coughing! When we left to go to work, he dropped me at the bus stop as usual, but dropped her off in Braamfontein, even though he knew she had an appointment to see the Dr in Richmond!! She waited 45 minutes for a bus and it never came, only managed to get to the Doc by walking through to Hillbrow and catching another bus. She was feeling really ill by now.

He's determined to do his own thing, no matter what. Working hard on the garden and making a rockery with a curvy path down to the gate, to make the garden seem bigger.

A man came in the evening to discuss bricks for the path. He insisted on interviewing him in the sitting room, switched off my favourite programme 'Perfect Strangers' on open time MNet. He could have taken him into the dining room. He's aiming to show off how much he's done to the property to his snobbish sister and her friends and wants to sell the house for a profit. We are married in Community of Property with accruals, I don't suppose I will fare very well if our marriage breaks up. Everything is fine, as long as I agree with him. It would appear that my only use to him is as a companion on his holiday.

Saturday 25th August – We go to Sun City and we see 'Celebrations' a 'girlie' show with semi-nudity, the dancing is good. 'And God Created Women' a new version with Rebecca de Mornay, but prefer the original with Brigitte Bardot! Win R94 on the one-armed bandits, helps to pay for dinner. Fri 31st – Watch 'Anthony and Cleopatra', Wits Student production by Maggie Heale in the Downstairs Theatre, quite good.

Sunday September 2nd – My birthday braai at our place, my family plus the Anglo crowd. Mon 3rd – Ist read – through of 'Inherit the Wind 'at the Summit Club. It's the story of the Scopes Monkey Trial in the US, when teachers began to teach Darwin's theory of Evolution at a school in the deep South, Bible Belt. Jimmy Borthwick, Mike McCabe, and Jacqui Singer are the leads, I play Mrs Blair, one of the townsfolk protesting against his theory! Maureen England is another protester, (a folk singer – Bryan said she used to have an affair with him, before I met him), she told him she was allergic to her husband's sweat, so she divorced him . . . one very eccentric lady. She's very thin, extremely funny and I like her.

Fri 14th – Gala Opening night of '84 Charing X Road' and we have a good audience. Eris battles with her lines as Helen Hanff, it's a huge part! I wear a mink fur coat, flimsy Fifties style dress with large hat and gloves, my scene goes well. H manages to stay awake in his scene in the bookshop, Eris leaves out a whole scene and there's panic stations, but she manages to get back on track somehow!

Sat 15th – Rehearsal of 'Inherit the Wind'. Art Gross, who raped me years ago when I was at RADA is one of the crowd. Now fat and bald, but I see his name on the cast list. He doesn't appear to recognise me, but he must feel my loathing. I say nothing to H or anyone. Mon 17th – We rehearse every evening, but Art does not re-appear, must have realised who I was after all. Thur 20th – Do three shows of '84 Charing X Rd.'

Sun 23rd – Collect my old saggy bed from Sally and take it over to Roger's house for Boo. Thur 27th – Write to Michael for the third time, but have had no reply?

Monday October 1st – Catch a combi van at Windybrow for rehearsal in Pretoria. Tues 2nd – H's birthday and Boo gives him a Moody Blues Tape.

Thur 4th – Preview at State Theatre with an invited audience. I'm enjoying the travelling in the combi, we swop food, sing, tell jokes, have drinks, (alcohol allowed only after the show, of course)! Nick has a dry sense of humour, Maureen is a scream! We share a dressing room. Fri 5th – Actual Opening Night, go with H and Boo in his car and come back in the combi. Marius Weyers is at the after party, a director of PACT. Everyone is very good. Sat 6th – Start recording a new book 'Killing in St Cloud'. H can't get any sound, something wrong with the system? Wed 10th – H goes to Cape Town and stays with his daughter, Sarah. Fri 19th – Opening night at the Alex theatre. Tues 30th – A Farewell Party for H at Anglo-American with speeches, flowers and cheques. One is for R500-00 and he very unexpectedly buys me a sewing machine with it!

Friday 2nd November – Show cancelled, as Mike McCabe has hurt his back. Ray from GAPA takes a photo shot of me for the Nedbank Advert. See 'The Freshman' at Cresta shopping centre with Marlon Brando is good, but huge. Sat 10th – Last night party at the Alex and I'll miss them all.

Tues 13th – At last, a letter from Michael! He says he's written a few times, but I received nothing. He's on an English course and learning the guitar in the evening – he met up with Angus McNair, when he was in UK. Wed 28th – Opening night of Franklin Players home – grown cabaret. We do 'Take Back Your Mink' with strong Bronx accents, pink satin sheaths, sequinned feather headdresses, long pearl beads, sheer black net stockings. After the last verse we pull apart the poppers on our dresses, drop them, revealing droopy twenties undies and drawers! For the 'Bridesmaids 'song we wear pink net party dresses and rosebud s in the hair. The Twits is a skit on earnest choral groups, ie 'Cherry ripe' and 'Flora's Holiday'. Pretty corny stuff, but the audience seem amused!

Saturday December 1st – Adin Scheepers moves into spare back bedroom. We advertised at Cresta. He does his own cooking and seems a nice boy, very religious. Sun 2nd – Spedag Christmas Party at Wemmer Pan in a lapa (open covered area). Nadine brings her ghetto-blaster, Hans Schaeppe our elderly Swiss Director, dances very energetically . . .

Sat 7th – H has gone away. Ian Clark-Dearing and his wife take me to meet Molly van Loon. She is a Buddhist and lived out East for many years. Her whole house is full of wonderful Tibetan artefacts, tankas (wall hangings) and statues. She appears to be a calm and a wise woman. Wed 12th – H is back and we have words, I must look for a flat, can't stand his bitchy remarks. Apologises, says he'd been drinking. Persuade him not to go to a Scientology meeting, Bryan had warned me how dangerous they are. (Yvonne works for one and he never pays her).

Tues 18th – Dinner party, Shelagh and husband, Rosalie, Peter Lotis and Zia – we listen to F.W. De Klerk's speech. Fri 21st – 'A Nativity' at the Market Theatre. Wacky, wonderful play! Nic Ellenbogen and Ellis Pearson are given a standing ovation!

Sat 22nd – Have invited a few people for drinks, his sister and David, Eris Malan, Rosalie and Peter. H is in a funny mood, keeps on hiding and popping out at me. He serves a variety of drinks. Tidying up the sitting room the next day and I find a full glass behind Eris's chair. Knowing just how much she likes her 'dop' (drink), I'm puzzled. Taste it, it seems to contain a mixture of whisky, gin, brandy, coke . . . I ask him about it. He flares up, we have a full-scale row! He finally admits he's an alcoholic, he thought he could beat it and then agrees to go to an AA meeting. Goes that evening and I lock the drinks cupboard.

Mon 24th – Dine at the Sutherlands with Boo, a 'slap-up' meal! Tues 25th – My family come to me, plus Jason. Thur 27th – Back to work, Boo leaves, I give her some of my clothes, she doesn't have many . . . Mon 31st – New Year's Eve party at Rita's house and we bring our own food and drink. Sit out side in the moonlight, a half-circle of chairs – no one says anything, it's cold and there's no party spirit.

1991 Diary for this year is lost – So can only pick out certain events.

Spedag started to reduce it's staff, preliminary to a business take-over. I wasn't sorry to go, it was a dreary company. Typing accounts was soul-destroying. Found a job in Rosebank – the United Building Society, working as a switchboard operator/service support in the Enquiry section and they were now made into a Bank. Thank God they never made me a Teller, although one of my duties became adding up the day's transactions and making sure they balanced! It was a really nice building with a lovely internal garden, near the shops and easy to get to by bus from almost anywhere – except Windsor East! H had to give me a lift every day, to which he objected . . . I got on well with the staff, especially my relief, a charming little Portuguese body, Aurora.

One Saturday H and I came in to do our weekly shop at Pick n Pay in the Firs shopping centre. I had a black leather handbag hanging in front of the trolley. Suddenly noticed it was missing, went to the manager, raised a hue and cry, but by the time it was found, empty on a shelf, the thief was long gone. I had a whole trolley load of shopping and no money to pay for it. H had scampered, as soon as he saw there might be trouble. Found him skulking around nearby shops. Went to my bank's ATM – the thieves had already emptied my account. My bank manager was wonderful, allowed me a R600 loan and also gave me enough cash to pay for the shopping. H was merely embarrassed and seemed to think it was my fault . . . , but you don't expect that to happen in such a reputable area . . . , we trundled unhappily home.

Our lodger Adin fried some sausages one night and nearly set the place on fire, he didn't know you only have to prick the skins and add a little water, not pour oil on the frying pan! Somehow that was my fault as well. Lying in bed one night he said – out of the blue, 'You know, you are not a good wife', so went to see Angus, this was the third divorce he'd instituted for me! I told him about H's drinking, odd behaviour, constantly going away on trips with his buddies, his meanness, nastiness to Boo in particular and his sister's snobby attitude.

We started to lead separate lives. I found a flat in Craighall, (easy to get to work from there). Clive phoned me one day, then took me out to lunch. He was a louse in many ways, but at least he seemed to like me! I still belonged to Franklin Player's. We won an award at the Drama Festival, with Edward Albee's 'The American Dream', a theatre of the absurd play, I was 'Mommy'.

On the 8th of December – I went to the Supreme Court for my divorce. The crotchety old Judge said, 'You've only been married two years, aren't you being a bit childish'? I insisted that we had irreconcilable differences, so it went through. Zia went with me and her dog Muffin snuggled into her handbag. He was very good, not a sound! We had agreed to keep whatever we had owned previous to marriage, plus I kept the sewing machine. All quite amicable really, we still continued to see each other, as friends, just didn't live together.

Saturday January 25th 1992 – Braai at Jane's, Roger comes over and belatedly opens his Christmas presents! Next day H brings over Millie's TV, carpet and evening bag, donated by Gillian, but only on loan. (Reg and Millie died at the end of 1991).

Saturday 15th February – Tea Party at Zia's flat and Joan Blake is there, frail, but beautifully made-up of course. She was a marvellous revue artiste. She died soon afterwards. Mon 24th – Start my 15 day holiday. H and I catch the Greyhound Bus to Durban. It's very misty and stay at the Golden Sands, it's deteriorated over the years . . . . The night porter insists we must pay R900 cash in advance . . . , so we have to find an Autoteller open at night, draw half each from our own banks at Mangrove Beach centre. The flat is grubby, sleazy and not a great start to our stay. I treat us to a meal at the Elangeni Hotel, delicious kingklip to cheer us up! Next day we go to the Indian Market in Grey Street, buy lovely curry spices. Films at the Wheel,

H sees 'Frankie and Johnny', I see 'Deceived'. (It's good that we can choose different films without a row)!

Thur 27ᵗʰ – Lunch at the Elangeni with Guy Bradley, H's old architectural friend, he's charming, but terribly old and frail.

Sunday 1ˢᵗ March – H leaves for JHB with his backpack, walks to the station, what a tough old nut he is! Tues 3ʳᵈ – Clive now works in Durban office, meets me for lunch, then in the evening to the Maharanee, then an extended pub crawl, not my idea of fun . . . he gets drunk, of course. Durban a big disappointment . . . and he is tied up with his son all the time. Catch the Translux bus back to Jo'burg and H meets me. Yang is very glad to see me! Flat stinks of garbage, Boo only stayed for three days, Jane looked in and fed Yang. Mon 9ᵗʰ – Back at work. Sat 14ᵗʰ – H takes me for a meal at Hunter's Pride in Blairgowrie, Tom, Rita and new baby are there. Mon 16ᵗʰ – Boo now has two jobs, one running an ice-cream parlour in Yeoville and the other, a waitress in the evening.

Tues 17ᵗʰ – Hooray! Referendum Day! The Yes votes win – I tried to vote, but was not allowed to as am not a South African Citizen. Fri 20ᵗʰ – Tony from GAPA phones, books me for the Telkom Advert. Sat 21ˢᵗ – Film in a lovely house in Melville. Hans Kuhle directs and know him from the 'Diggers' series. A simple plot, a couple in bed with their son phoning from overseas, simulate great excitement. Paid peanuts, but it all helps . . . Thur 26ᵗʰ – rehearse the 'Twits' at Joan's flat. Our 'cod 'choir was such a hit we've been putting it on at various old-age homes! Sun 12ᵗʰ – Braai at Jane's and take Easter Eggs for Ali. Thur 16ᵗʰ – Yang and I house-sit at Jane's and to make sure I know how to work all the alarms! Thur 23ʳᵈ – 'Dead Again' with Kenneth Branagh and Emma Thompson, go with Christine Roberts and used to know her when I was at Stuttafords. Sat 25ᵗʰ – With H to see 'Van Gogh' at the 7 Arts. Brilliant, but too long!

Sat 9ᵗʰ May – Rosalie Waugh marries Peter Lotis at St Francis Church. She looks lovely in a slim long oyster satin dress with an over blouse of sequinned ecru lace. Party at Dan Hill's house with all the old muso's in full force. Sun 11ᵗʰ – Mother's Day – Go with Jane to Gareth's Nursery School. Best pudding competition, spit braai and fun! Roger & Boo phone to wish me. He takes me to Dickens Inn for a meal.

Fri May 15th – Go with H to the Everard Reid Gallery for an Opening with drinks supplied. Dine at the Hunter's Pride Inn and changed it's image again, now it's a biker's hangout, the bikes arranged round what used to be the dance floor! Joshua Hunt has his first birthday party in the open air at Rhodes Park. His mother Janice is a sweet girl . . . I give him a blue jersey, he's very bonny. Greta ignores me, thinks I shouldn't have divorced H, but she was there on the occasions when he treated me shabbily.

Saturday 6th June – See 'Grand Canyon', Robert Altman's brilliant film, a series of inter-related cameos. Fri 12th – Fed up with the United and go job hunting. Sun 28th – Braai at Jane's, Roger and plus Boo with her lovely shiny hair is now in dreadlocks . . . discuss my moving in with Jane. I'll pay them R600 per month.

Sunday August 2nd – Roger's birthday, give him a nice Indian shirt from Kashgar. He gives us both a set of Shogun knives! Have decided I'll stay with Jane and Neil, until I've saved up enough money to go back to UK to live, as I'm now very homesick. Have sold the fridge, washing machine and no room at Jane's for the lounge suite, will sell that as well. Wed 30th – Move in to 34 Jean Road, Blairgowrie with Jane.

Saturday 5th September – Joan Blake is dead. Tea at Zia's – Molly Seftel, Olive King, Heather McDonald Rouse, the costume designer, Muff Evans, we have a great old gossip! Mon 21st – Boo has lost 4 and a half kgs at Weighless! She's moved in with Yvonne. Tuesday 6th October – Lunch with Clive at the outside pizza restaurant in Rosebank Mall. Such huge portions and give half of mine to a little black beggar. Wed 7th – On leave and he pops in, proposes to me again – I quite fancy the idea of living in Durban. (It's not easy living with Neil, he treats Jane so badly, but I have to keep shtum.)

Thusday October 15th – Skinheads Court case – Boo has been threatened, told not to appear as a witness. Her friends were attacked and their flat was vandalised.

Fri 30th – catch Flitestar to Durban and met by C. Sat 31st – All Hallows Eve, we are engaged and out to dinner at Bailey's in Umhlanga Rocks.

Sunday November 1st – Return flight to JHB. Sat 28th – Jane's belated birthday celebration at the Bayerisherhof and terrible smell of pigs and drains. The Kasson's and Kerr's with us, Neil refuses to come, as usual. We all put money (R60) in a tankard on the table as a sort of kitty, when we come back from dancing, a cleaner has pinched the lot, kind of spoils the fun.

Saturday 5th December – Ronnie Kasson's party, PJ, the Texas oil man and Stephanie are there, (their baby daughter had cerebral palsy and died), but they've now had another healthy baby, thank goodness). Thur 10th – Roger borrows R1000 from me and another R1000 from Jane, so he can buy a car. Wed 16th – Back in Durban, Michael is in JHB with his mother so C and I have some privacy and perhaps get on better! Go to the Edward to dance at the Causerie, but they've turned it into a Casino. Dine at Tong Lok, I choke halfway through the meal, but recover. Fri 25th Dec – At Jane's on patio for Christmas lunch with cold yellowtail fish, salad and turkey. Wed 30th – Hand in my notice, UBS won't give me a transfer to Durban.

Saturday 9th January 1993 – Jacques birthday and go to his farm. Lots of people, great fun! Dance with Gavin, a Jim Morrison look-alike. There's quite a strong attraction there – Jane is shocked that I can still appeal to a younger man? A very strong wind blows us all inside, we have to put out the braai fire in case the sparks set fire to the thatch. Fri 15th – Roger picks me up and we go to have dinner with Peter and Rosalie in Hunter Street, Yeoville. Most enjoyable evening. Sun 24th – Farewell braai at Jane's. Rosalie and Peter, Zia, Roger, Boo, Matthew Oates (the 'Nosh' choc bar ad man) and his girlfriend Winnie, the drummer from the 'Dyslexics'. Fri 29th – Drinks upstairs at Dewars with old friends from UBS. Jane and I go on to Rumours, expecting to hear jazz, Zane Cronje at the piano plays well, but not jazz . . . it's really drab there these days. Sun 31st – Rumours again. Roger takes Boo and I. Michelle Maxwell is singing, she's <u>so</u> good with Art Kelly on the guitar and Stan Jones on piano. She and I have a little hug and a weep, remembering the time when we were both in 'Madame de Sade'. Michael Keir is there, his gargoyle sneer has become fixed, it's like 'The Picture of Dorian Grey' in reverse. Boo whispers that once when he gave her and Georgie a lift, he tried to touch her up. He comes over all smiles, I ignore him.

Thur 4th February – The movers arrive on time, only charge R385. I arrive on the coach to Durban at 5pm. C and Michael met me. His flat is in Clarence Road, on the ground floor. It's big, old, terribly stuffy, heavy red curtains in the sitting room. Can hardly breathe at night. C leaves the bathroom door open, no privacy and the loo smells of men's wee. Clothes, bedding, towels all have a strange musty smell, I soon learn that Durban smells like that, especially when it's humid. I feel like an interloper. His son is off-hand, says virtually nothing, but they go off to his bedroom and have great giggles together. Tiger, their tom cat, is very boisterous, I hope poor old Yang will be able to cope with him when she arrives. Sun 7th – Go to the beach at Umhloti, blown to smithereens. Mon 8th – Meet their girl, a real tough bossy boots. She usually does all the buying and cooking of food. My being here has really put her nose out of joint! C says she overspends when she buys at the local Spar grocery (although how he thinks buying food for 3 instead of 2, plus another cat, could work out cheaper)? Agreed she probably buys extra for her family, as all the servants do that, it's understood. Wed 10th – Discover Tape Aids is just down the road! Go there and meet Stella the boss lady, very nice and she gives me two books to record straightaway!

Sat 20th – C drives us to Jo'burg for Boo's 21st birthday party. C drops Michael off with his mother. We go on to the 'Oribi' Pub (known as the 'Orrible'), near my old flat Sanview. It had a lurid reputation, frequented by biker's, but now it has a 3-piece band, old people are dancing, C is a bit boozed and goes into his lurching pelvic mating dance! Sun 21st – Jane & Neil host the party. I give Boo a thick-linked silver ID bracelet, C a porcelain perfume jar, Roger, Ali, The Sutherlands, Tanya and Mark, her new boyfriend are there. Mon 22nd – Pick up Michael and Yang. Heavy rain starts outside Pietermaritzburg. Yang wouldn't stay in the basket and got stuck under the driving seat, by the time we manage to coax her out she wee'd and the whole car stinks. All get soaked in the torrential rain when we unload the car!

Wednesday 24th February – Go job-hunting, C says I don't need to work, but I shall go mad sitting in that stuffy flat! Try Leisuretime near the Wheel, they work at weekends, so that's out, C expects me to be at his beck and call at the weekends . . . Sat 27th – Go to Makro, buy R500 worth of foodstuff, it's supposed to be very cheap, but some of the items are more expensive than in normal shops. Play Putt Putt with Michael.

Monday March 1ˢᵗ – Claim unemployment money from Manpower. Leave original resignation letters in their file, haven't made copies . . . they lose them, so only pay me for two years!! Tues 2ⁿᵈ – Record 'Words, words, words' for Don. Good to see Maureen Adair and Roger Service from the old days, (1964). Fri 5ᵗʰ – see film 'Last of the Mohicans' with Daniel Day Lewis, fantastic! Sat 6ᵗʰ – Raving Ron is on at the Cockney Pride Pub at the Beach Hotel, a very funny entertainer who sings ballards, plays guitar and drinks a series of 'wines 'lined up in rows. Tues 9ᵗʰ – Go to the Workshop, arrange to start at 'Juluka' a curio shop, next Saturday. C will just have to accept it . . .

Fri 12ᵗʰ – Reading 'Impersonal Affairs 'at Tape Aids. Sarah Payne is my monitor. She has the most glorious thick brown hair hiding a pinched and wan little face with huge specs. The hair appears to be taking nourishment away from her body.

Sat 13ᵗʰ – Work at Juluka with interesting ethnic stuff. Plenty of tourists wander in.

Sun 14ᵗʰ – C already moaning about me working. Discover they are only paying me R50, not the 100 promised. So I take the money and run! Wed 17ᵗʰ – No sign of my pension cheque from UBS. Buy a bathroom scale and electric fan at game. Dine at the Woodcutters, quite a nice place, Michael likes it (pretty young waitresses)!

Mon 22ⁿᵈ – Start a course with Computer Practices, Word Perfect and Lotus. C and I pay half each. Thur 25ᵗʰ – Course finished, but I can go back and practise if I want to.

Wed 31ˢᵗ – Collect Michael from DHS school and take Tiger and Yang to the cattery. Off to Cape Town and have to go via Bloemfontein and spend the night there, as too much banditry in the Transkei. Two meerkats sitting up and peering comically at us at the roadside, plenty of buck and so strange – two ostriches wearing balaclavas because of the cold!

Thursday April 1ˢᵗ – Arrive at Llandudno in Cape Town. Stay in a lovely little flat built into the rocks. Incorporating them as part of the wall with little pockets of flowers like a rockery. Very nice building constructor lives in the flat above – he designed and built both flats himself. If we crane our heads round to the left we can just see Sandy Bay, the Nudist Beach! Anyway, it's so chilly, not many nudes about! Happy just looking out to sea and the view is so glorious . . . Fri 2nd – Visit the Victoria and Albert new Waterfront Complex. Great place, all kinds of boaty things to look at, lots of outdoor pubs. Later visit C's relatives. Mon 5th – Hout Bay, Seal Island, stinking and writhing with seals. It's raining and go round the Castle, bend double in the dark little dungeons, horrible feeling. Upper rooms have beautiful furniture and portraits. It's dwarfed by the surrounding commercial edifices. Michael wants to buy an anorak, but he's hard to please. Traipse from shop to shop, haggling, sullenly settles on a purple and black number. A spoilt difficult adolescent. C wants us to pose together, I put my arm round him and smile, when the picture comes out – he's scowling!

Wed 7th April – Drive back non-stop and collect cats, they seem none the worse for their stay. Michael goes back to Jo'burg by bus. Thur 8th – Phone Roger, says Jane has had a letter from Michael – so he must be all right. Always worried about him . . . Boo and Roger had a wonderful time at the 'Rustlers Valley Music Festival'. Fri 9th – Good Friday, C and I go to a restaurant on the Greyville Racecourse, 'Déjà vu', cavernous place and no atmosphere. On the evening news – Chris Hani has been shot in Boksburg in his driveway, on his way home after an early morning jog!! So what will happen now – he has an enormous following?! Sat 10th – C went to bowls this morning, came back already sloshed . . . in the evening go to the Cockney Pride. C starts to insult the people near us. It seems he always picks fights and insists on going to another pub, starts insulting someone else, they appear to know him there, then chuck him out. Finally I manage to get him home. I've made a terrible mistake coming to live with this man and if I had a job I could move out.

Wed 14th – Michael's 14th birthday. C gives him a portable HiFi, I give him a Monopoly set. Out to Woodcutters restaurant. There are riots and looting in West Street, because of Chris Hani's shooting. Thur 15th – Quest have sent me to do temp work at Durban Transport. It's in Alice Street, a nasty part of town. C is almost an hour late to give me a lift home. It's very cold, aggressive crowds are milling around me, the mood is very anti-white. We play Monopoly in the evening. Fri 16th – Work with Monika, a very coarse crude person and she spends her time making personal calls, when not trying to sell Avroy Shlain cosmetics over the phone . . . Our nervous little boss seems afraid of her. C and I go to the Umhlali Hotel to visit Terry and Mary. He's supposed to be finding me a job at his Prospecton factory. The hotel is frequented by wealthy loud-mouthed young sugar farmers. Have an expensive meal, plied with exquisite wine, liqueurs, they want us to stay the night, but have a bad feeling about these people and feel there were sexual insinuations. He owes C's company money to do with import licences, but persuade him to take me home.

Thur 22nd – Collect another Manpower cheque. Surprisingly long queues of well-dressed white people down on their luck and a few vagrants. Sat 24th – Back in Jo'burg. It's Wendy's father's birthday. Big crowd, tables overflowing with food and drink. Collect Michael. Visit C's sister in Germiston and at mid day her alcoholic husband is still in his dressing gown. There's a group of AWB (Afrikaner Resistance) on a roundabout, complete with guns, flags, Nazi type uniforms, they are trying to drum up support for their loathsome army. They will probably do well, Germiston is a verkrampte (bigoted) area. Tues 27th – Roger has deposited the R1000 he owes me in my bank,

Fri 30th – Last day at Durban Transport, Told Quest I didn't want to work there again – that disgusting Monika!

Saturday May 1st – Workers day, all shops are supposed to be closed. Edgars is open however. C buys Michael a whole lot of clothes, he's growing fast. Fri 7th – C leaves with a friend for a Bowls Tournament in Jo'burg. I am left to entertain Michael, what an ordeal, he never speaks to me. We go to Game Centre and I buy him a TV game. Have lunch, I try to make conversation, he won't reply. Take him to see 'School Ties' with Brendan Fraser, he's catatonic, think he must hate me.

Tuesday 11th May – C is back and off work. I tell him I want to get my own flat. He seems surprised and shocked. Hasn't he noticed how miserable I am? We lie in the same bed at night and there's no communication. He doesn't even pretend to want to make love to me. He was filled with lust when I was married to another man and he was married to Wendy. It can only be the effect of all the alcohol he imbibes. I tell him what an awful time I had with Michael – the stony silence whenever I tried to talk to him. Next day, he goes off to Bowls, comes back very late, drunk, the food I cooked ruined. I sleep on a mattress in the sitting room. Can't stand being near him any more!

Thursday 13ᵗʰ May – Suppose this part should be re-named 'Starting again – in Durban'. Find a flat in the paper, Ottawa Court, corner of West and Gillespie Streets. It's on the 11 th floor and one bedroom with an enclosed balcony, (so Yang won't fall over). Parquet floor and partly furnished with a single bed (find out later it's broken)! Hideous orange velour 3 piece lounge suite, still beggars can't be choosers. Can just see the sea, squinting round the balcony. It's very busy in the street below. Fri 21ˢᵗ – C organises a truck with his company and piles my stuff on the back. See Mike the artist watching me, he's always lying about in the nude, painting himself and leaving the painting on his veranda for the old ladies to ogle . . . won't miss him! Meshek, the boss boy at the new flat finds a couple of helpers, we unload the truck. In the evening, I smuggle Yang there in a shopping bag, not supposed to have pets, but can't just leave her behind. She miauws a bit, hope she settles down. Perhaps she misses Tiger, although he gave her no peace. Bed sags at the head area and so had to fill it up with books. Noise from the clubs all night, shall just have to get used to it . . .

Sat 22ⁿᵈ – Free at last! Love Durban, the sea, relaxed atmosphere, just miss my family. Buy stuff for the flat. There is a phone, but it's locked. Contact Jane from the phone office nearby, she rings me back in the flat. Organise hiring a TV with Teljoy. Get the phone key. Wed 26ᵗʰ – Take my CV to the UBS in Smith Street. The manager says they are only employing black people now – it's racism in reverse.

Sun 30ᵗʰ – Long walk to the Amphitheatre at North Beach. There's a wonderful Flea Market there and buy two cups and saucers. Yvonne phones. Have a drink with C at the Beach Hotel. In the same way that H and I are still friendly. C doesn't hold a grudge and he's a very easy-going person.

Tuesday June 1ˢᵗ – Post a letter to Michael in UK. Work at Momentum Life for Quest.

Fri 4ᵗʰ – Record at Tape Aids. Mon 7ᵗʰ – Buy a double bed at Gain's R475 including transportation, turn flat around to fit it in. Phone Roger, he'll come and stay soon with Boo. Thur 10ᵗʰ – Nita's birthday party at Quest. Meet Linda, an English girl from Coventry, goes to UK every year to see his family – wish I could! Thur 17ᵗʰ – Go to the bank, change my Will, had left everything to Belinda, but it seems unfair now she is an adult, change it so now divided equally between all four children. (Not that there is much to leave)! Mon 21ˢᵗ – Play hooky, C takes me to the Wild Coast Sun. We get on so much better now he's cut down on his drinking. He plays roulette, has a system – places something on all the numbers, spends R500, wins back R780! Lovely scenic drive back and watch hundreds of birds following the sardine run far out to sea.

On Friday 2ⁿᵈ July – Jane and Ali arrive in the evening. Sat 3ʳᵈ – Jane and I go to the Durban July, the racing event of the year. Ali stays with Michael Meyer and his friends. I wear a stylish black and white number! We battle through the crowds to place our bets. Since neither of us know anything about 'form', we back the horses we like the look of, as they parade around the ring. I back 'Dancing Duel' for a place. Scream ourselves hoarse, it comes in 3ʳᵈ – we win R30! Back to C's flat, knock, but there is no answer – assume the kids are out. Wait at the nearest bus stop for an hour, by now it's freezing cold. Go back, turns out they were there all the time, but were using the back door? Collect Ali, catch a bus home, all rather disgruntled . . . Sun 4ᵗʰ – At Umhlanga Rocks, bleak weather, we sit inside while Ali explores the rocks and pools and at 11years old, he's impervious to chills. Mon 5ᵗʰ – He enjoys the film 'Aladdin' with Robin Williams's as the Genie and see it at the Wheel cinema. They catch the coach back to Jo'burg.

Sun 11ᵗʰ – Pulley over the bath breaks, as I'm hauling up the wet clothes, crashes onto my elbow, very sore. Meet Roy Titcombe in the lift. He commiserates over the injury, comes to have a look at the pulley and stays to tea. A very pious man, who lives with his mother.

Mon 12ᵗʰ – Roy pops in and says he'll mend the pulley. Sat 17ᵗʰ – Been working at Durban Fire Dept all week and battling with a cold and now in bed with flu! C turns up with Seija and her drunken mother. They leave, but he comes back and I make him supper, then finally he goes home. At 1.40am I'm asleep and he starts ringing my bell!! He's allowed in by another tenant and by now he's staggering drunk – says he was beaten up by thugs? Passes out in my armchair! 2 hours later he wakes up and has to go. On go all the lights, bumps his way out ricocheting from one piece of furniture to another. This is the end! Sun 25th – Walk along the sea front, waves are brown with sand. Look in Yang's mouth, her teeth look bad, the gums red. Mon 26th – Last day at Durban Fire job. They are a nice crowd and fun to work with. Thur 29th – Roy helps me take Yang to the vet and have to leave her overnight. Fri 30th – Collect her, she's had a tooth removed and others scaled. Roy comes to dinner.

Sunday 15th August – H is here. I buy an answering machine at the Hypermarket. Roy helps me set it up and leave my first message. Dinner at Gringo's. Next day he meets his friend Guy, now very bent and frail. Tues 17th – Goes back to Jo'burg. Roy comes over. Tells me he's single-handedly fighting the First National Bank for commission on a real estate deal he put through ten years ago and I think he's mad. He has epilepsy and his mother tells me she has to rescue him and revive him, even sometimes in the street or in the bath! She is quite frail having survived a serious motor accident a few years ago. He's borrowed another flat from a tenant who's overseas and both rooms are covered in piles of paper from his case! Now he wants me to write a book about him – the intricate legal niceties would befuddle a Supreme Court Judge – also it would be phenomenally boring!!! Thur 19th – Georgie and Boo arrive. They are staying with her brother. Tues 24th – At Tape Aids and now learning how to edit tapes. Roy finds out it's my birthday soon and insists on treating me to dinner at Gringo's. His friend Mannie has had a good idea, by putting handicapped people in information kiosks at strategic points in the main towns.

Thursday 26th August – Boo and Georgie come to stay with me and share the double bed, I sleep on the broken one. Sun 29th – Roger comes over, gives me a lovely dark blue duvet set with pink roses on it! Boo gives me music tapes, (which I choose at the CNA). Jane arranged for a lovely basket of flowers to be sent to me via Interflora, she and Ali phone and sing Happy Birthday! We all have a superb curry at the Westbrook Hotel, (used to be the Tongaat, of happy memory)! Monday, the kids go to Jam & Sons and Sand Pebbles. Tuesday, Boo comes back, but not Roger – he was wasted and spent the night in his car . . . lost all his money and my flat keys. I lent him petrol money to get back to Jo'burg. Have to get new keys made!

Wednesday 1st September – Yvonne phones, she's lost her job, Malherbe the scientologist cheated and constantly underpaid her . . . at 68 it will be hard for her to get another job. Thur 2nd – Interview with Mr Churchill at the North Beach Office for the Durban Recreation Dept, (Quest).

All over South Africa – at 12 pm, all people come out of their offices and stand in the street holding hands with strangers – we all wear blue ribbons and are silent for 5 minutes, praying for Peace – <u>maybe there's hope for this benighted country!</u>

Fri 3rd – Start work at North Beach office. I use a VHF radio for emergencies (ie drowning, muggings, to call the rescue helicopter, etc.). Share switchboard and reception with Wendy Milton, a plump self-satisfied woman, who's been there since Pa fell off the Bus (17 years)! Sat 4th – Today work at South Beach office and near my flat, luckily? Len Impey the manager, a pleasant chap with a great sense of humour. Also Pat Webber, a strange lady, as one minute she's nice as pie, the next grumpy as hell! She shows me as little as possible about her work. I'm supposed to be on a six month stint for Quest. I love it here. Mon 6th – Phone Boo to wish her luck with her new Course in Sound Engineering, which she paid for herself, out of the money she inherited on reaching 21 years old. This is a very positive step. Tues 14th – Record play with Don Ridgeway 'With Intent to Deceive'. Stuart Parker is there looking as sleepily, sleazy, as ever . . .

Wed 15th – Matthew Oates and Winnie get married, (she needs a work permit, he needs a British passport)! Thur 16th – See 'Rosenkrantz and Guildenstern Are Dead' at the Workshop theatre, very good local production. Fri 17th – Learn monitoring at Tape Aids with John Coldbeck. Roger phones and asks me to buy a Star newpaper, the wedding party at a restaurant are on the front page with him in the background, looking debonair as usual! Tell him to count the petrol money he owes me as a birthday present.

Tues 21st – At South Beach, a fisherman, half drowned, is brought in by the lifeguards and paramedics. He must have fallen off Veitch's Pier in a drunken stupor and bashed his head . . . he looks quite grey. Later I hear he died in hospital and a terrible storm blows up that night.

Tuesday 5th October – Phone Nazar the landlord, about the old fridge, which is rusty and iced up, says his father has one in the flat next door. I also tell him the glass towel rail has snapped and the pulley fell down, he says 'chuck it out'. His father dies the next day, so I don't want to hassle him. Thur 14th – He swops the 'frot' (useless) fridge for the one next door. Boo is still doing her course and has bought the P.A. Sound Bible.

Fri 16th – Saw Frank Churchill's 'At Home' and most enjoyable. Go with Dolores Niemand, a typist and others there are Allan Pembroke, a Director and his wife, Jimmy Anderson, a manager, Sanders Naidoo, Head of the Marine Inspectors, Basil Bridal, Manager of the Northern Life Guards, Dave Williams a tall and thin like John Cleese and Riaz Carrim our accountant. Frank has a plump jolly wife and like him!

Wed 20th – 1st day of rest. Erratic, doesn't fit in with normal working days, as I have to be on duty at the weekend. See 'Homeward Bound', a wonderful film about two dogs and a cat, who travel all the way across America to find the family who had moved and left them behind – based on a true story. Thur 21st – 2nd day of rest. See 'The Fugitive' with Harrison Ford, the train smash one of the most exciting stunts I've ever seen. Buy two 'Concert in the Park' Paul Simon tapes. Wed 27th – Inspector Elvis Govender finds me a small radio and looks more like a TV, because it uses such a large battery (it's so I have some music at work to listen too). The inspectors are all very helpful, Wendy sends them running in all directions for her, but I don't like to take advantage. (I gradually find out that they actually like being sent out, so they can do their 'own thing' and get off work). Roger phones, he's going to Mozambique to sell motor bikes! Dangerous there with Frelimo active (the guerilla uprising).

Friday 5th November – See 'Sleepless in Seattle' with Inspector Michael Govender. It was something he dared me to do to prove I'm not a racist! Not many people there, but the few that were, turned round furtively and made pointed remarks to each other – it appears that Durban is not ready for multi-racial friendships. Tues 16th – Roy asks me to go with him to the DP (Democratic Party) meeting, we are already late, but as we leave he sees a beggar, dashes back to his flat, comes out with a sandwich for him . . . Roy's a weird bloke. Meeting not very well attended, but the speakers, Colin Eglin and Chris April are really good. Tues 23rd – Phoned Michael in London to wish him happy birthday and he sounds strange with a cockney accent. He says he's very cold and sitting over a tiny fire in a huge factory room. He's with his buddies, Nick Fletcher, Simon French, etc. They are putting logos on T shirts. Thur 25th – Tape Aids Xmas Party and Harold Freed is there with his wife, Anne, who is very frail, we swop acting stories from when I did radio plays for them in 1964.

On Saturday 27th November – Bump into John Coldbeck, who tells me Maureen McAllister is living in Durban now, (I thought she was dead)? Also Nigel Kane is living in Pietermaritzburg with his ex-wife. He gives me her number. Tues 30th – Renfreight Christmas Pensioners Luncheon at the Elangeni. Only people I knew were Buddy Hawton, the Chairman, Piet Steyn, and John McDonald.

Wednesday December 1st – Nigel comes over in the evening and brings champagne. Go to Gringo's for a meal and swop reminiscences . . . Thur 9th – Maureen comes to my flat for coffee and has changed a lot with false teeth, (which she takes out after half an hour)! Thick short dyed brown hair with the same gravely voice and marvellous sense of humour. Her last boyfriend was burnt to death in a caravan they shared. (That must be why everyone thought she must be dead). Fri 10th – Life guards party at South Beach and join up with Wendy and Flo.

Thur16th – Day of the Vow, I work overtime. The Hare Krishna Float goes along Lower Marine Parade. A huge chariot full of priests and they throw flowers, I catch a carnation and get a beaming smile from one of the Swamis . . . hope it brings me good luck! They put on a marvellous firework display on the end of the pier in the evening. Peter Bendheim is arranging a local programme 'Radio Beachwise', phone Nigel to tell him, I know he's looking for work. Leave a message. Sat 18th – Nigel phones and not interested in Peter's 'Mickey Mouse' operation! I phone Boo, Yvonne has double pneumonia, Jane and Boo take her to hospital. Roger phones, he's now working for German TV. Fri 24th – C says he will take Yang to the cattery, as he's taking Tiger anyway. Catch the Translux coach to Jo'burg and staying with Jane.

Sat 25th – Christmas Lunch at Jane and Neil's house, George and Louisa with their kids Lauren and Gareth, Boo and her friend Jack, the Kasson's and their kids. After lunch Jack stands up, asks me if he can marry Boo, takes my shocked silence as assent, goes down on one knee and puts a zirconia and silver ring on her finger. It's a clever fait accompli, in front of all these people . . . I don't think he is in any way the right man for her (he barely speaks English and an Afrikaner), comes from a terrible home, violence, alcoholism, drugs, but how can I say no to the two young faces shining with love and hope. I nod agreement in a bewildered way. The hugs, pats on the back, toasts, help to shore over that my face must have shown my true feelings of shock and horror!

Sun 26th – Lunch at the Kesson's. It's raining, but they have a large covered patio. Ali has a great time playing with their girls jumping in and out of the pool. Mon 27th – Peter Blandy (my ex) is coming to lunch, so I arrange to be elsewhere. Meet Jack and Boo at the Pizzeria in Rosebank. See 'The Secret Garden'. It somehow underlines the great difference between Jack's lifestyle and the genteel, cultured English way of life. Tues 28th – Neil gives me a lift to the station. C is supposed to have collected Yang, he doesn't, and I have to pay for an extra day. He grumbles and won't ask him again. Fri 31st – I work and it's very tense on the beachfront – many muggings and robberies, most whites are afraid to go there now. I'm so tired and sleep through all the drunken New Year's Eve noise!

Saturday 1st January 1994 – Shots are fired on Brighton Beach, out at the Bluff near Durban. Many AWB right-wingers live there. Violence keeps breaking out all over the beach front and aggravated by alcohol. There's a stand-off at the North Beach Police Station, right next to us. The police fire rubber bullets and tear gas canisters . . . Wendy and I think it's tickets for us, frozen with fear behind our desk. A Commander faces up to the angry crowd, talks reasonably to them and manages to diffuse the situation, he's a very brave man. One of the Inspectors gives me a lift home at 7pm. It isn't safe for a white woman to walk alone now. Sun 2nd – Uneasy mood today, but better – they've all have got hangovers!

Tues 4th – Buy a micro-wave at Game (R599), paying it off monthly. See 'Mrs Doubtfire' with Robin Williams – hilarious! Next day Wendy's off with a sprained ankle so I have to work. Sat 8th – Roy's mother finds a turtle in their bath, it was dark and she'd gone for a midnight pee. Theirs is a seventh floor flat! Roy thinks it must have come from the Taiwanese guy's flat down the corridor – they own a restaurant . . . he must have been destined for turtle soup or maybe got apprehensive and toddled to the nearest wet spot? But how he got into their flat is a mystery. He takes it down to the beach to put back in the sea, but a lifeguard spots him and asks if it is salt water or a freshwater turtle? Roy doesn't know of course and finally takes it to the Aquarium. Sun 9th – Turtles again. This time a big one gets stuck in the shark nets at Brighton Beach and everyone thinks it's a shark – big fuss ensues! The lifeguards have to swim out and disentangle the poor thing and it swims safely away out to sea!

Fri 21st – Record at Tape Aids. Maureen and I go to the 'Cellar' downstairs in the Alhambra to see 'Brazil', Maureen Donne sings and a group of young men dance sambas etc . . . afterwards have drinks with Mervyn Goodman and David Lloyd Jones, who run the Cellar. Mervyn acted in School plays with Mo (Maureen). I chat with Maureen Donne. Sat 22nd – Sell my lovely grey Siberian squirrel jacket (ex David's mother) for R300 to Inspector Russell, as it's far to hot here for furs, so he'll give it to his aunt who lives in Jo'burg. Besides, there's been such an outcry against wearing furs ever since the advert came out showing models wearing real furs and blood spilling out from under them, as they're dragged along. He is a comical redhead and full of wisecracks. Fri 28th – Basil Bridal runs a Braai at South Beach in aid of a Lifesaving Event.

Monday February 2nd – Phone C asking him to bring Yang's basket. He says he's on the wagon now (oh yeah)?! Brings it to the office and order a taxi to take Yang and I to the Vet. She has fleas and must have caught them at the cattery – has scratched terrible sores on her neck. I tried flea powder and then nearly drowned her with the special shampoo. He gives her an anti-inflammatory injection and worm pills. Put a plastic collar round her neck. Sat 12th – Inspector Prakash comes to fix my cistern (he runs a private plumbing business on the side), he's also supposed to fix the dangerous plug in the sitting room, which is hanging out of the wall. Nazar refuses to let him touch it, but pays him for the cistern.

Tuesday February 15th – Nan phones and has discovered my cousin, Peter Ferguson is living in Cape Town! I write to him. Tues 22nd – Call from Peter and he had a stroke a while ago, had to retire and now paints for a living. His daughter Sarah is married to a Gascoigne and lives in Durban! We try to catch up all the years. Thur 24th – Roger phones, he's doing sound for the BBC in Pietermaritzburg and will stay with me Saturday. Go with Roy to see 'The Crying Game' with Stephen Rea and Jaye Davidson, thought she was a woman, until he flashes his family jewels! Very good, but a sad film. Sat 26th – Sarah comes to tea and a quiet, dark girl with frizzy hair, she must take after his wife, as Peter is fair like me.

Friday 4th March – Audition at SABC for Marketing, to do radio adverts.

Mon 14th – Speech and Drama Cocktail Party at the Elizabeth Sneddon Theatre in the University. John gives me a lift with his mother. Ellis Pearson gives a very amusing talk, illustrating it with masks and balloons, he's a marvellous mime! Meet a few teachers from the schools, where I shall be adjudicating – yes, have a new career possibility.

Sun 20th – Go to Greyville Presbyterian Church with Mo, as she has become very religious and on to the "Flea Market", sit on one of the huge logs stranded on the beach after the '87 floods. Reminisce about the old days, her boy friend, Lance Lockhart Ross is now a tennis coach to David Adams, the aspiring Wimbledon champion and has become a Baron. This reminds me of Rigby Foster, that camp old queen!

Tues 22nd – See 'Schindler's List' with Roy. So harrowing, especially when the camp commandant takes careful aim at a female prisoner working in the grounds and shoots her with the same objective air, as if bagging a deer. Liam Neeson excellent, as Oskar Schindler, Embeth Davidtz is also good, a South African actress, who's doing well in Hollywood. Roy is strangely unmoved, what a weird man he is! Fri 25th – Day of the ANC March in Durban City Centre – expecting trouble, all office staff are sent home at 12pm.

Wednesday 6th April – Public holiday and Inspector Harris Govender visits me. He is a tallish muscular man, very anglicised in his speech and behaviour. He had chosen Harris instead of the unpronounceable name he has. Wed 13th – Boo and Jack arrive by bus. We go to the beach, they swim and play around. Fri 15th – I'm off and read 'The Bridges of Madison County' for Tape Aids and was later made into a film with Clint Eastwood. See 'The Piano' at the Workshop with Boo and Jack, a totally brilliant film, glad Holly Hunter doesn't say a word, she has a dreadful voice! Music is wonderful.

Sun 24th – Inspector Danny gives the kids a lift to the station. When I came back, find a radio, tape deck, binoculars, electric fan, bottle of brandy and a new pair of black shoes are missing. Mon 25th – Phone Yvonne, tell her what happened, she says she watched them unpack and none of those things were in their baggage. So now its proof, the flat boy must have done it. He was noticed yesterday, he left carrying a lot of extra parcels . . . awful to have to quiz her, but I couldn't accuse the servants without proof. Must get out of this awful place!!

Wednesday 27th April – Election Day! Determined to vote and was never able to do so before. I'm working at North Beach and allowed to take the time off, so walk to Addington Primary School. Huge long queues and everyone is happy, all races mixing and waiting patiently. It all takes two and a half hours. Exhilaration is mixed with amazement and never thought this day would really come. Fri 22nd – Harris comes over and brings me a toaster. I've made chicken curry, but he says it isn't hot enough! Thursday May 8th – Roger phones and says he's on the front page of the Star – in the background behind FW de Klerk doing sound for the programme. Sun 9th – Mother's Day and Duanne, Roger's friend arrives and bringing a new iron and some lovely soap. Phone calls from all the kids. Harris gives me a rather yucky perfume and I say, 'I'm not your mother'(He is 20 years younger than me)! I like him, because he's very brave and the other's respect him. He's the most senior inspector, but refuses to be made a manager. He's divorced, his ex wife is a captain in the police and more senior to him. She refuses to let him see his son and don't know why? Anyway, he says he just likes to give me presents!

Tues 10th – Inauguration of President Mandela at Pretoria. We all watch it on TV. Planes fly past with all the colours of the new flag streaming behind them, then helicopters follow with flags attached to them and then a whole lot of doves are released. Winnie Mandela is in emerald green with a huge hat. Dignitaries from all over the world are crammed into the stands. Nelson makes a wonderful speech and its a fantastic occasion!

Tues 17th – Go to look at a cheaper flat near Addington, but it's right next to the ANC office, where there is always violence in the area. Inspector Tim Treffly-Goatly says he might take Yang if I find a flat, which doesn't allow pets. He has a house with a large garden and has cats and dogs. Yang is quite used to dogs, because Yvonne had one. (His is a sad case – he was a brilliant mathematician, designed systems for NBS, went sky-diving and landed on his head. He now has a steel plate in it and sometimes acts strangely . . .)!

Thur 19th – Go to look at 82 Wendover on North Beach Marine Parade. It's perfect, overlooking the sea, small bedroom with sitting room, separate kitchen and bathroom. I'd be so glad to get away from the screams of the street children, howls of drunks being attacked and injured. Of course the problem is – no pets! Yang is so miserable in my present flat. Still can't get rid of the fleas now, as they are in the cracks of the wooden floors and leap up and bite my ankle – have to walk on tippy-toes like Felix the cat in the cartoon, so trying to book the fumigators. Fri 20th – Pay deposit on new flat.

Sat 28th – Tim comes to collect Yang. I've put her few belongings together, tins of food, soft lining for her basket. Poor thing and she meowed a bit and shall miss her so much, but he seems a very kind person. Mon 30th – Tim phones, Yang has settled down well and she's even playing with the dogs!

Wednesday 1st June – Visit new flat and record 'Six Characters in Search of an Author' by Pirandello. Maureen Adair, Roger Service, John Simpson and lovely to see all the old crew! Fri 3rd – Rentokil come at last – They say it will take three days for the stuff to kill all the fleas with awful fumes and have to get out. When I come back everything is doused in a foul-smelling brown liquid.

Sunday 12th June – Moved to Wendover yesterday and the view is marvellous! Tired of unpacking and wander out to Bay Beach and sit on a log and eat a spring roll. Harris brings me my Sunday newspaper, but still no fridge and using a cooler bag and ice bricks at Spar. Watch the moon's reflection gleaming over the waves, straight into my window. At high tide the sea lulls me to sleep and no more screams and yells! Thur 16th – Harris has organised a fridge from the pawnbroker on the Bluff R625, a nice little 2 door Kelvinator and delivered at 3pm. Bless him for organising it. It's Soweto Day, but not a public holiday and streets are quiet. Wed 22nd – Buy a sofa bed at Gain's and the stripes are a bit loud, but will cover it with an Indian print counterpane. Fri 24th – Record an episode of "The Moon and Sixpence". Mon 27th – Jane phones, Humphry has had a stroke and his whole left side affected, so visited him in the Sandton Clinic.

Friday July 1st – Boo has fallen and broken her wrist in 3 places. Harris brings his big TV and carries it up the stairs with no effort. Sat 2nd – My phone is installed, Boo's arm is in a cast and Jack has to do everything for her. He now has a job as a barman at No 58, but now a gay club. Martina Navratilova wins Wimbledon. Sat 9th – Night Surfing Competition on at North Beach – wonderful sight, huge klieg lights high up on posts illuminate the bay, rolling waves an impossible blue with white crests, like Japanese paintings – one can barely see the surfers. Sat 16th – Mo's birthday, so we go to a party at a sugar farmer's house at Tongaat. Jackie Harris is there, she runs Speech and Drama, Alison Cassell and family. We play Pictionary and fun! Go for a walk in the veld (field), very dry, but many big trees. On the way home, Sue the nurse, interrogates me in hectoring tones about my Indian boyfriend . . . she doesn't find out his name though, Mo must have told her.

Sat 30th – Adjudicators Workshop, try to get the day off, but no – then Sipho Dludla, agrees to relieve me! Get off the bus more or less near the Institute. No way to cross the busy road, except by a narrow bridge over the dual carriage way!! The railing is below my waist level and walking across it, is one of the most terrifying things I have ever done. The traffic seems to lure me to the edge. I put one foot in front of another, advance with my eyes closed, holding on for dear life. An African lady gives me a funny look, when I finally reach the end, the bridge is so narrow that she had to wait for me to cross. (She must have heard my screams)! The Workshop is excellent and John Coldbeck gives an amusing talk. He then gives me a lift back.

Tuesday 9th August – Meet at Mo's flat, see 'Hamlet' at the Playhouse and Martin le Maitre in the title role. He's wonderful in the Player's scenes, but in the more serious parts he remains comical, a big shambling bear of a man, his soliloquy's addressed directly to the audience a` la Henry Irving. His forte is comedy. It's a strange modernistic noisy set, the Ghost of Hamlet's Father makes an awful row clanking over the bridge to the castle walls! In the bar afterwards we chatted, I told him what I thought, a bit cruel, but with hindsight, I believe it did him good, because his next role in a comedy sitcom is such a success and he never looks back! His wife is Megan Wilson (who was with me in Inherit the Wind).

Thursday 11th August – Boo and Jack came to stay for a while and her arm is very weak and Jack still having to do everything for her. Sun 14th – Have to work at the Rachel Finlayson pool, as a Cashier. They have no one else to do it, so up at 5am and to be there at 6pm. A terrible storm is raging and trip trying to get inside the gate and twist my ankle. Its very quiet all day, because of the awful weather and still have to stay till 6pm. Mon 15th – Have a row with Boo, we were watching a news programme, two whites have been arrested for theft and Jack is in the bathroom, I mutter 'bloody Afrikaners' to myself, but she heard me – says Jack did too . . . he takes offence, of course. Tues 16th – He leaves in a huff!

Thur 18th – Get a lift to Clayhaven Indian Primary School and I adjudicating their Drama exams. Quite fun, some of the girls are good, but some have the typical 'singsong' intonation, which spoils the effect. One poor little soul is so nervous she wets herself. I try to make her feel better by telling her that the same thing happened to me once at primary school, but she's too upset to listen, a teacher bursts in and carries her off. They were terribly disorganised, mixed up the children's names and classes. Had to go to the loo, a mistake – no toilet paper, they have to wash their hands instead!

Fri 19th – Boo leaves early to catch the bus and is in a sulk (they just arrived and expecting me to cosset them, but I was very busy). I'm worried because of her wrist, but she just stomps off . . . At 5pm the Official Opening of the Re-decorated Office and in the entrance a little fountain runs over stones and plants, three goldfish swim in the bowl and a charming effect. Sun 27th – Harris comes over late, as his nephew has been in a terrible car accident, he's very upset (later the nephew died).

Wednesday 7th September – Roger phones and says I must watch 'Ordinary People' on TV, he did the sound. Friday 9th – Audition for 'Oliver' at the Playhouse, Murray McGibbon the Director says 'Why haven't we seen you before'? In an almost accusing tone! I sing 'A Nice Cup of Tea' from one of Noel Coward's Revues. He said, I'd get a call back . . . (if I got a part I would have to leave this job, which I love). Mon 19th – 2nd Audition and have to sing 'Where is Love', which is Oliver's song and it's too slow and high for me. Then had to do a very energetic dance with the other young chorus dancers, quite puffed after that! In the end Noreen Swanby gets the part of Mrs Bedwin, already does costumes for the Playhouse, so they don't have to pay extra.

Sun 25th – Spend time at South Beach, handing out 'muti' (medicine) for bluebottle stings (they are a kind of jellyfish). There are many lost children at the beach, people often leave them behind, when returning to the homelands after a holiday. Many of the gangs of street children start off this way. The South Beach office has moved to Bauman Road Depot at Victory Park, which is cramped and smells damp. Tues 27th – Record an Advert for Musgrove Centre at SABC. Fri 30th – Hear Boo and Jack have gone to Sun City to see Sting! Wish I could have gone!

Friday 7th October – Finish recording 'The Bridges of Madison County' and loved reading it, we had additional voices and music, a real production, well worth doing! Bump into Mo, she's off to the Kruger Park. Thur 13th – Humphry phones, Guy Bradley has died. Says he's anaemic and is thinking of moving to Durban. Fri 14th – Boo has bronchitis and wants to use my medical aid. She has a job managing a 'Photolab' shop.

We had a huge storm last night with driving sheets of rain and even came through the closed sliding windows which face the sea, so not much sleep. The carpet under the window is sopping wet, even with magazines and saucepans soaking up the moisture. Looked out at the collection of ships anchored at the roadsteads, even the big tankers were rocking visibly and their lights flickering up and down!

Mon 17th – Jane phones and having a bad time with Neil. His mother came from UK to stay with them and he got drunk as usual, so started being abusive to her, but forgot his mother was watching him . . . Jane is going to see our lawyer, Angus. Tues 18th – Tape Aids and supposed to be reading 'The Fountainhead'. Funny how impressed I was, when I read it in the Fifties! Now we will have to cut it extensively if it's worth doing. Wendy is expecting to get an award as Best Telephonist in the Council and comes in 3rd. Sat 29th – Roger arrives late and we go to El Cacador in Point Road, its dark, noisy and good food. He's been filming a Hindu wedding for 'Ordinary People'. Tell him about Harris, takes it well and he's open-minded.

Wednesday November 2nd – 1st day of Diwali and an appointment with Peter Gardiner's Agency, so leave photo and CV with him, but don't expect much in the way of work, everyone says he only finds work for himself and his wife, Caroline Smart, have done radio with her, she's a bit like Miss Piggy. Thursday, eclipse of the sun. Watch the Hindu wedding on Roger's documentary. What a business! Painted toe nails and hands on both bride and groom, special patterns drawn in the sand. Sat 5th – Harris and I watch the fireworks on the end of the pier, through my window until rain stops the display! Sun 6th – Give him R20 for a lazyboy armchair. He hauls it in – spiders everywhere, springs sticking out underneath. Put bits of sticking plaster on the torn parts, give it a good wash with handy andy cleaner – I really do need a chair! Tues 8th – Wendy off sick, Tim comes over to collect Len Impey's old typewriter, stays to supper and tells me Yang is OK.

Sat 13th – A female tourist is mugged, so I call the SAP. The muggers hide in the bush near the Snake Park and called the Dog Squad to flush them out. In another incident, a drunk young African woman attacks the IRB (Inflatable Rubber Dingy). A crowd prevent the Inspectors from arresting her. Another African woman has an asthma attack at Bay Beach and lifeguards give her oxygen, but Swiftcare Ambulance Service refuse to come, because she has no money. The Natal Paramedic Ambulance do finally come, but they take their time and quite a day! Thur 24th – Tape Aids Party and meet Cecil Northcote, a charming old man and a well-known radio actor in his day. Roger phones, has heard Michael has moved again and will let me know where.

Friday 25th November – Lovely weather today and not too choppy. Sean King from the Lifeguards wins the Endurance Swimming Race. Prizes and cups awarded at the braai at the South Beach Clubhouse afterwards. Tues 29th – Renfreight Pensioner's Lunch at the Elangeni and sit next to Gary Hopcroft from Swaziland, Buddy Hawton rhapsodizes about meeting Princess Anne, when she came out here recently.

Thursday 1st December – World Aids Day and wear a red ribbon. Thur 8th – Go with John Coldbeck to see 'Oliver'. Patchy show andClive Scott disappointing, as Fagin, Jamie Bartlett excellent, as Bill Sikes. Brenda Radloff, as Nancy and the boy who plays the Artful Dodger are good. Mrs Bedwin is really fat with a fruity contralto (not that I would have been an improvement)! Read 'Vivian', a biography of Vivian Leigh, there's quite a lot about her daughter, Sue Holman, who was at RADA with me. Thur

15th – Hare Krishna's put on a georgeous firework display at the end of the pier.

Wed 21st – Jane, Neil and Ali arrive and the next day go present shopping. Ali chooses an elaborate watch with all it's insides showing from the Turkish Bazaar. Drive to Umhloti and swim in the tidal pool. Neil sulks in the car! We have a wonderful lunch at the Westbrook Hotel. Fri 23rd – They leave 8ish and arrive at Port Edward safely. Sat 24th – Ali has been in hospital, vomiting and blood in his urine. Sun 25th – First time ever without any family at Christmas – at least there's lunch at the Office with all the trimmings. Mon 26th – Jane phones, Ali is better.

Saturday January 7th 1995 – Catch a bus to Jo'burg and Jane picks me up at 4am! Bless her! Have a braai with family and friends. Sun 8th – At Rosebank Flea Market to buy belated presents, a nice Indian shirt with toggle buttons for Jack, a one-piece short's dress in a patchwork design for Boo, an Indian skirt for Yvonne. Mon 9th – Take Ali to the Zoo, he's amazing, knows the names of all the birds and we have fun! Tues 10th – Ali and I watch 4 episodes of 'The Darling Buds of May'. Roger takes me to see 'P.J. Powers' who does Janis Joplin songs. Meet up with Tim Parr and Karin Jerg in the bar afterwards. We give them a lift to 'Mojo's', then back to their townhouse. They play and sing their new song, great and discover they are both Buddhists! Sat 14th – Kasson's Fancy Dress Party and I go as a Priestess in my long blue kaftan with a turban, Jane as a puppet with string tied on her fingers and toes, Ali as a painter with beret and a palette, Neil refuses to go as anything, but it's a good party (Someone went as a condom, swathed in yards of see through plastic).

Mon 16th – Back in Durban and see urologist, as have embarrassing moments, when laughing or coughing.

Wed 1st February – Nigel and Mo come to dinner and we discuss people we have loved. Nigel mentions Mirella, why her son was a weird child – he gets red in the face and becomes aggressive, as usual. Tues 21st – Boo's birthday and deposit R100 in her account. Phone the British Consul re renewing my Passport. Mon 27th – Speech and Drama Party at Liz Sneddon Theatre with John. Aldo Brincat does his thing, a very clever and funny man, a bit like Ellis Pearson.

Saturday 4th March – Very daringly, Harris and I decide to go out to dinner together to the 'Fragrant Dragon' and all the other diners stare, of course, but we ignore them. His table manners are awful, but that is something I may have to accept, if we are to continue a multi-racial relationship . . . I surreptitiously hand him money to pay on the way out. The staring and whispers get to me, as this is supposed to be the "New South Africa".

Sun 12th – At last have Michael's new address and phone number. So good to hear his voice, even more cockney than last time! Tells me I must buy Spirulina for my health, it's made of algae green stuff and takes me two years to find any, taste it – it's horrible!

Mon 13th – Booked into St Augustine's Hospital for a prolapsed bladder operation. Wake up full of drips, a catheter taped to my thigh. Sat 18th – Jane has come to stay with me while I recover. Tues 21st – Human Rights Day and toddle to the Blue Waters Hotel with Jane for coffee and scones. Fri 24th – Have stitches out and all is well. We watch Queen Elizabeth's yacht sail slowly past North Beach to the harbour – an historic moment, she is feted everywhere she goes! Sat 25th – Harris collects us and takes us for a drive past the docks and see the yacht all lit up, a wonderful sight! Carry on to the Bluff and have tea with Tim, see Yang and she's fine. Harris drops me at home and then takes Jane to the bus station to catch her bus back to Jo'burg.

Sunday 2nd April – Go to visit Mo, as she's moving to a PortaHome (like a permanent caravan) in Pennington. Lance has given her money for the deposit. Tues 18th – I phone British Consul in Jo'burg re non arrival of my passport. Sun 23rd – I have another row with Wendy and go up to Stephen Naidoo the Manager, to explain the situation and take the rest of the day off. He arranges for his relative, Savy Naidoo to work in my place on the days, when Wendy and I overlap. She's very pretty and he's grooming her to take my place – they call it affirmative action. They don't want any white faces on reception, so getting rid of us gradually!! Thur 27th – Freedom day and have been told my passport was sent to Jeppe Street PO on 3rd April, it must have been stolen, there is a lucrative trade in stolen passports. I will have to apply and pay again! Sun 28th – Phone Yvonne, she was attacked and burgled last week, her TV was stolen, she says she's all right, but wants to leave Hillbrow!

Thursday June 1st – I have a day off, but need the money, so work at a temp job for Quest. On the late bus coming home, the ticket box falls off and careers on down the road. Driver stops the bus and runs down the road after it! When he comes back he tells us all to get out – but changes his mind, when we protest. It was at the beginning of West Street, a dangerous crime area too. So no more buses due that night! Tues 13th – Union meetings everywhere and they're demanding a basic R900 for everyone, even the lowliest litter pickers. Harris's cousin Michael, vociferous as ever with his grating voice (he's known as 'exhaust pipe'). They all march to the City Hall, trashing bins, pulling down trees, damaging cars and threatening passers-by an awful sense of disintegration. Wed 14th – Mo visits me and has to stay the night, as her car got broken into, but luckily the Zulu night watch man spots the man and gives chase (No one faces up to an angry Zulu)!

Wednesday 14th June – (contd . . .) He doesn't catch the thief and it was only the side window that was broken, so not too bad . . . The other day, I met a man on the late bus, who plays the guitar at the Blue Water's Hotel nearby. He says that nowadays people are afraid to walk or even drive at night – the hotel used to do a roaring trade, but now he only has a scattering of die-hards listening to him. A man was shot on Bay Beach last week. In contrast on Saturday, a large crowd watch the Rugby World Cup, NZ v SA on TV in a huge marquee and we win 15 – 12! All seem merry and good natured, but little violence!

Tuesday 4th July – Send off another passport application. Sun 9th – Watch the local TV production of 'Titus Andronicus' and can never understand why anyone would want to put on such a gory play? It's in modern dress with Anthony Sher and is good looking like Castro, Jennifer, Roger's girlfriend resembles a thin-lipped 'boere meisie' (Afrikaans farm girl) and even with hands and feet cut off, manages to be moving! Audiences stayed away in droves, but it was worth doing for the SA cast, if only so they could put on London performances on their CV's . . . Sun 16th – Watch the Gunston International Surfing Finals and watch from the pier and then visit Harris on duty at CAC.

Saturday 19th August – I buy 2 tickets to the 'Wet Wet Wet' Concert. Persuade Harris to go with me. Marti Pellew is amazing and hits one high note and holds it so long, the audience erupt in cheers. Harris doesn't enjoy it at all, only likes Hindi music. He strides ahead and leaving me to scramble behind him – he doesn't want anyone to see us together. Apparently their men folk always do that (I think it's rude)!

Sun 20th – Roger and Jennifer phone, she met Michael when she was in London and says he's thin and his hair is in a pony tail, but he seems happy.

Tues 29th – My birthday and take cake, etc. down to the office. Roger comes over to give me a copy of Nelson Mandela's book, 'Long Walk to Freedom'. He's written on the frontispiece that it was really hard to get into the President's office and ask him to autograph his book, but as they had met a few times, Nelson graciously took the time to do so. He writes :

To Sheila,
Compliments and best wishes
N Mandela

Sunday 24th September – Nigel takes me to visit Mo at Pennington and her tiny home is nestled beneath huge trees. There are many birds and even monkeys, she loves it there. The only problem is when the leaves fall, they cover the house and garden! She has a beach nearby and absolute privacy. Mon 25th – Nigel and I breakfast at the Workshop restaurant, then walk to the Expo. His daughter-in-law, Beth Freeman-Kane is exhibiting her wild-life miniatures there. People are riding camels all over the place-bizarre! Find some more of her statuettes in the Natural History section and he goes back to Pietermaritzburg the next day. My renewed Passport has arrived at last!!

Wednesday 4th October – Alison of the Streetwise Agency takes a video of me, but doesn't seem very clued – up . . . and drinking wine at 9am . . . I don't think I'll be getting much work from her? Wed 11th – Watch a fantastic display of formation flying by the Red Arrows, heart – in – the – mouth stuff! Fri 21st – Fascinated by Kevin Kostner's expensive Sci-Fi futuristic film 'Waterworld'. It's been panned by the critics, but the novel idea of a whole world built in the middle of the ocean appeals to me! Impressed by the opening shots – he pees into a bottle, a tube runs out of it, then it's re-cycled, he drinks the result – a very clever and practical idea, literally a foretaste of things to come, when we have run out of fresh water!

Wednesday 1ˢᵗ November – Sherin from the North Beach Office tells me they've advertised my job at last – after two years! Must be the longest temp job ever!

Sun 12ᵗʰ – Roger phones and I tell him about the advert – says the whole family want me to go back to Jo'burg and share a house with them. Wed 15ᵗʰ – See 'The Bridges of Madison County' (the book I recorded for Tape Aids), Clint Eastwood a bit too crinkly, but Meryl Streep is good! I give two months notice at the flat. Mon 20ᵗʰ – Jane phones and has to go into hospital for a Hysterectomy. Friday 24ᵗʰ – Phoned Neil and she's fine. Go to Farewell Braai at Baumann Road for Officer's Moses and Prakash – they are being boarded (retired). Moses battles with sore feet, but Prakash has his own business and is fit. Sat 25ᵗʰ – Braai at new Kings Park Pool with Prize awarded for the Best Kept Pool. It's immense and beautifully clean!

Thursday 14ᵗʰ December – Quest Farewell Party. Wed 20ᵗʰ – Everything ready, boxes packed, labelled, movers come, wave them goodbye ! Look out at the lovely sea view for the last time. Harris fetches me in the evening and waits with me till the bus arrives. Usual curious glances from the other passengers and I've given him my standard lamp, hotplate and plus his own TV back. The reclining chair we gave to the night watch man.

Neil meets me at 5am and stay with them until my new flat is ready. Mon 25ᵗʰ – we are all together again. Sat 30ᵗʰ – Hear Boo has been mugged in Hillbrow and another black helped her up, luckily she's uninjured, but her handbag was taken.

Monday 8ᵗʰ January 1996 – At Senior Citizens Employment Agency for a job.

Tues 9ᵗʰ – Catch an Eyako (Putco) bus to Rivonia for a temp job with Stocks & Stocks. Normally, the bus would be for blacks only, but we are now able to mix races on buses and trains! It's a tinny, square cornered old bus with very thinly upholstered seats. Thur 11ᵗʰ – Putco on Strike! Just my luck! Manage to catch the only one running in the morning, but none in the afternoon . . . ring Angus and he collects me and runs me home. Find I've been burgled! Taken my radio and all drawers opened, thank God the wardrobe was locked with my jewellery inside. Couldn't get the TV out, as the outside security door was locked (they got in by forcing a window open)! Phoned the agent, he said another flat was also burgled, which is no comfort to me! Start working at Thompson's Tours in Dunkeld West.

Friday 19th January – Roger just back from Maputo, Mozambique where he went on holiday and has contracted cerebral malaria!! He nearly died up there and went to hospital, tossing and turning in his delirium and a syringe of fluid fell out of his arm. The nurse picked up the filthy swab off the floor and went to dab at his arm with it – he screamed at her not to use it, but she didn't understand English! He somehow survived, but looks like a grey ghost. Sat 20th – Georgie, Boo's best friend is going to UK and have a farewell dinner, Boo, and Jack also come and lovely to see Maureen and Ian again. Sun 28th – Nigel comes up from Pietermaritzburg and we go to the Waterfront in Randburg with his son and his wife. Roger phones later and he's very ill again and we get lost looking for his house. Nigel becomes very irritated! Mon 29th – Roger is now in Rietfontein Hospital for Tropical Diseases. In the evening, a nurse says he's better and has a rare strain of malaria, but they can treat it.

Saturday 3rd February – Harris arrives by bus and stays at a City Lodge. Jane drives us to the Waterfront, dine at the Fishmongers, where they serve the food in frying pans, it's fresh and fairly cheap! Harris takes Ali to the 'Cyber Show' and buys him lots of sweets. I stay over with him at City Lodge, but can't sleep in a strange bed, so sit up watching TV all night. He helps Boo and Jack move with Jane from a Hillbrow flat to a house in St Georges Street in Yeoville. The area has gone down since, I shared a house with Heather in '76 and it used to be a quiet little Jewish enclave . . . now the brothers drive up and down, shooting and playing radios very loudly. Wrecked cars are slewed up on the pavements and garbage everywhere. The house is very dilapidated with all the buttons on the gas stove missing? There's an old sangoma (witchdoctor), who lives in the back garden in a shed – Moses with a white fuzz of hair on his head and chin. Roger knows the landlord.

Thur 8th – Jane hears that her old friend Stewart, (who lost his leg under a train, as a schoolboy) has gassed himself in his car in Magoebaskloof!. He had just found out that his ex wife Mara and now separated, had formed a liaison with a man who lives on a nearby farm. Terrible news, especially for his two children! Sat 17th – Take Boo her card and present and the next day have a braai at Jane's. Roger comes and sneezing a lot. Also he was bitten by a tick in Graskop, where he was filming and now has 'flu' like symptoms – seems to be accident prone these days!

Friday 1st March – Give a month's notice at Thompson's, as can't stand the bitchiness, what a spoilt bunch! Sat 2nd – Ali's 14th birthday Bash with his friends from school, plus Gareth from Port Edward and his parents have come back to Jo'burg, as it's become too dangerous down there. Thur 7th – Have photos and a video taken at Characters agency. Also visit Cani Radio on the next floor and Andrew the engineer, records a tape of me doing various accents and dialects. An idiot who says' he runs the station' makes faces at me through the glass door, while I'm recording!? Sat 9th – My phone's out of order.

Thur 28th – Big Zulu march in the centre of town, everyone is apprehensive – nothing awful happens.

Saturday April 6th – House sitting for Jane. They have been staying with Mara up north, she's very upset by Stewart's suicide. Mon 8th – Ready to go home and lock my self in between the front door and the lounge and Jane did warn me about it . . . thump on the door, shout and scream. Eventually Fiona from next door hears me and she comes to the door – tell her I'm locked in! She phones for the locksmith to come, R200 later I'm free. Otherwise would have been without water or a loo for 48 hours!

Mon 15th – Start working at Salesearch in Jan Smuts Avenue. It's an employment agency for sales staff and answer the switchboard, do interview applicants and give them forms to fill in. Problem is – I have my back to the door and have to swing round to see who's rang the bell, then I press a button to let them in and later suffer from neck pain. Thur 25th – Roger has arranged a job for Jack, painting murals for film sets. Fri 26th – Harris flies up, as he has no transport, but expects Jane to ferry him around, she refuses to do it, he can use public transport like everyone else, after all he invited himself to stay . . . he sulks all weekend and we have a big row.

Tues 7th May – See physio re my neck pain and helps a little. Fri 10th – Boo is interviewed by Myra, a pleasant down-to-earth woman. She looks nice, I'm so proud of my lovely daughter! Sun 12th – Neil's birthday and also Mother's Day. Jane cooks oxtail potjiekos in a three-legged pot (like an old fashioned cauldron) over a fire. Delicious, the secret is to cook it in a pressure cooker first! Thur 23rd – Gillian phones and her father, Peter Ferguson has died of a heart attack. His widow, Honor is heart broken. They were entertaining guests and he was in a jolly mood, but suddenly fell down. They had been married 40 years. Phoned Nan in Broadstone to let her know too and I'm sad I didn't see him again. We send flowers to the family in Cape Town and I wrote an extract from a Walt Whitman poem, which I hope will comfort them.

Saturday June 15th – Roger and Judith (his friend from UK), meet up with Rosalie at the Civic Theatre to see 'A Tale of Two Cities'. An excellent production with Mike McCabe as Dr Manette, Jennifer as Lucy Manette. A large cast, Maggie Heale is in it as well. Life size puppets are carried on stage in the crowd scenes! Madame Dufarge is too young and not at all sinister. Go backstage to the Greenroom and chat to Mike and Jennifer.

Maggie's dressing room has a gold star on it and we remark on it, she says she has had it removed several times, but they always put it back! Why not – she is a star! She's looking a bit puffy, but seems to have shrunk in height. When we come in she's lying down, exhausted from running up and down the stairs in the multi-level set!

Friday 5th July – It's freezing! Humphry comes round with fish, chips and wine! He leaves early, because it's so cold. I've moved the TV into my bedroom and it's warmer to watch from my bed! Wearing bed socks, leg warmers and ankle warmers too! The one bar heater is not enough! On Saturday I watch tennis with Steffi Graf beating Sanchez Viccario and a terrific match. Next day, Richard Kraijicek beats Malivai Washington! Temperature at night is 4degrees and there is black ice on the roads.

Monday 15th July – Roger, Judith and her children collect me, as she's flying to UK tomorrow and we make a tape at Jane's for Michael. Roger and Neil sing and play guitar. I put my bit on it, but get emotional – can't stop the tears – it's been so long since I saw him – where do you start?! There's a power cut in the middle of it! Mara, her son Jarrod, and Alistair arrive and we light candles . . .

Saturday 3rd August – Zia throws a luncheon party and her flat looks wonderful, full of flowers, she sports a hot-pink velvet track suit! A Muslim cook arrives with marvellous dishes, pots of tandoorie chicken and not too hot! A gaggle of actresses – Shirley Friedberg, Fiona Fraser, Val Donald Bell (my old buddy from Stuttafords days & now TV's 'Too Many Cook's'), Molly Seftel and her equally tall thin daughter with masses of long hair, Angela Doughty (Megan's mother), Andre Hattingh, in one of her wacky creations, Reinette Maasdorp a good actress, now an accountant and Beryl Gordon.

Shirley is telling a story, waving her arms exuberantly and knocks Fiona off the slippery sofa! She is not amused. Roger arrives to take me to Jane's for his birthday braai. I tell them it's his birthday and they mob him with offers of food, champagne and pudding! He's embarrassed by all this attention and they want him to stay. He's 36, but looks ten years younger. Zia tells me later that we missed one hell of a party, but I couldn't stand anymore of the cackling din!

Fri 9th – Meet Boo in the Mall and go shopping for business-type clothes for her. Earlier she went on a 'dummy run' to see if she could get to the interview in Wynberg, that Myra had arranged. It's a very dangerous area and she had to take two African taxis, then a white man ran over to her, as she was walking along and told her a white woman had been mugged last week on the same bridge she was crossing – he insisted on giving her a lift to his factory, it was good of him to care. I tell her not to go to the interview and it's not worth risking her life. She goes off to her evening job at Spur in Highlands North and on the Monday, I explain to Myra what happened, she understands.

Sat 24th – Take a taxi to be at the Carlton Hotel early to see the Dalai Lama. The walls of the big ballroom are decorated with a series of tankas, (Tibetan tapestries). He wears toga – type red and yellow robes, is a small man with a lovely smile and an unexpectedly deep voice. The lecture is in Tibetan, pretty esoteric, translated by a young Tibetan man in a suit. The Lama's English is basic, but he makes himself understood. I'm lucky to get a seat in the first row with the contingent from the Kensington gompa (group). After the lecture, he walks along our row greeting and blessing us. I bow and say 'Namaste', with my hands raised in prayer form and at 2 pm he gives a free lecture in English. Boo meets me and we find seats further back. This time the audience is allowed to ask questions, but its mostly about the Chinese occupation of Tibet. He is a wonderfully serene man – Boo and I fall under his spell! I'm given a yellow cord that he has blessed and buy Boo a black T shirt with a gold circle symbol.

Thursday 29th August – I bring cake to the office, Olwen, the manager is back from New_Zealand and gives each one a little round cheese board made from a special Kiwi wood and drink a hurried glass of wine before closing.

Sunday 1st September – All the family come to the braai at Jane's including Humphry, Rosalie and her mum, Doris. Go to see 'Independence Day', but cinema very hot. Terrifying special effects. The water at the waterfront smells awful. Wed 5th – Third day off sick and sure it's that hot cinema and fetid lake. The phone rings at 9.40 pm – I get a fright! It's Michael, my son! He's played our tape, he plans to come out here soon, I can hardly believe it's him and can't think what to say, forget to ask for his phone number and address!

Sun 8th September – Horrifying news, Yvonne has been attacked by one of her tenants!

We hear a black woman, Miriam, lay apparently dead and her small daughter had called on Yvonne to help. The woman rose up and beat Yvonne with an ironing board, bit her on the face and hands, threw her on the floor and locked the door, so no one could get in, at last the door was battered down. Yvonne is found lying unconscious on the floor in a pool of blood. One of the other tenants runs to the nearby Rand Clinic, an ambulance is sent to rescue her. The heavily drugged woman says a monster attacked her – little Yvonne, 73 years old!?

Jane rushes me to the General Hospital and we wait 4 hours in A&E. Finally they say we can see her for a moment – A young doctor is stitching the wounds on her face with fine catgut, he's injected painkillers into her skin. We are not allowed to look at her face, it's too ghastly . . . Mon 9th – Visit her in the afternoon and we are prepared for the facial injuries, but not for the bruised, bitten, battered arms. She tries to mumble her story. Kevin Joseph the manager of Investec, the company who own the block of flats, goes to see her. Later has her transferred to a private clinic in Midrand, (the company will pay, thank god). Tues 10th – Go to see her and she's in a lovely private ward with beautiful soft sheets and more to the point, kind and caring nurses. Her poor hair is stiff with blood still and Jane wants to wash it, but the nurse says they'll do it tomorrow. Sun 15th – Move Yvonne's belongings and furniture out of Sunkist flat to Boo and Jack's house in St Georges Street, Yeoville. We have to catch the three cats first and put them in baskets. When we check on them later at the house, two have gone missing and find out they've gone up the chimney! Pack feverishly all day with Boo, Daphne, her daughter Tubby, Neil, Roger and a friend. Between us all manage the move, as Yvonne is still in the clinic and she will be surprised! Thur 19th – Her operation goes well and she has had a skin graft under her right eye. We visit her in the evening, she's quite chirpy and looking forward to the move.

Sat 5th October – Jane says Yvonne is getting better and can have a bath now, as most of her bandages are off. She's now living in the Yeoville house and Boo is taking great care of her. The case against Miriam comes up next week, that's if they can find her, she's disappeared, of course!!

Wednesday 13th November – Meet the cast of the Escom Film Advert outside the Holiday Crown Plaza in Sandton. Zia is there with Muffin and keeps on losing things, sometimes she even loses Muffin (it's become a standing joke amongst the actors)! We board the so-called luxury bus to Middelburg and staying at the Halfway Inn. I share a room with Pat Parr-Burman. Turns out she's deaf and why I found her a bit peculiar . . . , but she's a really nice person. Next day we lark around amongst the cows and cowpats, waiting to work, but the rain persists and boiling hot in the bus, freezing out side in our tiny shorts! The crew is always served first, of course, so we are tired, grumpy and muddy by the time we get back to the Inn. We do have a slap-up meal however! The pipes have burst and so no hot water! Late at night they've got the water going, bathwater – lukewarm and brown! Fri 15th – More waiting around and they film some tracking shots up and down the interior of the bus. The story is about a group of 'Ndebele maidens making pots, spraying them and selling them for exorbitant prices to unsuspecting tourists (us), as hand painted artefacts (the ad is for a spray-gun). We have to come back for another shoot when it's sunny.

Saturday 23rd November – Jane and Michael's Birthdays, but he is still in UK. When I get home in the evening I have a severe coughing fit and lungs won't take in air, take 2 puffs of my inhaler, no good, struggle through the security gate to get outside and lean over the balcony to get some air and at last a hoarse howl emerges! Phone Roger and he contacts Dr Osbey, who books me into the Sandton Clinic. They hook me up to penicillin and a saline drip – I'm too whoozy to protest and that I'm allergic to it. After many physio sessions, I'm more or less back to normal.

Sat 30th – Start working at the Forest Life Gift Shop and Cindy, the owner is rather touchy and busy with customers. A doctor and her family come in to buy presents and I'm in the back looking for a box to pack a decanter in . . . Cindy's left a large broken crystal vase in the middle of the floor . . . I turn quickly, cannon into it! Gouts of blood pour out of my ankle! The doctor takes me back to the Sandton Clinic and 7 stitches and an anti-tetanus injection later. Cindy pays and takes me back home (I pay her back half from my Medical Aid – she shouldn't have left the vase on the floor)!!

That evening – another crisis! Boo has finally admitted to herself and us that her engagement to Jack must end . . . he is abusing her physically and has been for some time! I had noticed blue bruises on her cheek, but she had 'bumped into a cupboard' or some such evasion. We must think of a plan to get her, Nana (Yvonne) and the pets, out of the house and I suggest she goes to UK.

Friday 20th December – The latest arrangement is, Roger will employ Jack on a film on the 3rd January, while he's away his belongings will be deposited at his parent's flat, plus a letter from Boo. Meanwhile Boo, Nana and the pets will have moved to my flat for a short while, until the dust has settled, so to speak. Wed 25th Dec – Lovely relaxing day at Jane's and have a cold lunch on the patio, then lie on the grass watching the two Siamese cats play with a stalk & a cushion, barbets and shrikes dart in and out of the feeder in the Syringa tree. We drink J.C. Le Roux Champagne and reminisce. Boo is with Jack at his parent's flat.

Friday January 3rd 1997 – D Day! Roger takes Jack to work at one of Roche`'s Flea Market's. Meanwhile Mini-Movers take all Jack's stuff to his parent's flat, most of it is broken, due to his violent fits! He then has been told Boo has gone overseas, so she has to keep a low profile in the meantime. Roger and Jane move Yvonne, Boo and the pets to my flat – this lasts only a few days before the menagerie, it's messes and the cramped conditions, because Yvonne pleads with Roger to move them back to the house! Jack protests to Jane, 'where has she gone, what did he do wrong'? Boo is upset, regretting her decision. Thur 9th – We try to re-shoot the Escom Advert, but once again rain pelts down, at least the farmers are pleased, they call us the rain bringers! So we all have to go back in the bus to Sandton!

Sat 25th – I have given notice at my flat and we all move back to St Georges Street. The driver has to tape his door shut there's so much stuff! Mon 27th – Moses and Pay (a helper), are busy painting the rooms and it rains like hell – my room is virtually dry, thank God! Roof leaks badly elsewhere though. Wed 29th – Interview with Quest agency, as have left Salesearch. Roger takes Boo to the British Embassy to collect her British passport, photos and copies of her Birth certificate.

Tuesday 11th February – Roger takes us to the SPCA and looking for a companion for Julie (who is to be spayed), which will also be a watchdog, we look at various breeds, big dogs have to have a six foot wall to stop them jumping over. We don't want an aggro type, which might turn on us!? The house is beginning to look quite presentable. Stopped the leaks and cistern fixed, the garden is cleaned up with plants and seeds sown. Boo has finished packing her boxes. She's collected her SA passport and ready to leave for UK.

Thur 20th – Zia collects me, to join the bus for the third re-shoot of the Escom Advert! This time the weather's fine, the shoot goes well with no hitches! (A lot of the original cast are either ill or have passed away) . . . Maureen Donne, Andy Bowman, Pat Parr-Burman, Blyth, Zia and I have a group snap taken. A helicopter takes aerial shots of the bus. A comical moment, when the bus is moved along and we are all discovered sitting in deck chairs with our backs to the road, (we were trying to find some shade)! Officious traffic officers trot up and down preventing cars from spoiling the filming. On the way back, I look at Maureen's flat in Clarendon Heights, where we used to live. It's spick and span, tastefully done up in black and white. She says she's marooned there and won't be able to sell it, because the other tenants urinate, vomit and spit in the lift and passage ways, have a threatening attitude and says her friends are afraid to visit her.

Fri 28th – Start working for Jo'burg City Council in Braamfontein, for the Quest agency.

Saturday 1st March – Celebrate Ali's birthday, they have been away on a fishing trip. Cook the trout he caught in the microwave with cling wrap, herbs, lemon and olive oil – simply delicious! It's the last family get together before Boo leaves. Thur 13th – A bag snatcher is caught by the lunchtime crowd in Jorissen Street, shop keepers applaud, he's black and even the black pedestrians cheer!

Monday 15th March – Take Boo to the airport and we meet up with Roger and her friend Samantha. Other friends were supposed to come, but we some how missed them.

Boo is very keyed up, excited, we have a drink in the bar. All around us are other young people. She's flying with Virgin Airlines and supposed to be a 'fun' flight, her backpack has been sealed in thick plastic. All of us are tearful and sad, but I'm confident she'll 'find her feet' there. We have all contributed towards her funds, plus travellers cheques. I wish it were me going back home . . . she's 25, older than I was, when I first flew out to Africa, but then I had a husband with me.

Tues 16th – She phones and arrived safely, Michael met her. Thur 25th – Phones again, is bubbling, happy and has a new boyfriend, Steve Bailey, an Irishman. He's talking about her moving in with him and ask her to find out more about him before she does.

Tuesday 29th April – Nan phones, her husband Colin died yesterday of prostate cancer. She is devastated, the poor soul. They were married for 47 years and at one point he was the youngest Major in the British Army. He had a marvellous war record and when a Signals Officer with the Chindits in Burma in 1944, he discovered a Japanese line direct to their HQ and so was able to intercept vital information. After the War, he served in Palestine, Germany, Cyprus, the Gold Coast and Singapore. (I give her Michael's address so they can go to the funeral, if they wish). Wed 30th – I tell Jane and Roger, we arrange with Interflora to send flowers. I've recently read an autobiography by John Masters, he was in the same campaign as Colin, as was my old Headmaster, Freddie Spencer Chapman, who wrote 'The Jungle is Neutral' (he later committed suicide).

Thursday May 1st – Have lunch with Maggie Heale at her house in Westdene, Zia and Rosalie also there. One-armed Tim arrives after an outing on his motor bike. He's an amazing man! We all have a good giggle about our adventures and foibles over the years. Tim works with Hal Orlandini in a flooring company. They've replaced their kitchen floor (which was being eaten up by white ants), with parquet made of old railway sleepers. Fri 23rd – See 'The Odd Couple' with Neil Simon's 60's play at the Market, Martin le Maitre plays the slob, Graham Hopkins the pernickety one, both excellent! Mon 26th – Some hail overnight, snow, slush and it's zero degrees! Roger buys us 2 electric blankets. He sells his beat-up Beatle and which has been reposing in our back garden.

Sunday 8th June – For two nights our neighbours have played very loud music all night!? Discover we've been burgled and Julie barked, Yvonne got up in the night, but noticed nothing and went back to bed . . . Our bedroom windows were yanked wide open, thank God for burglar bars! All they managed to steal was a kettle and a bowl out of the kitchen window. Julie must have scared them off! Wonder if the music was a ploy?

Thur 12th – Razor wire has been fixed on top of our fences now and a big padlock on the gate. Moses has cemented bits of broken glass on top of the adjoining walls. Neil attaches a bell on the gate, so our visitors and Moses's many clients can alert us they are there.

Fri 20th – Meal at Jane's and Roger back from his overseas film job and gives us lovely perfumes from Dubai. In Egypt he wangled his way into the main Pyramid with charm and a tip! Gives me a piece of stone from the tomb of Ramases 11!

Thursday 26th June – Jane has had a letter from Michael and he says I should go back to UK, thinks I could get points for a Council house?

Saturday 5th July – Letter from Nan says – 'How is it that after three husbands, you still have to work?' What does she know about life outside her sheltered 'Army wife' existence? I didn't marry for gain, but because I was in love . . . just not very good at choosing men! Discover Michele Maxwell is living in a house next to me and has been there for three years, so we have a great re-union! She's off on tour with her one-woman show 'Full Gallup'! Sun 6th – Lunch with Jane and meet Neil's mother, who's out here on holiday. Very tall, slim with twinkly blue eyes. Is an anti-smoker, very intelligent and not afraid to speak her mind. Neil is irritated by her! We watch the Wimbledon Finals. Pete Sampras wins with a succession of aces and no volleys – boring to watch.

Tues 15th – Serge the landlord has popped in and most impressed by our improvements, (especially as he paid nothing towards them)! Dinner with Humphry at the Black Steer and just got back from UK, where he spent some time with his son Arnold in Weybridge. His usual 'el cheapo' tour, staying with old ex – lovers, etc . . .

Saturday 2nd August – Zia's birthday lunch with Molly and Philippa Seftel get there early and prepare wonderful food – Mexican chilli soup, exotic salads, pita, guacamole, puddings galore, ice-cream cake with crushed biscuit topping, cold rice pudding with butterscotch ditto . . . I at least help with cutting up the salads! Give her an Angel card and R50 (she asked for money rather than a present). All the acting ladies there, as before. Sun 3rd – Jane and I go to the Flea Market and buy blue and yellow plates, the colour scheme for Roger's little house. Mon 4th – I get home from work to find an adorable puppy, wrinkled brow, black muzzle, slanty eyes and a sandy colour – reminds me of our lovely boxer, who died of tick fever in Uganda, so call him 'Butch' in memory of him. He's a mixture of Pitbull, Ridgeback, Boxer and Labrador.

Sat 9th – Woman's Day and find a pet shop nearby and buy doggy things and a cow's foot to chew on, a ball, strong collar and lead and find out about the correct food. Fri 15th – Roger, Jane and I have a conference at the Radium pub. I've been given notice by the Jo'burg Council (it was quite a long temp job). I plan go back to UK for good next year. Rog and Jane may move to Cape Town? Wed 20th – Go to Pension HQ, an official looks at my ID Book and says I can only get a pension, if I become a South African Citizen! This is a new law now, previously Permanent Residents were able to receive pensions and am rather shattered! Thur 21st – Temp at Cross Colours. The Cosatu Strike is on, so-called 'rolling action', which means they can go on strike, whenever they feel like it! Wed 27th – Go to Home Affairs. Get photos taken and should have taken my passport, but am not going to let it out of my sight, not since the last one was lost in the post. I have made copies of the relevant pages. An official says I shouldn't have signed myself as Ferguson Ward on all the forms, as my passport is just plain Ward – it would cost R220 to change my name, all my accounts are in the double-barrelled name, (my stage name). I'll have to join another long queue, buy more photos, it then occurs to me – I don't want to become a South African Citizen – I'm British! I don't think they'd give me a pension, even if I did change my name, so I treat myself to a slice of carrot cake and a coffee at the Carlton – in celebration!

Friday August 29th – Dinner at Roger's new house in Auckland Park, he shares it with Jackie Oates and her partner. Her parents are there and her mother has the most marvellous cheek bones that Matthew inherited!

Delicious Beef Stroganoff – Roger's cooking! Sat 30th – Lunch at Cranks with Maureen, Zia, Rosalie and her Mum and have lovely cashew chicken. Sun 31st – Braai at Jane's and Roger arrives wearing a Gorblimey cap, which goes well with his Dodge car with fake cow skin seats! The clutch fails only once . . . Back home in St Georges street and we're watching TV, a news flash comes on – Princess Diana has been badly injured in a car crash in Paris! Later we hear that she died in hospital!! Dodi Fayed and the driver Andre Paul also died. Her bodyguard was badly injured.

Monday 1st September – Daphne finds little Tottie, the wildest of our cats, dead and her head wedged in our gate towards the house, as if she was trying to get in. Now the news reports state that Di crashed into a tunnel wall at high speed in Paris, the driver alleged to be drunk and trying fleeing the paparazzi?! Mother Teresa has died, but instead of mourning for a genuine Saint (albeit an ugly one), the beauteous and shallow Princess, has the whole world weeping! A sad reflection on the values of this media-influenced era! Sat 6th – The funeral, I wasn't going to watch it, but Yvonne wanted to and so we end up crying buckets, as we watch the hearse with flowers thrown on it, as it goes slowly through the out lying parts of London. The service in the Abbey is beautiful, but Earl Spencer's eulogy criticising the Royal Family's reaction or lack of reaction, is a mean spirited.

Tuesday 9th – Working at Anglovaal. President Mandela is visiting Basil Hersov, a Director. He holds court in the Interview Suite, says he wants to meet everyone who works there. He's wearing a yellow and grey Mandela style shirt and has a most charming personality. I shake his hand and it's dry and thin, he says, 'How are you'? I stammer out that he knows my son Roger, who asked him to sign a copy of his book, 'Long Walk to Freedom', he says he remembers him (I'm sure he was just being polite), I'm blushing from the emotion of the moment and back away, he's surrounded by cell-phone carrying security men.

Thur 11th – Zia phones and says Maggie has fallen and broken her right arm, fortunately she's left handed. She's staying with Hal and Lynda for a few days. Phone Lynda's number and Maggie answers and offer her a place to stay, if she needs it. Fri 19th – An interview with ACI (Applied Communications) in Sturdee Avenue, Rosebank and just the usual work for reception, switchboard and sorting mail. Sun 21st – Sunny day, Zia collects me and visit Joan Brickhill's garden and every shrub is in bloom, well worth the R10 entrance fee in aid of the Theatrical Benevolent Fund. Chat to Brian Bales and he says, 'You used to be an actress didn't you?' A bit taken aback . . . surely people don't say to him, 'You used to be an architect/designer didn't you?' Dr Friedberg (Shirley Firth's husband) is there, sporting a shocking pink shirt, black and white striped jacket and carrying a walking stick covered in beads. Molly Seftel is like an elegant giraffe in harlequin patterned skin-tight top, leggings and asks us back to lunch. We go to buy pizzas, then on to her palatial house in Emmarentia with great big trees, manicured lawns, big patio and lovely pool. Drink wine out of tall cobalt blue glass goblets, eat the pizzas with tossed salad, avocados and olives. She tells us about her days in their pharmacy.

Sun 21st – (contd . . .) One day Winnie Mandela came in and she's tall and beautiful with a low sexy voice, ordering some make-up. Later on, after all those years of being on her own, she became a bitter shrew. The story is that when Nelson arrived at their home after being released from jail, he shook hands with all the servants and asked them how they were, she burst out of her room, screaming at the top of her voice, 'You stupid old man, stop spying on my servants'! Molly later left the pharmacy, when she became 'Mayor of Johannesburg'. Zia drops me at St George's Church and it's Bert Raphael's Memorial Tea Party. Rosalie, Maggie and Tim (her arm in a splint), Val Dunlop, Will Bernard and his wife, Gay Lomberg, Darren Coetzee, Corinne Willoughby and Patrick Mynhardt are there. Bert's lover, a sweet man is a bit overcome and red-faced, ginger hair, very Afrikaans and nothing like poor Bert, who was a smooth sophisticated person. I liked him a lot and he was quiet, reliable and a good actor. After the others have left, Rosalie and I sit in rectory garden watching the birds – hadedas, louries and catching up on our lives.

Mon 22nd – Boo phones me at work from UK and needs her SA passport. I send it via Postnet. Sun 28th – Walk to Natal Street to pay rent, it's very hot 29 degrees. On the way back, I see a man sitting in the street on the edge of the kerb, he says, 'Please help me, Madam'? I show him that I have no money with me – he says he doesn't want money, just help. As I walk on I think, wasn't that a pool of blood on the pavement beside him? The drops I thought were fruit from the overhanging tree, were they drops of blood? Now I'm feeling thoroughly ashamed of myself, go into the telephone office and ask them to help the man, they say to phone the Police, but I have no money for the phone, so ask where is the Police Station, one of the men lounging near the office shows me the way. When I finally get there, they tell me someone has reported the incident, an ambulance is on the way and just hope he recovers, as he was so quiet and polite . . .

Sunday October 5ᵗʰ – Jane comes over, we weed and plant seedlings and brought big bags of dog food, too heavy for me to carry. Bless her! Butch is growing so fast and always hungry. Boo phones to say she's received her passport at last. Has made up the row she had with her boyfriend and will not be coming home yet. Roger is OK, thank God! His car was impounded in Swaziland at the border, as the previous owner had installed a new engine and never registered it, so they thought he had stolen it. He had to pay a bribe of money to various officials and then had none left! So he managed to stay with friends, who have a farm there.

Mon 20ᵗʰ – Start working at ACI. Sunday 2ⁿᵈ November – Meet Lily Sklaar (Sam's ex wife), have tea at the Coach (literally a coach from a train), which is moored alongside the centre of Hunter Street. It's owned by a Chinese woman, her daughters' act, as waitresses. It's a charming concept and you can look down at the people walking in the street as you sip tea! Very popular with the Yeoville gentry! Artists and actors have made it their 'local'. Later at home, Moses and his tribe of followers drive me to distraction – toddlers run rampant through our hard won vegetable patch, trampling the seedlings, while an adult female stands helplessly by and Butch barks at the teasing children. He's only a puppy! Moses ignores this, as he chats to his male admirers (he isn't even paying rent)!!

Saturday 29ᵗʰ November – Buy a two plate cooker, in expectation of Maggie and Tim possibly coming to lodge with us. We happen to meet Joan Tudhope in the Checkers queue and she's living in a kind of African church home for indigent women in unbelievable squalor! I tell her to come and have a look at our spare room. I move furniture around to make it more 'lived in'. She's an ex-nursing Sister and seems pleasant enough, (also her skill might be useful in view of Yvonne's increasing frailty). Sun 30ᵗʰ – Maggie and Tim arrive and I'm in a fluster and misunderstand Jane's estimation of R500, she meant for both of them and I said each! Consternation! Later I phone Tim and correct the amount, but the damage is done and they won't be coming. It must be awful to go from living in their own charming house to depending on the charity of friends. We are all having to cut down on our lifestyles, as incomes plummet.

Monday 1ˢᵗ December – Joan moves in, and pays me R170. Thur 11ᵗʰ – Roger back at last and he gives Moses notice to leave at the end of January, Moses is pretty upset. Humphry phones and his sister Gillian has cancer of the spine and hips!! Sun 14ᵗʰ – Yvonne happens to mention that she has a lump in her breast. Jane is there and we look at it – It's big, red and the skin is puckered (all the bad signs). Poor soul, she smokes very heavily, her bedroom is brown from it all. Wed 17ᵗʰ – The lump is malignant and she's going to the Clinic, so she asks Joan to feed the dogs – a blazing row follows. When I come back from work, I try to solve the animosity between them and promise to feed the dogs before I go to work and in the evening.

Sat 20ᵗʰ – Belinda's friend Clara and her mother have arrived from London. I give her a letter for Boo telling her what has happened to Yvonne – she will be very upset! Also send her some assorted gifts, as Clara goes back on 27ᵗʰ· On Xmas Day at Jane's, special attention is paid to Yvonne and she gets lovely thoughtful presents, a lovely warm dressing gown and a pretty nightie. Roger gives me 'Fingerprints of the Gods', by Graham Hancock – much food for thought there – will the world ended in 2012?! (According to a Mayan prophecy)! Is Antarctica the real Atlantis and is the world's outer crust going to move, causing total destruction? Fri 26ᵗʰ – No longer called Boxing Day, now the 'Day of Goodwill'. Go with Zia to see 'Titanic', fantastic effects, the passengers sliding inexorably down the tilted deck! Kate Winslet and Leonardo di Caprio are so good! Wed 31ˢᵗ – Yvonne and I drink a champagne toast early in the evening, Joan declines to join us . . . lots of crackers and fireworks over in Hillbrow, but not much in Yeoville.

Thursday 1ˢᵗ January 1998 – Take Butch with me to pay rent and he's getting so strong he almost pulls me up the hills and he still learning to lift his leg when he has a wee and now stops at every tree to show off his skill.

I've had a letter from Freda Evans and she's now living with her son Dik, my old boyfriend in Hastings. Fri 2ⁿᵈ – Day off and take Yvonne to the Breast Clinic and what a maze of floors, the 5ᵗʰ level is on the ground floor – of course! Boo phones in the evening and worried about her, but tell her she feels no pain.

January 18th – Go with Rosalie to the Bahai Meeting in Acorn Road. Very quiet, people stand up and read a piece from either the Bible, the Koran, Buddhist scriptures or other religions. Nice atmospheric music plays and a jolly Negress sings a psalm. An elderly Canadian, Lowell Johnson seems to be the prime mover there (he was a notable broadcaster and journalist in his day). Fri 23rd – Yvonne is now on a special programme, run by Eli Lilly, she's a guinea pig in other words. Sat 31st – Pay Tim Heale R500 for their twin tub washing machine, looks in good condition, although its 15 years old. Maggie has thoughtfully left a list of instructions . . . I show Yvonne how to use it, but she's very nervous and looks at it as though it might bite!

Monday 2nd February – Daphne refuses to use it and prefers to slog it out in the bath. Jane comes in the afternoon and re-organises the kitchen, so the machine fits in. Thur 5th – ACI have arranged for me to do a 2 Day Course with Kelly Greenoaks to learn Word 97. Another woman is there to learn Excell and they've mixed us up and we both have to do our courses at the same time! Fri 6th – Pass with 90% score – amazing!

Fri 13th March – Drinks at work and our MD Chappie, celebrates 8 million profit in the first quarter of this year. It's also his birthday and is given a ship's bell, which has some mystic significance for him. Thur 26th – Phone Serge re-felling of the huge tree in the back garden, says he'll come over next week with a backi and a couple of boys. Mon 30th – Joan moves out at last, as she and Yvonne were no longer speaking to each other!

Saturday 11th April – See 'Seven Years in Tibet' with Brad Pitt as young Heinrich Harrer, a German climber stuck in Nepal at the beginning of the war, who ends up teaching the Dalai Lama and only goes home ten years after the war is over. Has the most wonderful, evocative music! Fri 17th – Tarot card reading at the House of Isis in the Rosebank Mall.

For Jane – A change of lifestyle soon, but will have a positive outcome. Michael – Things will improve in 2 months and next year even better. Roger – Life's a bit flat, but will improve after his birthday.

161

Belinda – Has an emotional problem, needs to get away and have a break!
Me – Sees a red-headed grand daughter with a big voice!

Sun 26th – Serge arrives to cut down the tree, which is leaning over into the next garden.

He has a big row with the old Jewish lady next door and shouting in Greek, she's yelling in Yiddish – it actually sounds very funny!

Friday May 1st – Roger moves most of his stuff into the house. Fri 8th – I notice blobs in my right eye and go to see Stephen Muller the optometrist. He says I have a cataract starting, but isn't 'ripe' (ready) yet. Says I have code 4 eyesight, quite bad and should always use glasses. Sun 10th – Mother's Day and Jane comes bearing gifts for us both! Go to a Meeting at the Yeoville Forum to discuss the increased violence on the streets. Some Nigerians attend, the locals look at them askance – they muscle in on the street traders and push drugs!

Friday May 15th – See 'Twelfth Night' at the Market theatre, have left tickets for Zia at the door, as she's busy parking. She marches in with Muffin in tow and the show has already started . . . lots of shushing! The production is based on a Coon Carnival theme, Olivia played as a hoarse-voiced shrew, no poetry at all, the cast clowning around in a pool of tepid water by an artificial beach. The Cape Coloured accents are so strong it's hard to understand a word! Sun 17th – Natasha meets me very early, it's bitterly cold and a long walk to the Berea Spiritualist Church. A Swami in an orange blanket points me out – says there is a calm benign female spirit looking out for me . . . my mind races around, who could it be? My sister Pat or my Scottish grandmother? Tears are running down my cheeks and am deeply disturbed. The ones needing treatment go to a special healing room, where we lie down on trestle beds covered by a blue blanket. A bald male Swami asks me if I have had an injury to my knee – I have, of course. He puts his hand on my knee under the blanket, a nice warm sensation. Then he puts one hand on my chest, the other under my back and says I need a full massage and will have to be another time. On the walk back, she says she has had no more fits since she started going there.

Fri 22nd – Zia is at the Kenridge with viral pneumonia. Roger gives me a lift. Doreen Levin and Val Drummond-Bell are already there. We cheer her up and get her laughing! Dr Connell arrives (our old GP), it's amazing how a sickly woman can perk up, when there are 2 attractive men around! We wait out in the passage while he treats her and talk to a patient, who says she spent the night with another patient who was a mad, violent woman! (This patient seems normal enough, except for a compulsion to talk non-stop) . . . When we go back to Zia and she tells us about a mad woman, who shared her 2 bed ward the previous night. Roger and I look at each other in wonder and just who is the mad one?! Sun 21st – Humphrey takes me to see Stephen Fry, in 'Oscar Wilde'. Watch him collapse on the treadmill in prison, horrifying it's like an escalator that won't stop! What did it do, did it grind corn? Jude Law plays Bosie Douglas, his lover – excellent film.

Wednesday 17th June – Lunch with Pat Parr-Burman. She tells me they are only staying in SA because of their dogs and so many people are anchored here, because of their pets!

Tues 30th – Pay rent at the Bank of Athens and find out the Rand is now 10 to the English pound. I phone Nan and her voice is much deeper than it used to be. I ask if she would like me to live in the same area as her? She says, 'I don't know you.' True enough, but rather a shocking thing to say to your own sister. Boo and I can stay with her, but not the boys . . . I in turn ask her to come and stay with us in SA. Says she'll think about it and has just come back from a 2 weeks holiday in Croatia (how lovely to be able to afford a holiday like that).

Monday 13th July – Back at work. Later go with Yvonne to an interview at the Old Age Home (it used to be the Casa Mia hotel). Rooms are very small, but the dining and recreation rooms are huge. She'll have to pay for food, extra money for cigarettes and cat food (so she can feed all the surrounding strays) is another matter!

Sat 8th August – Maggie's Farewell party at Zia's flat and all the old crowd, but we seem to have shrunk! Wed 19th – Maggie and Tim fly to UK with her arm is in a cast, broke it just before the flight, poor dear!

Thursday 29th October – We have at last have managed to get rid of the drunken lodger, who plagued our lives for a period. I had very unwisely given him the benefit of the doubt and let him stay, but the last straw was when he stood at our gate discussing the sale of his car while he wet his pants . . . and was blissfully unconcerned!

Friday 30th – Roger has been in UK for some time now and seen Michael. Roger bought Boo and Steve a camper van, so they can start up a business, he says both are well. Yvonne is packing up and ready to go to the Home tomorrow.

Sat 31st – Jane, Neil, Roger, Daphne, Frans the gardener from next door all help with the move. Yvonne's flat is nice with a lovely view of the garden and pool below from her balcony. Her bathroom and kitchenette are compact and easy to clean.

Monday 2nd November – Go to physio to treat neck pain, it did not help my hefting stuff during the move. Pay Daphne R350, including an extra R50 for helping on Saturday.

Sat 7th – It's Louisa's 40th birthday party and they've built a new extension to their home, lots of lovely wood, big sliding windows and an extra bedrooms upstairs. Neil's brother, John has come over from UK. He's even taller than Neil and has more hair, older, but looks younger. Has divorced recently and has been touring around the world using up his teacher's pension. Within a few hours he's lined up a rich divorcee, Christine. Roger gives me a lift home early, he has to meet Natasha, who's very upset, her 3 year old niece has just died in hospital. Sun 8th – At Jane's, John is encouraging everyone to 'jam', all a bit hung over, but try to join in with bongos, maracas, guitars, etc . . . and it peters out when he has to leave for his assignation with the glamorous Christine. Little did we suspect the 'knock on' effect of his visit, on Neil. Mon 9th – Re-do all the rooms. Yvonne's room is re-painted, as the walls were dark brown with cigarette smoke and Roger will be moving in to her room.

Thursday 10th December – Go to the airport to meet Boo and Steve, they flew with Ethiopian Airways, the plane was delayed till 9pm. She is much thinner and Steve is tallish, slim and completely bald from having alopecia, as a child. Big hazel eyes, a pale skin, and a pleasant personality. He always wears a hat or cap of some kind. We have dinner in Melville at the Fishmonger. An African comes round selling animals made out of coke tins, very clever. I buy a buffalo and they buy a lion. Fri 11th – Back at work and commuters on the Putco bus give our driver, Daniel, a birthday present. It's a bright red satin duvet set! He's chuffed! (We're asked for donations, I give gladly he's a nice driver). Then all the people on the bus start singing and clapping to gospel songs! The bus truly rocks . . . this is the spontaneous side of Africa that I love and will miss!

Sat 12th – Yvonne comes over and Boo takes snaps of everyone. She gives me £1,000 from Michael. They go with Roger to a Rave and it's in a large hole where a meteor once landed. Wed 16th – Day of Reconciliation. Roger, Boo and Steve hire a car and go off to Cape Town. Sun 20th – Shopping in Rosebank Mall with Jane. Chat to old actor friend Ian Lawrence and jokingly ask him why he isn't in 'Isidingo' (a popular TV series). Quick as a flash he says 'They couldn't afford me!' Dec 24th – They are all back from Cape Town.

Friday 25th December – Go to Louisa's house. George's Dad is there, dapper in a sparkling white suit! Talks non-stop to Yvonne, looking fetching in silky emerald green. Neil and his brother are away, touring the Peninsula. A lovely sunny day and all the better without Neil's sulky nagging. To save embarrassment, we gave each other our presents before coming. Thur 31st – Roger's in Cape Town, so Pierre takes Boo and Steve to the airport. I stay behind, as he has to go straight on to a gig afterwards for work.

Friday 1st January 1999 – Boo phones at 12.30 am and they arrived in one piece, after many stops and starts! She never got around to sorting out her myriad boxes (which was why she came out)! Sun 17th – It's happened at last – Neil has managed to alienate Jane for the last time. He went to watch the West Indies play against SA at the Wanderers Club and stayed out all night. She was so worried and he never bothered to phone. Then when he eventually turned up, he boasted that he had 'got his end off at last'! She understood that vulgarism to mean that he had picked up a woman at the cricket and slept with her. It was the last straw! John was the catalyst, Neil was jealous of his older brother's freedom. The relationship had been worsening for years and Jane told him to get out! Now he has to find somewhere to live.

Sun 31st – Cut down that bloody tree in the back garden with a kitchen knife and a small pair of clippers. Serge did cut it down before, but it has shot up again and the stems are easy to cut, as it's really a pot plant gone mad (I can take out my frustration about the awful crimes that are being committed every day in this country). Jane comes over with Yvonne and Natasha! She tells me what happened with Neil.

Tuesday 16th February – My last day at ACI and Barbara Morgan, the coloured girl who's replacing me seems to have it all in hand. She's quite bossy and they'll come to regret me leaving! Howie gives me flowers, perfume and R370 a collected from all the staff, I'm very touched! Wed 24th – Zia drove past the house yesterday and noticed Butch is in a bad way with lumps on his groin and a swollen face. I'm working temporarily at GAPA, Jane picks me up on the way and we collect Butch and take him to the vet. It's an allergic dermatitis and some plant in the garden is affecting him. I must not give him tinned food, only chicken and rice – he'll be eating better than we do! Jane is in a state, because Neil isn't picking up Alistair after cricket as he used to.

Fri 26th – Go to Absa Forex and fill in a form to take to the Receiver of Revenue, so I can take my savings out of the country. Now all I need is my IRP5 from ACI. Zia and I see the film, 'Regeneration' based on the WW1 trilogy by Pat Barker. Brilliant!

Monday March 1st – I go to the Receiver, but as I feared they can't do anything without my IRP5, which will only be ready at the end of March. Start packing books and can't decide what to take, what to leave behind. Wed 3rd – End of the first week of Butch's pills and he's good about taking them, snuffles them out of my hand. I suspect he was allergic to the old dog biscuits . . . Mon 15th – Graham Armitage died at the weekend, only discovered this by listening to Alan Swerdlow giving a eulogy on Classic FM. He was at RADA with me.

Mon 15th February – (contd . . .) Pieter Toerien puts in his two pennyworth . . . he and Graham had a big barney years ago. Graham's father was dying and he wanted to leave a show of Pieter's to fly home. Pieter said no, but Graham went anyway. It was important to him, particularly as his vicar father disapproved of his being gay. I hope they were able to forgive each other. Phone Zia and she's also going to the funeral. Patrick Mynhardt gives a funny eulogy with many anecdotes. They were both members of Alcoholics Anonymous.

Mr Nel recalls his last days, a moving account. Graham virtually stayed with him and his family, as he lived next door. When the children came into the sitting room, he would say, 'What is your name'? He would be told and then a few moments later, would ask the same question. He died peacefully, sitting in his favourite armchair in their house.

Sun 21ˢᵗ – Maggie has written, 'Us Oldies can get cheap rail concessions', which is good to know and maybe I'll be able to go to Scotland to see Aunt Mary? Mon 22ⁿᵈ – There's a cloud burst and Ian Davidson gives us a lift to Jane's. On the way he's involved with a 'black taxi', they get aggro and drive at him and so he makes a quick getaway. They had stopped their car and were getting out. These people all carry guns and that's the way it is now . . . even if you are in the right, no one dares to stop them. Jane is surrounded by packing cases just like me!

Thursday 25ᵗʰ March – Go to Home Affairs and don't have to wait too long, so get my passport back in ten minutes. Now I can return to SA at any time if I want to. Jane brings her two cats over and I have to keep them separate from Butch in another room, while she moves (although he would only want to play with them, but they don't know that)!

Sat 27ᵗʰ – She moves to Bradley Place in Windsor West and collects the cats.

Thursday 1ˢᵗ April – The Rubble man comes to take away the tree branches and he's brought a 5ton truck and charges R120 instead of the R60 he'd agreed to for a small backi load. Just for the sake of peace, I pay him R120! Thur 8ᵗʰ – Chaim and Miri come to look at Butch, as they might want to take him when I leave (as I don't know Roger's plans). Their small son is afraid of him at first, but when they want to leave he cries.

Fri 9ᵗʰ – Jane has been getting obscene phone calls, she's very upset and the police have given her a new number. She doesn't like her new house, it has a very small garden, and she loves gardening! Calvert's Removals come to give me a quote for packing and sending my boxes overseas, it's much less than Elliot's, hurray! The news from Serbia is awful, lines of Muslim refugees leaving Kosovo to escape the Serbian bombs! Boo thinks there will be another World War!!

Sun 18th – Roger and Wayne come back from their trip to Swaziland. Michael phones from Kenya, loving it there and he's going to climb Mt. Kenya, then on to Lamu near Mombasa. He's met Mr Patel from the duka (shop) in Meru where we lived and farmed tea. He remembered us well, his wife taught me to make curry in a pressure cooker on their kitchen floor! Mon 26th – Humphrey says he's flying to UK in six weeks and so we can meet up there. Fri 30th – Go to Absa to arrange for Jane to have my Power of Attorney to pay my bills while I'm away.

Monday 3rd May – Roger's back, fallen, injured both shins and had to have stitches! Have been feeling more energetic these last few days, maybe it's the Chlorella pills that Michael insisted I should take? Have a cut and dye my hair golden brown, that's what it says on the bottle – but it's khaki! My new friend, Fuzzy phones and says he'll take me to the local Sanga (he's another Tibetan Buddhist). I was supposed to go with Zia to an adjudication, so cancel that and she's miffed! The Sanga has a hushed, incense-laden atmosphere, statues of Buddha, the Madonna (I think it's the Madonna), Lao Tse, even pictures of my old teacher, Rosa (she is now known as Shigre Devi – a Guru). The last time I met her, she told me she had reverted to her old faith and is a Roman Catholic . . . well, I guess you can be both?!

Wednesday 5th – Phone Zia and try to explain how much it meant to re-connect with a group that had so much spiritual influence on my life. She's still cross! Go to Rosebank to collect the Open Return flight ticket. Sat 8th – Roger flies to UK and takes my file of Memoirs and some winter jackets, so I can fit more into my luggage.

Sun 9th – Mother's Day, Jane collects Yvonne and I, we go to George and Louisa's.

She's bought us both some chocolates, flowers and wine, she's such a kind and a generous person, how I shall miss her! Sat 15th – Farewell party and Zia comes, but is still upset with me. Rosy is away, Pat, Val, Maureen and Jane come. The huge carrot cake I bought was awful and quite dry, but the champagne was OK! Zia rushes away to see an early film and quite spoils the atmosphere! Tues 18ᵗʰ – Order traveller's cheques. Calvert's come to collect the boxes and is wonderfully efficient, re-pack everything, including the ones I'd packed and labelled myself! Wed 19ᵗʰ – Re-confirm flight booking. Lunch with Val at Hyde Park and always enjoy her company, as she's such a cheerful person.

Fri 21ˢᵗ – Wayne takes Natasha, Jane and I to the airport. She and I hug and cry a lot – such a wrench! The trip is pleasant and uneventful. Have to wait 6 hours in Brussels! Buy duty-free wine for Steve, scarf for Boo. Arrive in Gatwick on the 22ⁿᵈ – Buddha's birthday – auspicious or what?! Catch the Virgin Express to Heathrow. Boo and Steve meet me there in their old camper van. I can't quite believe I'm back in England . . . have an embarrassing longing to kiss the earth like the Pope, to lie on the grass picking daisies!

They live in Holloway in Mercer Road in London. My flat is on the mezzanine floor with two rooms, kitchen en – suite. Have to share a shower and loo.

It takes months for me to fill in all the correct forms and to find out how many years Humphrey worked in UK (4 and a half). Try to get a job, but seem to be too old and try to get a pension, but have to go before a Tribunal. The Chairman is a woman. A Mr Tooth represents the Pension people. Boo and I sit waiting for their final decision. Finally, they call me back in and the lady chairman gives me a lovely smile . . . they have decided to allow me to remain in UK and accept me as a Citizen of the UK. Boo and I creep dazedly out of the imposing building and suddenly start to dance a jig for joy!

Lightning Source UK Ltd.
Milton Keynes UK
UKOW040606050613

211802UK00001B/13/P